D0537326

Business Insights:

China

Every UK company with an international outlook now needs to develop a China strategy.

The **China-Britain Business Council (CBBC)** is the UK's leading independent source of China business information, advice, consultancy and services for UK industry.

As an independent, business-led organisation, we support British companies of all sizes by providing **Business Services, Practical In-Market Assistance** and **Industry Initiatives.**

Our membership scheme offers enhanced benefits including discounted prices for services, special member-only events and information – essential for those realising the time is right to get actively involved in the China market.

For more information, or advice on developing your China business, call our London office on
+44 (0)20 7802 2000 or visit **www.cbbc.org**

China-Britain
Business Cou
英中贸易协会

Helping you do business in Ch

China

Practical Advice on Entry Strategy and Engagement

Consultant Editor: Jonathan Reuvid

RECOMMENDED BY
INSTITUTE OF DIRECTORS

THE CULTURE
PARTNERSHIP

**KOGAN
PAGE**

London and Philadelphia

This book has been endorsed by the Institute of Directors.

The endorsement is given to selected Kogan Page books which the IoD recognises as being of specific interest to its members and providing them with up-to-date, informative and practical resources for creating business success. Kogan Page books endorsed by the IoD represent the most authoritative guidance available on a wide range of subjects including management, finance, marketing, training and HR.

The views expressed in this book are those of the authors and are not necessarily the same as those of the Institute of Directors.

Publisher's note
Every possible effort has been made to ensure that the information contained in this book is accurate at the time of going to press, and the publishers and authors cannot accept responsibility for any errors or omissions, however caused. No responsibility for loss or damage occasioned to any person acting, or refraining from action, as a result of the material in this publication can be accepted by the editor, the publisher or any of the authors.

First published in Great Britain and the United States in 2008 by Kogan Page Limited

120 Pentonville Road
London N1 9JN
United Kingdom
www.kogan-page.co.uk

525 South 4th Street, #241
Philadelphia PA 19147
USA

© Kogan Page and individual contributors, 2008

The right of Kogan Page and the individual contributors to be identified as the author of this work has been asserted by them in accordance with the Copyright, Designs and Patents Act 1988.

ISBN 978 0 7494 5062 5

British Library Cataloguing-in-Publication Data

A CIP record for this book is available from the British Library.

Library of Congress Cataloging-in-Publication Data

Reuvid, Jonathan.
  Business insights China : strategy, planning and marketing analysis for
international business / Jonathan Reuvid.
    p. cm.
  ISBN 978-0-7494-5062-5
  1. Investments, Foreign--China--Handbooks, manuals, etc. 2. China--Commerce--
Handbooks, manuals, etc. I. Title.
  HG5784.R48 2008
  330.951--dc22
                                                      2007042291

Typeset by JS Typesetting Ltd, Porthcawl, Mid Glamorgan
Printed and bound in Great Britain by Cambridge University Press

It is reported that twenty years ago counterfeiting and piracy (IP crime) business was 1 percent the size it is today. It seems that everything about it has changed – except, the way we fight it.

The extraordinary growth in intellectual property crime has created one of the most devastating problems facing world business. It is underpinning serious and organised crime and allows criminals to accrue huge finances by stealing others' creative efforts.

Over the past 10 years widespread access to sophisticated technology, E-commerce and increased world trade have resulted in more open borders that make it is easier to manufacture in one geographic location and distribute elsewhere. In addition we have seen a shift from cottage industries, producing poor quality fashion accessories and luxury goods, such as Rolex watches, to massive manufacturing plants that have the capability to turn out everything from bogus home entertainment products and electrical appliances, to sometimes extremely hazardous consumer fakes such as pharmaceuticals, automotive parts and household goods.

Unfortunately while globalisation offers greater stability and prosperity, many transitional and developing countries find themselves exposed to organised counterfeiting networks. It is important to understand that criminals have targeted emerging economies and have been quick to exploit economic mechanisms aimed at more effective trade. In the People's Republic of China for example, despite hard work by the Government and enforcement authorities, there has been an explosive growth in counterfeiting and piracy as a result of the shift from public to private enterprise systems.

Often it is claimed that the growing market in fake goods is a simple response to consumer demand; satisfying the bargain-hunter mentality that has been seemingly insatiable since the 1980's. But how well the sinister aspects and effects of counterfeiting and piracy are understood by consumers and even those in government, enforcement and the judiciary is debatable and sometimes doubtful. As in many countries the UK judicial and enforcement systems have sometimes proved to be unsatisfactory in discouraging infringers. There has been a definite lack of awareness. Such a large and growing trade cannot exist unless it is organised; thankfully it is more accepted that the high profit and low risk principle has attracted criminal networks that have access to complex distribution networks and work in collaboration across borders.

So what harm is it really doing? A plethora of statistics and figures have been used over the past ten years to estimate the damage and potential effect on business and the economy. Most are startling and illustrate a dramatic growth that virtually outstrips other forms of criminality. The financial cost of turning a blind eye is huge but the harm is much wider. Yes it is true that businesses, communities and consumers are all hit, but there is an equally damaging consequence. Many of the products we take for granted have been developed as the result of someone's innovation and creativity. If we ignore this and allow the pirates to enjoy the fruits of someone else's hard work we run the risk of destroying our instinctive desire to progress. Why should creators bother if there is no protection of their inventiveness and ultimately their livelihoods?

The UK Government has clearly recognised the importance of creativity and inventiveness as the country's greatest asset, has commissioned several reports and a Minister to lead the innovation agenda across the whole of Government. The Gowers' Report in particular set out a clear detailed strategy for government action to improve the UK's innovation performance and protection of rights.

The Gowers' Report and the recent Review by Lord Sainsbury "The race to the top" make it clear that Intellectual Property rights underpin innovation by providing a tool for businesses to protect their creativity and make a return on investments. The UK Government's response has been to announce its intention to invest £1 billion into programmes to boost business innovation and applied research over the next three years. One focus of the Government's new Innovation Programme which is of interest to universities will be to give more support through the Higher Education Innovation Fund to business-facing universities, setting targets for knowledge transfer from Research Councils, doubling the number of Knowledge Transfer Partnerships, and extending these to Further Education Colleges.

But no matter how innovative or how large a company's financial assets are, often its brands are even more valuable and to ensure clean and fair markets there is a need for effective enforcement. As the seat of IP in the UK, the UK-Intellectual Office has been tasked with a number of actions in respect of better enforcement of intellectual property rights; the main objective being the formulation of a first National IP Crime Strategy.

Work on the strategy began in February 2004 and we immediately brought together government agencies, industry and enforcers to develop a cohesive plan. The "Counter Offensive" strategy was published in August 2004 and produced three main deliverables:

- The launch of a multi agency IP Crime Group (including a structure of Expert Groups to look at specific aspects that affect enforcement);
- The establishment of a central intelligence and information gathering team within the UK-IPO;
- The publication of National (Annual) Reports on Counterfeiting and Piracy (available on our website);

In brief the "Counter Offensive" strategy has been based around the introduction of a more co-ordinated approach where public and private enforcement resources are targeted more effectively to produce tangible results.

Most recently we have strengthened our own framework in this area by the introducing a specific Copyright and Enforcement Directorate which is developing collaborative approaches between operational enforcement work and broader policy and support activities. As a result we have established regular training programmes for enforcers and launched a number of interactive training publications and CD's aimed at assisting enforcement officers and brand holders to build successful prosecution cases. Our training tools are provided free to enforcement officers and those involved in the fight against counterfeiting and piracy and brand holders.

Of course we are very aware of the international aspects of IP crime; the Office is a member of the Interpol IP Crime Action Group and has Chaired the UN Economic and Social Advisory Group on the Protection of IP Rights, which offers technical assistance to assist transition countries. This fits extremely well with out own objectives, as we have a long established record of bi-lateral assistance to transition economies.

To help keep a clear focus an bring together out international emphasis, this year we have introduced a specific International Coordinator and we are in the process of developing our work, identifying appropriate partners and mechanisms, to look at how we can assist vulnerable countries to enforce its IP legislation.

Of course China is key country for the UK. It has the fastest growing economy in the world and offers huge opportunities to business.

To help encourage creative and innovative inward investment in China, its government has been placing increasing value on intellectual property rights (IPRs) and is adopting an increasingly proper approach to protecting entrepreneurs holding IPRs there.

For example in 2001 China began a comprehensive revision of its laws and regulations in relation to IP and clearly began to take on seriously obligations to protect and enforce IP rights.

China has also accepted the World Trade Organisation's TRIPS (trade-related aspects of intellectual property rights) agreement which sets minimum standards of protection and enforcement for IP internationally in respect of administrative, civil, criminal and border measures. China has made and continues to make significant progress, bringing its IP framework into compliance with TRIPS.

Nevertheless many Western business sectors maintain that high piracy rates continue to exist in China. It is claimed that China has decided on an IPR system that it considers appropriate to its particular national economic situation, aiming to balance the interests of rights' holders and consumers.

However, it should be noted that the damaging effect is not lost on Chinese authorities who recognise that China also faces considerable losses. Therefore to combat the growing threat of IP Crime the Chinese government has shifted emphasis away from the development of legislation and towards how current legislation can be effectively enforced. In January 2005, the State Council approved the establishment of the Leading Group for National Intellectual Property Strategy Formulation of P.R. China. Wu Yi, deputy premier of the State Council, headed the leading group and Ministers from almost 30 ministries are members.

The authorities themselves feel they have made real progress and cite many recent successes as a result of their drive for better collaboration in IPR enforcement. .

I am pleased to say that the UK-IPO works very closely to assist China's progress in this area and this year published a Road Map for businesses seeking to invest in China and protect their IP rights.

But China isn't our only interest; the UK-IPO has a long established record of technical assistance to transition economies. We work with the G8, the Commission, the United Nations, the US PTO, Interpol and through bi-lateral agreements to help raise awareness and standards in IP legislation, use and the enforcement of rights. Our work extends to countries such as Romania, Bulgaria and Serbia but also stretches to emerging states in the Balkans and further afield as far as Latin America, Turkey and Kazakhstan. Indeed our recent work with China, Romania and Bulgaria has proved successful in improving the law and the approaches adopted by enforcement officers and those in government and the judiciary.

Unfortunately it is plain that counterfeiting and piracy has emerged as a clear and serious threat. The traffic in fake goods threatens to overwhelm honest business throughout the EU. Losses of jobs, higher taxes and increased prices are all passed on to the taxpayer who ultimately meets the extra costs of greater policing and rises in insurance premiums and interest rates. To counter this we need to drive co-ordinated approaches and to use the skills and expertise that exist throughout enforcement, industry and government. Like the criminals we face, we need to work together to develop effective communication chains that eradicate waste and avoid duplicated effort. Without joint action and a policy to dissuade consumers from seeing it as a "victimless crime" a cycle of destabilisation could occur with control slipping to the criminals.

Contents

The Centre for Intellectual Property Policy and Management at Bournemouth University

Innovation and creativity are at the heart of all enterprise. The Centre for Intellectual Property Policy & Management (CIPPM – **www.cippm.org.uk**) is a unique combination of academics, practitioners and industry colleagues committed to an interdisciplinary approach to the governance and application of intellectual property rights. The recognition of intellectual property management as an enterprise skill, and regulatory impact analysis are at the heart of the Centre's mission. It operates under the joint directorship of Professor Martin Kretschmer and Professor Ruth Soetendorp.

Founded in 2000, CIPPM has rapidly achieved national and international recognition. Research and consultancy projects have been commissioned by the Leverhulme Trust, European Commission, UKIPO, European Patent Office, Arts Council, Social Science Research Council (New York), World Intellectual Property Organisation, the Arts and Humanities Research Council and the Higher Education Academy. In addition, CIPPM offers professional IPR management education to government departments, public institutions and commercial companies.

Studying intellectual property at Bournemouth is a rewarding experience. PhD students from all over the world contribute to a lively environment of research and enquiry. Since 2006 IP courses at Bournemouth have been accredited by the Joint Examination Board of The Chartered Institute of Patent Attorneys and The Institute of Trade Mark Attorneys. Successful completion of the LLM IP, or the Post Graduate Certificate IP (newly available via block and online delivery), gives full exemption from their foundation unit examinations. Dr Gurpreet Bhambra, a recent graduate now a trainee Patent Attorney with AstraZeneca plc writes "The course provided an added advantage by increasing my employability profile and I am currently using the knowledge gained at Bournemouth in my daily working life. I would say that the IP qualification from BU has given me an 'edge' over other graduates entering this profession." Intellectual Property Management is becoming recognised as a career path in its own right, for which you can prepare with confidence at Bournemouth.

2005/06 The Centre for Intellectual Property Policy & Management collected the Informa World Leaders award for Intellectual Property Education.

Bournemouth University

For further information about the centre, please contact the Centre Administrator Emily Cieciura on **+44 (0)1202 965197**.

'excellent innovation' 思佳

Joan Turley: BA (Hons) PGCE, M `es L

How you can succeed in trading with China

Understanding the Chinese culture

The Culture Partnership is a cultural training, facilitation and mediation consultancy specialising in China. We enable both UK and international companies to build trading, educational and professional relationships through understanding the Chinese culture and how they communicate.

Enhance the likelihood of success

The Culture Partnership can enhance the likelihood of success for clients by accompanying them at every stage, helping them to understand and manage the differences in business culture, process and exchanges; the important ways in which different cultures approach meetings, negotiation, teamwork, deadlines and finance.

Fifteen years experience

Fifteen years experience in working with multi-nationals and governments worldwide has provided us with a privileged position to assist our clients with contacts, cultural knowledge and cultural communication skills, ensuring a smooth passage to international success.

Products and services

The Culture Partnership can offer special expertise and experience in the areas of;
◆ Mediation ◆ Training ◆ Briefing ◆ Cultural Trade Facilitation ◆ Seminars ◆ Master Classes.

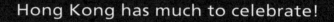

Hong Kong has much to celebrate!

2008 marks the Olympic Games in Beijing.
Hong Kong is a proud co-host city
and will stage the Equestrian Events.

2007 marked the 10th anniversary of
the Hong Kong Special Administrative Region.
'One Country, Two Systems' is working well,
and the economy is booming.

Hong Kong is riding high!

Asia's world city

HONG
KONG

Recognising China as the dominant economic force it was to become **Xanadu Productions** was formed over 10 years ago to make independent broadcast programmes specifically on China.

Employed regularly by BBC programme strands like "Correspondent", "Panorama", even "Blue Peter", all have benefited from the unique respect Xanadu holds, on the ground, in mainland China.

When selling into the vastness of China there's never been a better time to employ video, delivered on CD or DVD as a powerful communications medium.

British television production, whether broadcast or corporate, is still deemed to be the best in the world. Utilise it to impress your Chinese colleagues.

For more information please contact Maggie Still:
mstill@xanadutv.com or visit our website **www.xanadutv.com**

Xanadu's long term experience and depth of cultural knowledge about China puts it in a truly unique position, to help exporters or potential investors achieve their desired goals. Have you, for example, considered how important it is to your Chinese colleagues to communicate your company information in their language? Or recognized the potential of a video business card possibly with a translated message from your CEO, as a DVD leave behind or to be sent by mail or email?

Networking with tried and tested Chinese colleagues, Xanadu can showcase your business effectively in China. Business relationships are all important in China and the building of trust is the first step. At Xanadu we understand and utilise the concept of "guanxi" (business relationships) and the other guiding principles of building trust with Chinese colleagues and potential clients.

rouse & co. internation

intellectual property is key to business success in China

We have more than 10 years' experience in China and provide the full range of intellectual property services from offices in Beijing, Guangzhou and Shanghai.

Asia   Europe   Middle East

www.iprights.com

China Association of International Trade was founded in 1981 to promote research on international trade and China's open-door policies, and is now the leading association in the field of international trade studies, training and consulting, with institutional and personal members around the country.

http://gmxh.mofcom.gov.cn/index.shtml

Mission

CAIT aims to be a thought leader in the field of international trade theories. AIT is committed to promoting academic exchanges and training in international trade esearch and practices within China and with the outside world through its association with domestic and international partners.
CAIT is dedicated to improving the well-being of the world trade community by enhancing the understanding between China and the rest of the world.

An affiliate of the Ministry of Commerce, P.R.China
中国国际贸易学会
China Association of International Trade

We bring minds together in research, training and consulting

Research: CAIT undertakes research projects from both government and non-overnment organizations in the field of international trade policies, theories and ractices. CAIT also initiates research in its capacity as a national academic association. . holds, on annual basis, national research conference and announces "international esearch excellence awards" , which are regarded as one of the top research awards in :hina. CAIT also sponsor/co-organises research seminars.

Training: CAIT offers a diverse range of training programs for international trade ractitioners, including certification programs that develop skills in international usiness and move up international trade career ladder. CAIT now works with over 00 training centers throughout China to deliver the training programs.

Consulting: CAIT advises both domestic and international companies on their narket entry strategies, partner selection and negotiations, cultural management, overnment relations, etc.

Contact us

Email: cait@yahoo.cn

China Association of International Trade
2, Dong Chang An Street
Beijing 100731, China

Tel: +86-10-65125843
Fax: +86-10-65128257
    +86-10-65123234

**WE'VE BEEN
EXPECTING
YOU ON
█ LATITUDE 31°N**   Cairo, Egypt   Beiji

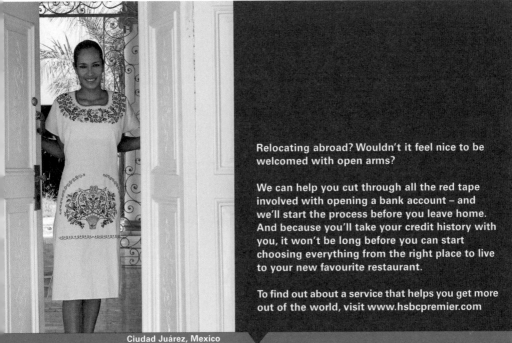

Contributors

Peter Budd is a director at Arup. He has extensive experience in the design and supervision of civil engineering, structural and multidisciplinary projects both in the United Kingdom and overseas – in East Asia, the United States, the Middle East and Central Africa. Peter leads Arup's global airport business and has been involved in the planning and design of airports worldwide, most recently in China, the Philippines and the United Kingdom. He sits on the Airports Advisery Council, which advises the British government on matters relating to airport policy and is a board member of the British Airports Group (BAG), a trade organization that represents over 200 UK companies exporting their skills and products worldwide.

The China Britain Business Council (CBBC) is the United Kingdom's leading source of China business information, advice, consultancy and services for UK industry. The CBBC supports British companies of all sizes by providing business services, practical in-market assistance and industry initiatives via its network of six UK offices and presence in 11 Chinese cities.

Guy Facey is a Partner with Withers LLP and is based in their Hong Kong office. Formerly of KSB Law LLP, he acts for corporate clients, developing international business particularly with China.

Ian Faragher has held both regional and country manager positions in China including Hong Kong and Taiwan, Thailand, Singapore and Australia. He has also held senior underwriting and management positions in the United States. With 30 years' insurance experience, the most recent of which includes 13 years in Greater China, he has a strong track record in successful leadership and management of organizations at various stages of development, including start-ups, joint ventures, mergers and acquisitions and complete company restructuring.

Stephen Gill runs his own engineering and business consultancy, Stephen Gill Associates. An experienced business manager and company director with a strong engineering background, he has developed into an accomplished all-rounder with a proven track record in technical design, sales and marketing, general management, business law and management accounting.

Amanda Gu is a manager at the China Affairs Division of HSBC Holdings plc.

John Lee is Senior Taxation Partner at KPMG in Greater China and is based at the KPMG Shanghai office.

Linda Lin joined KPMG's China Transaction Services team in 2003 from KPMG Vancouver, Canada, focusing on serving the needs of multinational clients investing in China. Since joining the China Transaction team, Linda has provided clients with due diligence, valuable assistance and timely advice and support throughout their transactions. She is a Financial Advisery Services Partner.

Mark Michelson is a long-term Hong Kong resident and is Associate Director-General for Investment Promotion at Invest Hong Kong, the government agency responsible for attracting foreign direct investment. He is a past Chairperson of the American Chamber of Commerce in Hong Kong and serves on Hong Kong's Fulbright Advisery Committee.

John Miles is on the group board of Arup, the engineering and design business consultancy that has a 30-year history of doing business with China.

Luke Minford is Head of China Operations at Rouse & Co International. A New Zealand qualified lawyer, Luke has lived in China for over 15 years. He has been with Rouse & Co since 1997, and manages diverse IP portfolios across many industries for some of China's largest foreign companies.

Tim Moore is CEO of SGAI Tech, a joint venture between Automatic Manufacturing Ltd (AML) of Hong Kong and Sagentia of Cambridge, United Kingdom. Tim joined Sagentia in 2001 to work in new product development. Previously, he was Technical Director of Phenomenon Group and OnMedica Group. He graduated with a first class honours degree in Physics with Electronics at the University of Birmingham and in 1998 he received a PHD from Cambridge University in Microelectronic Engineering.

John Pickup founded Avington Systems after gaining a master's degree from MIT and a career in IT sales and marketing management. Assignments have included the establishment of the UK office of a Canadian/Chinese software company. He has addressed IT industry events and has taught a software marketing course in Beijing. Avington Systems works with UK companies to take advantage of the huge benefits of outsourcing software development to identified software companies in China with the reputation of good work completed on time.

Jonathan Reuvid has more than 20 years' experience of joint venture development in China. An Oxford MA, he worked first as an economist for the French National Oil Company, Total, before moving into financial services and management consultancy. He became Director of European Operations for a Fortune 500 US multinational before engaging with China in the mid-1980s. In 1989 he started a second career as a writer and editor of business books for Kogan Page and has more than 30 titles to his name.

Ruth Soetendorp is a National Teaching Fellow, joint Director of Bournemouth University's Centre for Intellectual Property Policy and Management (www.cippm. org.uk). Ruth works globally to promote intellectual property education. Partners include European Patent Office, World Intellectual Property Organization and academic and business institutions. Funded research includes: The Leverhulme Trust, UK Intellectual Property Office, Financial Services Research Forum and the European Commission.

David Steeds qualified as a Chartered Accountant with PriceWaterhouseCoopers. After a period in private equity he joined Serco Group plc and was part of the team that built it up to be one of the United Kingdom's leading support services companies. He is a former Chief Executive of the Private Finance Panel, the UK government agency previously responsible for the Private Finance Initiative and corporate development director of QinetiQ Group plc. An experienced non-executive director, he has helped four companies to list on AIM.

Joan Turley began her career as an academic specializing in modern languages, having previously won the French Government Medal for her undergraduate language studies. Having acquired a Masters through the French Postgraduate system, Joan began a lifelong fascination with the rigours of relating well to other cultures for work and business. After her PhD studies she specialized in the application of English for the international business community, followed by three years with a global strategic research company applying cultural values to the analysis of business and competitive information. For the last 10 years, Joan has specialized in applying extensive cultural skills to enhancing clients' business performance. Her current work involves promoting empathy and effective intercultural dialogue between Western clients and China across education, finance, media and government.

Joshua Whale holds degrees in Law, Politics and Chinese from the University of Otago, New Zealand. Since joining Rouse & Co earlier in 2007 he has helped establish Rouse's China Research Unit, and now coordinates IP enforcement in the pharmaceutical, FMCG, transport and bathroomware industries. Joshua speaks Mandarin and German.

Ning Wright is a Risk Advisory Partner for KPMG China and has over 15 years' experience in risk management and advisery work including system implementation review, project management, enterprise high availability, system integration, system selection, margin enhancement and IT governance. Before working in China, Ning also worked in the United Kingdom and Hong Kong.

Foreword

Miles Templeman, Director General,
Institute of Directors

As China continues to evolve as an economic hotspot, directors in the United Kingdom are recognizing the potential opportunities and looking for ways to exploit them. We are seeing a shift in attitude, with British businesses feeling less threatened by this vast emerging market, and more inclined to explore its potential.

But they must proceed with caution. While there is no shortage of opportunities, the simple message is to have a clear business objective, identify the markets and sectors with the biggest potential and utilize all the information and support resources available.

The key to success in any foreign market, emergent or established, is detailed research. Feedback from the Institute of Directors' Business Information Services suggests that members are increasingly requesting 'an inside track' – that is, real practical advice – on doing business in China.

While language, legal and financial difficulties certainly exist, by far the largest barrier to trade is created by the different business culture. Perhaps the single biggest issue for companies in China right now is intellectual property theft. It is a huge problem, and although the Chinese government is trying to tackle it, until China has established its own global brands, it will continue to be a problem. Finding the right trade partner is always a crucial stage in overseas trade, but for companies going into China, for this reason, it is doubly important. Get as much help as you can and don't try to go it alone.

Cost is a huge driver, but moving your manufacturing processes to China will not make you a fortune overnight. There are huge economic disparities between the

Chinese provinces. Where wages are lower, skilled staff are much harder to find, while in the areas where skilled staff are plentiful, demand is driving up the wage inflation. It is certainly not a get-rich-quick opportunity – in fact, it may not work for your company at all – and that is something all companies need to bear in mind.

China's wage inflation is rising, and while this will inevitably make the region less financially feasible as a manufacturing base, it will become more attractive to British exporters. The potential consumer market in China is enormous, and this will present real opportunities for retail and service sector companies.

This book will provide practical advice on setting up in business in China as well as pointers to support organizations that can help. Readers will get an insight into the internal economic climate and the incentives available to UK companies. The book will also include case studies from companies that can recount first hand their experiences of setting up business in the region, and highlight the benefits and the potential pitfalls.

For any business thinking of doing business in China the information in this book will make it a 'must read'. The practical advice it contains, written and edited by experts, will be of enormous assistance – and I commend it to you.

Introduction

Jonathan Reuvid

When I set out to plan the contents of *Business Insights – China*, I had in mind a book that would focus almost exclusively on experience-based advice and case studies from some of us who have worked on developing business in and with China in recent years. These intentions are carried out in Parts 2 to 5 of the book you are now reading.

However, attendance at the Institute of Directors' seminar, 'International Insight for Business: China & Hong Kong', in London in June 2007, convinced me that the ongoing debate on the future of China and, specifically, as to whether its economic performance is sustainable, could not be ignored. In the prophecies of doom that circulate in the English language press, and in the many books on this subject, one can detect more than a whiff of *schadenfreude* – an underlying sense of hopeful satisfaction that China might stumble and that its uncomfortable global presence might be diminished. I decided that this issue, whatever prior conclusion readers might have reached, ought to be addressed in our book.

The contents in summary

I have tried to lay out the evidence rather fully in Part 1 for the benefit of those who are not fully conversant with the economic facts and, in Chapter 7, to arrive at reasoned conclusions based not only on historical, economic and political data but on alternative scenarios of how the patterns of global trade and investment might alter throughout the 21st century. After all, as entrepreneurs engaging in China, you need to have a clear understanding and make your own appraisal of the macroeconomic risks that may affect your venture over the span of its likely duration.

For those who are ready to make a commitment in China, Part 2 explores the basic business issues that all businesspeople will encounter. These chapters are overviews and do not attempt to offer comprehensive advice. Most of them are covered in more depth in *Doing Business with China*, published originally by Kogan Page but available now in more recent editions from GMB Publishing, London, and updated at intervals online from www.globalmarketbriefings.com.

Part 3 is written for the benefit of readers intending to invest in China either in a wholly owned enterprise or a joint venture with Chinese partners. As before, the chapters of this part are more overviews than detailed professional advice.

Parts 4 and 5 are case-study-driven but include chapters from experienced professional organizations active in China. Part 4 is concerned with joint venture management, Part 5 with service provision and trade. Experiences are mixed and the many case studies include failures as well as successes. What readers may find of greatest interest is the description of the problems in practice, both those that proved insurmountable and those that were solved.

Acknowledgements

My personal thanks are due to those contributors who have written specifically for this book. The individual authors and their backgrounds are listed in the contributors' notes. Their organizations include Arup, Bournemouth University Business School, Stephen Gill Associates, HSBC. The Culture Partnership, Invest Hong Kong, KPMG, Lloyds of London, Rouse & Co. International, Sagentia, Steeds & Co. and Withers LLP. My grateful thanks also to Humphrey Keenlyside of the China Britain Business Council (CBBC) for furnishing me with so many case studies from CBBC members' experiences.

We are grateful to the sponsors of the book, HSBC, Rouse & Co. International and Sagentia, whose participation has helped to underwrite the book. We also acknowledge with gratitude the role of the Institute of Directors (IoD) as our associates in the publication of *Business Insights – China*. Finally, I offer my particular thanks to Miles Templeman, Director General of the IoD for his Foreword and for his encouragement for this project from the inception of the book.

Whatever predictions for the further development of China may come to pass, we can be sure that the coming decades will continue to be as eventful as the last 30 years. As the practical experiences of those businesses that have engaged with China multiply, you may expect further editions of our book. In the meantime, I hope that this first edition is of practical use to those who set out on their personal long march.

Part 1

The economy

1

The economy – China's long march

Jonathan Reuvid

There is an unresolved debate about the sustainability of China's amazing economic growth that continues to fascinate academic economists and journalists, and is of increasing concern to government strategists on both sides of the Atlantic and the international business community. The Chinese government is discussing quite openly the long-term issues arising from the imbalances not only of its foreign trade, but also of the living standards between the comparatively wealthy urban populations of China's eastern seaboard and hinterland and the agrarian population of Central and Western China and its less developed cities.

Throughout the past 23 years that I have been engaged in China, both as a businessperson until recently and as a regular commentator since 1993, the siren voices among China watchers have regularly forecasted a 'hard landing' for the economy, every time that there has been a dip in the world economy or a regional financial crisis. So far, the prophets of doom have been proved wrong; either the landing has been 'soft' or the Chinese economy has marched on with scarcely a blip. However, the present debate about medium-to-long-term sustainability arises from China's extraordinary economic renaissance and the resulting structural and social pressures within China, and on its relationships with the rest of the world. For these reasons, the downside scenario has to be taken seriously by those businesspeople planning to engage with China for more than a short-term trade opportunity. Before committing to investment and management time in China, readers need to form a clear opinion on this issue.

This chapter, and the two that follow, focus on the key features of China's domestic economy and foreign trade and are intended to provide readers with sufficient evidence to arrive at a balanced view of its economic future. Then in Chapter 7, as the conclusion to the first part of the book, the doomsday scenario, championed by Will Hutton in his well-argued book *The Writing on the Wall – China and the West in the 21st Century* (2007, Little, Brown, London) is challenged by a more positive scenario that offers an alternative outlook, more favourable to China although equally uncomfortable for present OECD member states.

Population growth

At more than 1.3 billion, China's population is still growing at a comparable annual rate to the population of the EU15 ('Old Europe'), much less than the OECD countries, less than half that of the United Kingdom and the United States and, more significantly, also less than half of the population growth rate of India, the world's fastest-growing large country. As Table 1.1 shows, China's population was growing at 2.7 per cent annually in 1971, and had fallen to 1.3 per cent in 1979, the year when Deng Xiaoping's 'open door' policy was introduced. After rising again to almost 1.7 per cent in 1987, population growth fell back steadily to the 1 per cent level over the decade following and latterly down to 0.26 per cent in 2005.

China's 'one child' policy has had an effect on population growth, but, over a period of unprecedented growth and rising living standards for city-dwellers, working parent families have also been motivated to invest in the best education achievable for a single child rather than attempt to raise a larger family. Either way, population growth is now contained, but the widely held impression that it is almost static is seen to be false.

The domestic economy

Gross domestic product (GDP)

In 2004, on the basis of China's national economic census, the first since 2002, the National Bureau of Statistics (NBS) adjusted GDP growth estimates from 1993 onwards by an average of 0.5 per cent per annum upwards. These revised figures have been incorporated into OECD statistics and its time series of real GDP growth is reproduced in Table 1.2, which compares China's performance with the OECD, the euro area, the United States, India and the United Kingdom for the period 1979 to 2005.

OECD estimates for 2006 and forecasts for 2007 and 2008 are rather less than those of the composite index of *The Economist*, which have been adopted for those years in an extension of the table on the basis that China registered GDP growth of 11.1 per cent and 11.9 per cent respectively in the first two quarters of 2007.

Table 1.1 Comparative population growth rates 1971–2005

	Annual growth (%)						
Year	World	OECD	EU15	USA	UK	China	India
1971	–	1.33	–	1.27	0.49	2.7	2.27
1972	–	1.18	0.68	1.08	0.31	2.29	2.40
1973	–	1.12	0.59	0.96	0.29	2.33	2.35
1974	–	1.11	0.57	0.92	0.03	1.85	2.29
1975	1.87	1.06	0.47	0.99	(0.02)	1.72	2.24
1976	1.81	0.94	0.32	0.96	(0.02)	1.40	2.36
1977	1.75	0.93	0.35	1.01	(0.05)	1.34	2.14
1978	1.71	0.92	0.34	1.07	(0.02)	1.35	2.26
1979	1.70	0.94	0.36	1.11	0.11	1.33	2.21
1980	1.71	0.95	0.38	–	0.18	1.19	2.47
1981	1.72	0.89	0.33	0.99	0.05	1.39	2.26
1982	1.72	0.87	0.26	0.96	(0.12)	1.58	1.92
1983	1.73	0.83	0.20	0.92	0.04	1.33	1.21
1984	1.73	0.78	–	0.87	0.17	1.31	2.12
1985	1.74	0.78	0.21	0.89	0.26	1.43	2.21
1986	1.75	0.77	0.23	0.93	0.23	1.56	2.17
1987	1.75	0.76	–	0.9	0.21	1.67	2.12
1988	1.74	0.8	0.34	0.91	0.20	1.58	2.21
1989	1.69	0.84	0.42	0.95	0.28	1.51	2.16
1990	1.63	0.42	0.55	1.14	0.28	1.45	2.11
1991	1.57	2.55	–	1.35	0.35	1.30	2.07
1992	1.51	0.93	0.46	1.40	0.25	1.16	2.03
1993	1.46	0.84	–	1.33	0.23	1.15	1.87
1994	1.43	0.83	0.34	1.23	0.26	1.13	2.29
1995	1.41	0.91	0.30	1.20	0.28	1.06	1.56
1996	1.39	0.60	0.27	1.17	0.24	1.05	2.20
1997	1.36	0.75	0.27	1.21	0.26	1.01	1.94
1998	1.34	0.73	–	1.18	0.28	0.92	1.90
1999	1.31	0.70	–	1.16	0.36	0.82	1.97
2000	1.54	0.71	0.40	1.13	0.34	0.76	1.83
2001	1.28	0.74	0.46	1.03	0.39	0.70	1.80
2002	1.25	0.71	0.49	1.01	0.35	0.65	1.77
2003		1.43	0.69	0.46	1.00	0.39	0.60
2004		1.20	0.67	0.46	0.97	0.47	0.59
2005		–	0.69	0.56	0.94	0.26	0.59

Source: OECD Factbook 2007: Economic, Environmental and Social Statistics

Table 1.2   Comparative real GDP growth rates from 1979

	Annual growth (%)					
Year	OECD	Euro	US	UK	China	India
1979	3.8	3.8	3.2	2.7	7.6	(5.2)
1980	1.3	2.1	(0.2)	(2.1)	7.8	7.2
1981	2.0	0.6	2.5	(1.5)	5.3	6.0
1982	0.1	0.8	(2.0)	1.9	9.0	3.1
1983	2.7	1.6	4.5	3.5	10.9	7.7
1984	4.5	2.4	7.2	2.6	15.2	4.3
1985	3.7	2.4	4.1	3.5	13.5	4.5
1986	3.0	2.5	3.4	3.9	8.9	4.3
1987	3.4	2.4	3.3	4.5	11.6	3.8
1988	4.5	4.2	4.1	5	11.3	10.5
1989	3.8	4.0	3.5	2.2	4.1	6.7
1990	3.0	3.5	1.9	0.7	3.8	5.6
1991	1.4	2.7	(0.2)	(1.4)	9.2	1.3
1992	2.2	1.5	3.3	0.2	14.2	5.1
1993	1.3	(0.8)	2.7	2.3	13.9	5.9
1994	3.1	2.4	4.1	4.3	13.1	7.3
1995	2.5	2.4	2.5	2.9	10.9	7.3
1996	2.9	1.5	3.7	2.8	10.0	7.8
1997	3.5	2.5	4.5	3.0	9.3	4.8
1998	2.6	2.8	4.2	3.3	7.8	6.5
1999	3.3	3.0	4.5	3.0	7.6	6.1
2000	4.0	3.9	3.7	3.8	8.4	4.4
2001	1.2	1.9	0.8	2.4	8.3	5.8
2002	1.6	0.9	1.6	2.1	9.1	3.8
2003	2.0	0.8	2.5	2.7	10.0	8.5
2004	3.2	2.0	3.9	3.3	10.1	7.5
2005	2.6	1.4	3.2	1.9	10.2	8.4
2006*	n.a.	n.a.	3.3	2.8	11.1	9.2
2007#	n.a.	2.6	2.0	2.7	10.3	8.1
2008#	n.a.	2.2	2.7	2.5	9.3	7.6

Sources: 1979–2005 OECD Factbook 2007: Economic, Environmental and Social Statistics
2006* *Coface*
2007/2008# *The Economist,* 30 June 2007

This staggering performance is remarkable both for its relative consistency and resilience. Following the introduction of open-door policies, notably China's 1979 Joint Venture Law, the economy took off through the 1980s until the blip of 1989/90, reflecting international fallout from the Tiananmen Square incident. After picking up in 1991, the economy powered ahead, risked overheating in the 1993/94 period and suffered a modest setback only from the Asian financial crisis 1998/99. Once again in 2007, there is a present risk of overheating and some of the corrective action being taken by the government is described below.

In the absence of some unforeseen dislocation to the world economy causing a halt to its onward progress, China's GDP in absolute numbers will inevitably overtake that of the United States in the next three or four decades. On a purchasing power parity (PPP) basis, China's GDP, estimated at US$10.17 trillion for 2006, is already creeping up on the United States' at US$13.13 trillion.

However, in terms of prosperity, China has a long way to go. GDP per capita at PPP in China stands at US$7,700 compared with US$44,000 for US residents and US$31,800 for residents of the United Kingdom. Nevertheless, in PPP terms, China's GNP per head is US$6,600 against an emerging country average of US$5,540 and regional average of US$5,210 that includes Hong Kong at US$37,300.

GDP per capita and personal incomes vary widely from East to West within China. Per capita income in Shanghai was estimated in 2006 to be more than US$15,000 at PPP, reducing to only US$1,247 in the rural West where poverty is worst. Moreover, even in the wealthy coastal cities and provinces of the East there is a marked differential between the prosperous middle classes and workers who have migrated from the countryside. In 2005, 13 of China's 31 provinces and the four municipalities still generated around 70 per cent of total GDP.

Sector contributions to the Chinese economy

The statistical revisions of 2004 added US$300 billion to 2004 GDP, of which 93 per cent was derived from value-added for the tertiary industry, largely in the hands of private enterprise and previously under-reported. The post-revision contributions to GDP as value-added were estimated to be:

	Value-added (US$ billion)	% GDP
Primary industry	260	13.2
Secondary industry	977	45.2
Tertiary industry	806	40.7
Total	2,042	100.0

In the tertiary sector, new value-added products and services, notably in the ITC sector (such as computers, software, the internet, satellite transmission fixed line and mobile telephones), together with leisure products, transport and storage, wholesale and retail trading and real estate services, where the private sector holds the lion's share, contributed about 70 per cent of the additional value-added.

Sector analysis data is also available for the relative contributions of private and state-owned industry. Some of the production performance statistics available are collated in Table 1.3.

Some of the 2007 Quarter 1 numbers imply a diminution of activity but this impression is misleading since the period includes the Chinese New Year (Spring Festival) holiday when agriculture and industry come to a halt.

Table 1.3 Industrial sector performance data

Sectors	2003	2004	2005	2006	2007 (Q1)
GDP at current prices (yuan bn)	13,582	15,988	18,387	20,941	5,029
Agriculture, forestry & fishing	1,738	2,141	2,307	2,470	363
Industry	6,244	7,390	8,736	10,200	2,555
Services	5,600	6,456	7,343	8,270	2,110
Production indices					
Total industry (excl. construction) (SPPY=100)	116.7	115.9	115.4	116.3	110.1
Crude petroleum (Year 2000 = 100)	105.0	107.7	111.5	113.2	113.6
Coal (monthly ave. mn tonnes)	109.4	130.4	150.8	172.0	164.9
Crude steel (ma. mn tonnes)	18.3	23.3	29.5	35.3	38.1
Cement (ma. mn tonnes)	68.0	78.2	85.0	100.8	80.6
Electricity(ma. GWh '000)	152.6	176.2	199.8	229.1	231.7
Building construction (ma. m²mn)	32.9	35.4	40.7	44.2	20.6

The most recent report of industrial enterprise profits for the period January to June 2007 is summarized in Table 1.4.

Table 1.4 Chinese industrial enterprise profits – January to June 2007

	Profits (billion yuan)	Growth over 2006 (%)
State-owned and State holding	419.3	42.4
Collective enterprises	22.3	24.0
Joint-stock companies	484.5	39.5
Private enterprises	137.9	48.6
Hong Kong & Macao registered companies and FIEs	241.9	38.0

Source: http://www.stats.gov.cn/english
Note: Sectors with superior rates of profit growth (2007/2006) include: construction materials (70.1%); chemicals (69.4%); special equipment manufacturing (65.3%); transportation equipment (60.0%); power generation (60.0%)

The same National Bureau of Statistics of China (NBS) report for January to June 2007 also identifies changes in profits over the year for China's 39 industrial sectors. Strikingly, sectors where private and foreign-invested enterprises are strongly invested such as chemicals, special equipment manufacturing, transportation equipment (which includes the automotive industry) and power generation show profit improvements of 60 per cent or more. By contrast, sectors where state-owned enterprises (SOEs) are dominant, such as the steel industry, show minimal profit increases, while oil and gas exploration profits decline 18.3 per cent and oil and gas processing has managed to convert a previous year loss to better than break even.

These variations between the state-owned, local-government-owned and private sector enterprises show that the private sector and foreign-invested enterprises (FIEs) have gained an increasing share of economic activity in China and point to the relative inefficiency of state-owned enterprises. This disparity is encouraging but also emphasizes the major problem that the Chinese government continues to face in converting China from a command to an open-market market.

We shall see in later sections of this chapter that the low productivity of SOEs is reflected not only in the poor utilization of labour but also in the inefficient utilization of investment.

Inflation

Inflation has not been a problem for the Chinese government since the Millennium until the current year 2007. Indeed, there has been a reverse problem of stimulating domestic consumption to overtake foreign direct investment (FDI) and export demand as a main driver of the economy. In fact, in 2002, China suffered from disinflation for a time before modest consumer price inflation was restored in 2003 to a level of 3.2 per cent. In 2006, the 12-month inflation rate was 2.8 per cent but inflation in June 2007 stood at 4.4 per cent, nearly 2 per cent higher than a year earlier. The increase has been attributed by the NBS to buoyant consumption in the first half-year with retail sales of consumer goods increasing 15.4 per cent, the fastest rise for a decade, while food prices rose 7.5 per cent in the same period. In July, the inflation rate rose again to 5.6 per cent.

The government, already on alert against overheating, has taken a series of measures to dampen the economy so that full-year inflation for 2007 would not exceed the 2006 level. It has marked up interest rates on loans by 18 basis points from 6.84 per cent to 7.02 per cent and deposit rates from 3.33 per cent to 3. 6 per cent, a bigger increase of 67 basis points.

Employment

The labour force was estimated at 798 million in 2006, of which 45 per cent were said to be employed in agriculture, 24 per cent in industry and 31 per cent in services (Central Intelligence Agency, *The World Factbook 2007*, Washington, DC). Overall employment is growing at only a little more than 1 per cent annually.

According to *The Economist* (30 June 2007), unemployment in 2006 stood at 9.5 per cent but this is widely regarded as an underestimate. Taking into account migrant workers in transit from rural areas seeking urban employment, and the 'disguised' unemployment of those without jobs in SOE workforces, it has been suggested that unemployment at any one time could be as much as 170 million, representing 21.3 per cent of the labour force.

Herein lies the root cause of China's socio-economic problem, of which the Chinese government is fully aware. The Deputy Director of the China Development Research Council was quoted in *Financial Times China Supplement*, 8 November 2005, as suggesting that China needed to 'create about twenty million new jobs a year' for students leaving universities and school, those unemployed as a result of SOE rationalization and migrants from the countryside, implying an annual increase in jobs of more than 3 per cent. For this reason, China cannot let up on its job-creating export drive until more jobs are generated from rising consumer demand and accelerated investment in the lesser and underdeveloped regions. Only in this way can the inequality in standards of living be addressed.

Savings and consumption

In its summary report of the 2007 Second Quarter Survey on Urban Household Savings (to be found on www.pbc.gov.cn/english) the People's Bank of China reviews householders' expectations and the recent trend towards reduced savings ratios. Conducted between the two interest hikes of 18 March and 19 May, the survey found that there had been a cumulative fall of 15.7 per cent in the share of savings deposits in households' main financial assets from 2005. The proportion of households choosing to 'save more' had fallen over the three previous quarters to a 26.3 per cent, a record low in the past six years.

For the first time, the proportion of households choosing 'to invest more in stocks and mutual funds' overtook savings deposits as the preferred investment choice, rising to 40.2 per cent. In contrast, consumers' willingness to spend disposable income on large-value items had fallen from 28.2 per cent in the third quarter of 2006 to 19.5 per cent in the second quarter of 2007; in particular, willingness to buy large durable goods and automobiles.

Interest rates and monetary policy

Historically, the Chinese government was slow to use monetary controls implemented through the People's Bank of China to regulate the economy. The first hike in interest lending rates for nine years was introduced in October 2004 with a 27 basis point rise to 5.38 per cent. However, since April 2006 there have been seven increases to the benchmark one-year deposit and lending rates with the most recent increase of 67 basis points in August 2007, bringing the one-year savings rate to 3.33 per cent and the one-year lending rate to 7.02 per cent (a lesser increase of 18 basis points). The previous hike, introduced to 'help to adjust and stabilize inflation expectations' – a classic central bank governor's statement – was accompanied by a same-day announcement that tax on bank interest income would be cut from 20 per cent to 5 per cent from August 2007. The most recent increase was prompted by the further rise in inflation in July recorded above. The effect has been to narrow the gap between inflation and savers' returns and to halt the recent decline in bank savings. The measures may also keep some funds out of the overvalued stock market.

Since 2004, the People's Bank of China has also adopted the conventional monetary tool of squeezing credit by imposing higher reserve ratios on Chinese banks in the form of increased deposits with the central bank, in place of some of the government's more draconian 'stop-go' temporary bans on investment in selected industries, notably construction, previously favoured.

Investment

For 2006, gross fixed capital formation ran at 43 per cent of GDP, having increased steadily from a 30 per cent level before 1992. Over the three decades of reform, investment has been the main engine of China's economic growth.

Foreign direct investment (FDI) has played an important part in this progress, rising steadily year by year from 1992, with the exception of 1999 and 2000 when the Asian financial crisis impacted, to a total of US$79,127 million in 2005, ranking third behind the United States and the United Kingdom.

Although the share of FDI in the total level of domestic investment has been relatively insignificant in absolute terms, it has played a critical role in the development of the economy. Most FDI has taken the form of foreign-invested joint ventures and other foreign-invested enterprises (FIEs) that have deployed their funds efficiently, realizing above-average returns on capital employed and generating a large part of China's export of manufactures.

The SOE sector is heavily criticized for its poor output/capital investment ratio. Hitherto, SOEs have not been required to pay dividends and have been encouraged to plough back any cash surplus into capital investment often unnecessarily, without any prospect of an enhanced return, or into plants that are running well below capacity. Investment into property, and sometimes the stock market, has also taken place. Of course, those SOEs that have been converted to joint stock companies and floated on stock exchanges are obliged to pay dividends in order to meet stock market expectations. Now, in a recent announcement, the government has given notice of a requirement in a pilot programme for SOEs to pay dividends. Details, including the formula for quantifying dividends, have yet to be announced. It is hoped that this measure will help to raise the productive utilization of capital generally. The World Bank has estimated that a 4.8 per cent dividend payout from state industries in 2002 would have covered all the school fees for children that year. The State Council has said that funds raised now through dividends would be applied to support the welfare system and the funding of high-technology industries and industrial development.

Other macroeconomic indicators

In relation to the more pessimistic forecast for GDP growth in 2007–08 on which the Coface statistics are based, Table 1.5 records the five key ratios that illustrate the management of the Chinese economy.

Together these ratios present a picture of a robust economy under conservative management. Indeed, in its most recent commentary, the OECD suggests that there is scope for the Chinese government to run a higher public sector deficit to fund social programmes or support the rural economy outlined in the new Five Year Plan.

Table 1.5   Macroeconomic indicators (US$ billions)

Indicators	2002	2003	2004	2005	2006	2007(f)	2008(f)
Real GDP growth (%)	9.1	10.0	10.1	10.4	11.1	10.6	10.5
Public sector balance (% GDP)	(2.6)	(2.2)	(1.3)	(1.2)	(0.7)	(1.1)	(1.4)
Current account balance (% GDP)	2.4	2.8	3.6	7.2	9.5	10.8	10.6
Foreign debt (% GDP)	12.8	12.7	12.8	12.5	12.3	11.1	9.9
Debt service (% exports)	7.1	4.7	3.1	2.9	2.3	1.7	1.5
Foreign currency reserves (in months of imports)	9.9	10.4	11.7	13.3	14.8	15.9	16.3

Source: Coface (http://www.trading-safely.com) 23 July 2007
Note: (f) = forecast. Figures in brackets indicate deficits

The current account balance ratio and foreign currency reserves are discussed in Chapter 3 in relation to China's external economy.

2

China's foreign trade

Jonathan Reuvid

The most worrying aspect of China's rapid rise as the dominant global source of many manufactured goods is, of course, the impact that its dizzying export growth is having on the traditional manufacturing bases of the Western world. These concerns increase as the focus of Chinese manufacturing climbs the value-added ladder of more technically sophisticated products, leaving other emerging economies of South East Asia to take up an increasing share of global demand for cheaper consumer goods such as textiles and clothing.

Other concerns surround China's massive imports of raw materials, notably oil and base metals, needed to sustain its manufacturing and the long-term import and exploitation deals with oil-producing countries in politically sensitive regions to secure its long-term supplies.

A further concern is the overhang of US$1.2 trillion of China's foreign exchange reserves, a by-product of the trade surpluses over many years, which are held mainly in US dollars and the potential impact on the US economy of their redeployment.

The United States is the most strident critic of China's trade policies, followed to some degree by the EU in specific areas of merchandise and intellectual property (IP) issues. US demands on China relate mainly to claims of particular breaches in its obligations as a member of the World Trade Organization (WTO), infringements of IP and a more extensive revaluation of the Chinese currency. There is an underlying complaint that China is the primary cause of the US trade deficit.

However, not everything is quite as it seems at first sight and this chapter, like the previous chapter, is intended to provide readers with the data necessary to form their own judgements on these issues and how they might affect their involvements in China.

Foreign trade in merchandise and services

In Table 2.1, China's exports and imports of goods, the trade balance of goods and the services trade balance are compared with those of the OECD, the EU15, the United States and the United Kingdom for the 10-year period from 1996 to 2005. Data for 2006 is not yet available on a comparative basis.

Table 2.1   Exports, imports and balance of merchandise trade, and services trade balance

	OECD	EU15	US	UK	China
Exports of goods					
1996	3807.5	2075.2	622.8	258.9	151.0
1997	3958.4	2081.8	687.5	281.2	182.8
1998	3993.4	2154.5	680.4	273.4	183.8
1999	4103.7	2163.4	692.8	270.7	194.9
2000	4432.7	2210.9	780.3	282.9	249.2
2001	4290.7	2224.5	731.0	272.6	266.1
2002	4438.0	2360.5	693.2	280.6	325.6
2003	5110.9	2809.8	723.7	307.7	438.2
2004	6078.0	3339.8	817.9	348.2	593.3
2005	6640.9	3586.3	904.3	384.4	762.0
Imports of goods					
1996	3856.2	1968.4	817.6	287.6	138.8
1997	4001.4	1972.0	898.0	307.5	142.4
1998	4078.5	2078.1	944.4	320.3	139.5
1999	4327.7	2130.3	1059.2	323.8	165.7
2000	4816.4	2225.6	1258.1	339.4	225.1
2001	4633.7	2207.1	1180.1	338.0	243.6
2002	4771.8	2285.0	1202.3	359.4	295.2
2003	5522.7	2741.8	1305.1	393.5	412.8
2004	6590.3	3282.8	1525.3	461.3	561.2
2005	7380.0	3611.4	1732.3	515.8	660.0
Trade balance of goods					
1996	(48.7)	106.8	(194.8)	(28.7)	12.2
1997	(43.0)	109.8	(210.5)	(26.3)	40.4
1998	(85.1)	76.4	(264.0)	(46.9)	44.3
1999	(224.0)	33.1	(366.4)	(53.1)	29.2
2000	(383.7)	(14.7)	(477.8)	(56.5	24.1
2001	(343.0)	17.4	(449.1)	(65.4)	22.5
2002	(333.8)	75.5	(509.1)	(78.8	30.4

Table 2.1 *Continued*

	OECD	EU15	US	UK	China
2003	(411.8)	68.0	(581.4)	(85.8	25.4
2004	(512.3)	57.0	(707.4)	(113.1)	32.1
2005	(739.1)	(25.1)	(828.0)	(131.4)	102.0
Services trade balance					
1996	nk.	nk.	86.9	17.4	(2.0)
1997	82.1	nk.	90.2	23.1	(3.4)
1998	84.3	nk.	82.1	24.3	(2.8)
1999	63.6	(7.9)	82.7	22.1	(5.3)
2000	63.6	(5.8)	74.9	20.8	(5.6)
2001	53.1	(0.2)	64.4	20.8	(5.9)
2002	62.0	16.9	61.2	24.9	(6.8)
2003	76.4	24.9	52.4	31.3	(8.6)
2004	114.3	37.9	54.1	47.5	(9.7)
2005	140.4	44.4	66.0	42.6	(9.4)

Source: OECD Factbook 2007: Economic,Environmental and Social Statistics

Over the period, China's merchandise exports increased fivefold and imports 4.75 times. After 1996, the trade surplus varied between US$22 billion and US$44 billion until 2005 when it soared to US$102 billion. By comparison the OECD, United States and United Kingdom have run trade deficits throughout, rising continuously each year. Other than China, only the EU15 has maintained trade surpluses in 8 out of the 10 years. OECD exports increased 74 per cent (imports 91 per cent) and EU exports by 73 per cent (imports 83 per cent).

In contrast, US merchandise exports grew by only 45 per cent while imports more than doubled, highlighting the United States' foreign trade weakness. The United Kingdom performed rather better, at least up to 2003. However, over the 10-year period, exports grew by 48 per cent while imports increased by 79 per cent. The United States (US$66 billion) and the United Kingdom (U$42 billion) both run consistent substantial services trade surpluses against China's relatively tiny deficit, but the trade in services is not significant in the overall pattern. The question posed by Table 2.1 is the extent to which China's upsurge is the root cause of the much more substantial United States, United Kingdom and two trading bloc deficits.

In answering this question, account should be taken of assessments made in 2006 that over half Chinese exports are accounted for by foreign invested enterprises (FIEs) with possibly as much as 80 per cent in the high-tech sector. In its November 2006 working party report, the Organization for Economic Co-operation and Development (OECD) reported that FIE exports accounted for 58.2 per cent of the 2005 total exports and FIE imports represented 58.8 per cent. The report noted that the FIE proportion of manufactured exports is noticeably higher than in other newly industrialized Asian countries at a comparable point in their development. For example, in the mid-1970s, FIEs accounted for 25 per cent of Korean exports and the ratio in Chinese Taipei (Taiwan) was only 20 per cent.

Pattern of world merchandise

The balances and imbalances of trade between one selected country or region with another are explored in Table 2.2. The three years 2003 to 2005 are surveyed in terms of exports from each country or region of origin to the countries and regions with which they trade. For the purposes of the analysis only the export data from and to the United States, other North American territories, South and Central America, the EU25, Japan, China and Asian territories are included. China's trade with other territories is relatively minor.

The United States is confirmed as China's biggest export destination (2005: US$205 billion) followed by the EU25 (US$176 billion), Japan (US$102 billion) and other Asian countries (US$151 billion). However, the United States is a much greater market for other North American (ie, Canadian) goods (US$485 billion) and the EU25 (US$309 billion). Exports to the United States from Japan and the rest of Asia combined (US$333 billion) were 62 per cent more than exports from China.

In terms of US exports, its major destinations were the rest of North America (2005: US$332 billion), the EU25 (US$186 billion) and Asia other than Japan and China (US$126). Exports to Japan and China were only US$55 billion and US$42 billion. By tracking through the cross-trade for the same regions and countries we arrive at a simplified summary in Table 2.3 that identifies the major sources of their surpluses and deficits in terms of their exports and imports with key trading partners.

In light of this analysis, it now becomes clear that although China's growing trade surpluses with the United States and EU25 (further increased in 2006 and the current year) are of cause for great concern, the United States is running a chronic trade deficit with most of its trading partners. Indeed, the 'China issue' is proportionately more of a problem for the EU25 than the United States. In theory, without regard to other considerations, as good a case could be made for devaluation of the US dollar as for revaluation of the Chinese RMB yuan.

It seems likely that the focus of the US Congress on China and its pressure for revaluation of the currency is a reflection of its general discomfort with China, not just in terms of the economic imbalance but in broader political terms. China's growing military might and, above all, its non-democratic form of government are perceived as threats. Human rights and environmental issues also play their part in the general sense of unease.

Merchandise trade by product and partner

Analysis by product group is the next step towards forming a more complete picture of China's foreign trade with its key partners and Table 2.4 provides an overview of China's trade in the key sectors with the same key partners as in previous tables except for 'Other North America'. There is an additional column this time for 'The World'.

Table 2.2 Pattern of world merchandise trade – selected regions and countries (US$ billions)

Origin		US	Other NA	Destinations S&C Am.	EU25	Japan	China	Other Asia
US	2003	–	267.70	51.48	154.63	52.13	28.43	107.18
	2004	–	300.64	60.73	173.04	54.46	34.73	120.89
	2005	–	331.97	71.54	186.50	55.41	41.84	126.28
Other	2003	381.03	–	9.68	19.91	6.43	3.87	6.94
NA	2004	434.72	–	10.81	24.04	7.11	5.56	8.40
	2005	485.35	–	15.15	29.46	8.99	6.96	10.13
S&C	2003	65.11	10.51	49.55	42.78	5.97	10.12	11.70
Am.	2004	80.26	13.04	67.86	54.76	8.29	13.36	15.58
	2005	101.02	16.91	86.23	62.72	10.11	17.21	19.28
EU25	2003	253.73	41.75	39.47	2125.01	45.38	45.19	117.90
	2004	288.48	53.44	47.30	2523.06	52.58	58.61	143.33
	2005	308.82	50.97	54.34	2672.86	53.18	63.61	157.59
Japan	2003	117.54	11.06	6.46	75.62	–	72.86	146.72
	2004	128.69	13.81	8.14	89.21	–	92.91	181.93
	2005	135.96	15.76	9.35	87.61	–	98.36	190.29
China	2003	119.16	11.23	8.44	95.84	70.83	–	86.17
	2004	159.73	16.45	13.02	132.97	89.63	–	117.00
	2005	204.88	21.09	17.72	176.45	102.38	–	151.41
Other	2003	161.61	15.23	11.91	140.94	23.20	126.10	294.34
	2004	185.74	18.44	16.51	172.91	29.28	153.00	374.04
	2005	197.20	19.83	22.84	186.20	35.10	175.78	434.02

Source: www.wto.org

Of the three basic product divisions of agriculture, fuels and mining and manufactures, manufacturing predominates. In 2005, manufactures accounted for 65 per cent of China's US$660 billion imports and 71 per cent of exports against 18 per cent and only 4 per cent respectively by fuels and mining. Trade in agricultural imports and exports represented only 6 per cent of imports and less than 4 per cent of exports.

Agricultural products

In food, China's predominant export markets are Japan and other Asian countries. Exports to the United States and the EU25 are comparatively modest, but the US

Table 2.3 Merchandise trade balances – selected regions and countries

	US	Other NA	S&C Am.	EU25	Japan	China	Other Asia
Origin			**Destinations**				
US 2005	–	(153.38)	(29.48)	(122.32)	(80.55)	(163.04)	(70.92)
Other 2005	153.58	–	(1.76)	(21.51)	(6.77)	(14.13)	(9.70)
S&C 2005 Am.	29.48	1.76	–	8.38	0.76	(0.51)	(3.56)
EU25 2005	122.32	21.51	(8.38)	2672.86*	(24.43)	(102.84)	(28.61)
Japan 2005	80.55	6.77	(0.76)	24.43	–	(4.32)	165.19
China 2005	163.04	14.13	0.51	102.84	4.32	–	(24.37)
Other 2005 Asia	70.92	9.70	3.56	28.61	(165.19)	24.37	–

Source: http://www.wto.org
Note: * Represents the inter-trade between EU member states

market accounts for a similar level of food imports as other Asian countries; Central and South America are the major source. In the case of food raw materials, the dominant sources are other Asian countries and the United States in proportions of approximately 2:1. The United States is a net exporter to China in both categories.

Fuels and mining

China is a heavy importer of all kinds of fuel, metals and other mined products with imports in 2005 running at nearly four times exports. In fuels, Middle Eastern trading partners account for all but US$18.8 billion of China's US$63.6 billion imports. The only other significant source of imports is the rest of Asia, providing US$14.6 billion of imported fuels and taking US$13.4 billion of China's fuel exports.

Trade with the United States, the EU25 and Japan in non-ferrous metals is at a relatively low level. Imports from Central and South America are more substantial but the bulk of exports as well as imports are to and from other Asian territories.

Imports of ores and other base minerals at US$38.6 billion greatly exceeded exports at US$2.7 billion in 2005, with other Asian countries the dominant suppliers followed by Central and South America, accounting for 74 per cent of total imports.

Table 2.4 China's foreign trade by product group with selected regions and countries (2005) (US$ billions)

Product group	US		S & C America		EU25		Japan		All Asia		World	
	Exp	Imp	Exp	Imp	Exp	Imp	Exp	Imp	Exp	Imp	Exp	Imp
Agriculture	3.1	9.1	0.3	8.6	3.9	3.4	8.3	1.5	18.1	15.4	28.7	45.2
Food	2.5	4.4	0.3	7.3	2.8	1.2	7.4	0.3	16.1	5.8	24.6	21.5
Raw materials	0.6	4.7	–	1.3	1.1	2.2	0.8	1.2	2.0	9.6	4.1	23.7
Fuels & mining	2.4	3.3	0.9	12.3	3.2	3.2	5.0	4.9	22.7	44.2	31.3	119.6
Ores/oth' mins	0.3	2.6	–	8.4	0.9	1.7	0.4	1.6	1.3	20.2	2.7	38.6
Fuels	1.1	0.3	0.8	1.5	1.4	0.1	3.1	1.3	13.4	14.6	17.6	63.6
Non–ferrous	1.0	0.4	0.1	2.4	0.9	1.4	1.5	1.9	7.9	9.4	10.9	17.1
Manufactures	157.6	36.2	11.9	3.1	136.6	67.0	70.3	93.4	305.5	363.4	542.4	428.3
Iron & steel	1.7	0.3	16.5	3.6	1.9	3.5	1.5	6.4	13.0	7.7	19.3	6.3
Pharmaceut'ls	0.7	0.2	0.2	1.0	1.0	1.3	0.3	0.2	1.1	0.5	3.8	2.3
Oth' ch'cals	4.1	7.5	1.4	0.5	5.3	7.8	3.6	12.7	17.0	50.0	32.0	75.4
Semi–m'fctrs	14.7	1.8	1.4	0.7	11.8	4.6	5.4	4.2	20.7	13.7	57.8	22.2
EDP/off. eqpt.	24.9	2.2	0.6	–	30.3	1.6	10.2	4.2	46.8	31.4	110.7	35.8
Telecoms eqpt.	23.9	0.9	2.0	–	19.4	2.3	6.3	4.7	42.5	25.7	94.9	29.4
Integr'td circs.	1.8	4.6	0.1	0.9	1.7	3.4	1.8	12.8	16.4	85.2	20.4	95.3
Automotive	3.0	0.9	0.3	0.1	1.4	4.4	1.2	4.9	2.6	7.9	10.0	13.6
Oth' transport	3.9	3.8	1.0	0.1	4.8	4.2	1.4	1.3	7.5	1.9	20.2	10.5
Powerg'n. m/c	1.0	1.9	0.1	–	0.8	2.9	0.8	1.5	3.2	3.7	6.0	8.1
Non–elec. m/c	6.6	5.1	0.8	0.1	19.2	6.6	3.7	16.2	14.7	13.0	35.7	56.1
Electrical m/c	10.1	2.4	1.1	0.1	10.1	5.4	5.8	10.6	27.7	33.0	54.4	41.8
Textiles	4.9	0.4	1.7	–	4.7	0.8	2.9	3.2	20.5	14.2	41.1	15.5
Clothing	13.7	–	2.2	–	13.8	0.2	14.7	0.2	29.1	1.4	74.2	1.6
Pers. & h/h g'ds	16.5	0.1	1.2	–	8.2	0.4	3.9	0.2	10.1	0.8	43.0	1.3
Sc./control instr.	1.8	2.8	0.2	–	2.0	1.1	2.1	5.7	12.1	34.9	17.0	41.4
Misc. mans.	9.3	1.6	1.4	–	12.9	1.7	4.8	4.9	20.1	12.6	60.0	16.6
TOTAL*	163.2	48.7	17.7	24.2	143.8	73.6	84.0	100.4	347.3	424.3	761.9	660.0

Source: www.wto.org – selected data

Notes: *includes unspecified products; '–' denotes values less than US$50 million

Manufactures

In all but three of the specific industry sectors, chemicals other than pharmaceuticals, integrated circuits and scientific and control instruments, China is a net exporter to the United States. Overall, China is a net importer in these three categories together with, automotive products and power generation and non-electrical machinery.

Products where China is a net importer

Dealing first with the categories where China is a net importer and that are targets of opportunity for Western manufacturers, 89 per cent of integrated circuits are sourced from Asian countries other than Japan, notably Singapore and South Korea, which also provide 79 per cent of China's imports of scientific and control instruments.

Pharmaceuticals and chemicals

The trade in pharmaceuticals is relatively minor, with China a net exporter overall and to the United States, although not the EU25. However, both exports and imports of other chemicals are substantial, with China importing US$75.4 billion and exporting US$32 billion in 2005. Two-thirds of imports were drawn from other Asian countries with Japan, providing a further US$12.7 billion and the EU and the United States almost all of the remainder in equal proportions.

Automotive products

Automotive products are imported predominantly from Japan, the EU25 and other Asian countries totalling US$13.6 billion. Exports are now climbing but in 2005 were still only US$10 billion. In other transport products, China maintains a small surplus with both the EU25 and Japan, as well as the United States, to which it is already a net exporter of automotive products.

Power-generating machinery

China's imports of power-generating machinery at US$8.1 billion exceeded exports by more than a third, with the other Asian territories, the EU25, the United States and Japan as suppliers in descending order.

Non-electrical machinery

Non-electrical machinery is another substantial category in China's foreign trade, both in terms of exports (US$35.7 billion) and imports (US$56.1 billion). Once again, the bulk of imports (US$29.2 billion) are sourced from Japan and other Asian countries, with the EU25 supplying rather more than the United States. In exports, the EU25 is China's largest export territory (US$19.2 billion) followed by the other Asian countries (US$14.7 billion). The United States is a net importer of non-electrical machinery from China as are the other Asian territories, but Japan exports less than a quarter in value of its export to China.

Electrical and electronic machinery

By contrast, China is a net exporter of electrical and electronic machinery with sales of US$54.4 billion against US$42.8 billion. Almost all imported equipment is sourced from Asia with more than three-quarters coming from countries other than Japan. China's main export markets are the other Asian countries (nearly 50 per cent) with most of the remainder sourced equally from the United States and EU25.

Semi-manufactures

China's exports of semi-manufactured goods at US$57.8 billion were over two-and-a-half times the value of its imports. The other Asian countries import one-and-a-half times the value of their exports of semi-manufactures from China emphasizing the value-added and re-export relationship with its trading partners. The high export–import ratio of China's trade in semi-manufactures to the EU25 and even higher ratio of more than 8:1 to the United States are also a reflection of those countries' engagements in joint ventures and processing agreements with Chinese suppliers.

Textiles and clothing

And so to the product sectors where Chinese products dominate world markets and are the principal bones of trade contention with the United States and the EU. In textiles, Chinese exports exceed imports more than two-and-a-half times, with almost 50 per cent going to other Asian countries, from where some 90 per cent of imported textiles are sourced. The two other major export markets in 2005 were the United States and the EU25, each accounting for more than 11 per cent of sales from China. However, China's global exports of textiles at US$41.1 billion are far outpaced by sales of clothing at US$74.2 billion. Although around 18 per cent each of clothing exports are sold into the United States and EU markets, a lion's share of 39 per cent is sold into other Asian countries and almost 20 per cent to Japan. Imports of clothing from the United States or the EU25 are negligible and from elsewhere are slight.

Personal and household goods

Similarly, Chinese exports of personal and household goods, which include the contentious sub-sector of toys, at US$43 billion dwarfed imports by 33:1 in 2005. Exports to the United States at US$16.5 billion dwarfed imports by more than 16 times. Sales to the EU25 were less than half those to the United States with an export–import ratio of more than 20. Exports to Japan were less than half again of sales to the EU25 and sales to other Asian countries combined amounted to US$10.1 billion against exports to the EU25 of US$8.2 billion.

Electronic data processing (EDP) and office equipment, telecoms equipment and integrated circuits

Finally, there are the three 'hi-tech' product sectors where China has climbed the value-added ladder, covering data processing and office equipment, personal computers, telecoms equipment, including mobile telephone handsets, and integrated printed circuits. Exports in these three categories together amounted to US$226 billion in 2005 compared with US$158.3 billion in textiles, clothing and personal and household goods combined.

In the two major hi-tech categories of EDP and office equipment, and telecoms equipment, China's largest export market are the other Asian countries, accounting for 42 per cent and 45 per cent respectively. Exports to the United States of the two categories totalled US$48.8 billion in 2005 compared with US$35.1 billion in textiles, clothing and personal and household goods; together they accounted for 24 per cent of total exports.

Similarly, exports of the two categories to the EU25 totalled US$49.7 billion – rather more than the United States in EDP and office equipment and rather less in telecoms equipment. Not surprisingly, exports to Japan are significantly less in both categories, which together accounted for only 8 per cent of China's exports. Overall, exports in these two categories accounted for 27 per cent of all China's exports.

As the counterpart to its strong export performance in these product groups, China was also a heavy importer (US$65.2 billion in 2005) of which US$57.1 billion are sourced from other Asian territories excluding Japan, of which much represents the purchase of components for use in exported products.

Integrated circuits are in a different sub-category where China imports US$95.3 billion (89 per cent from other Asian countries including Japan and South Korea) against only US$20.4 billion of exports. This is a product category where hitherto China lacks the most cost-effective technology and its low labour costs yield no advantage.

Table 2.5 Macroeconomic indicators of foreign trade (US$ billions)

Indicators	2002	2003	2004	2005	2006	2007(f)	2008(f)
Exports	325.7	438.3	593.4	762.5	969.6	1214.0	1460.0
Imports	281.5	393.6	534.4	628.3	753.6	907.0	1098.0
Trade balance	44.2	44.7	59.0	134.2	216.0	307.0	362.0
Current account balance	35.4	45.9	68.7	160.8	250.0	350.0	415.0
Current account balance (% GDP)	2.4	2.8	3.6	7.2	9.5	10.8	10.6
Foreign currency reserves (in months of imports)	9.9	10.4	11.7	13.3	14.8	15.9	16.3

Source: Coface (http://www.trading-safely.com) 23 July 2007
Note: (f) = forecast

Current outlook

The overall outlook for 2007 and 2008 based on Coface forecasts is summarized in Table 2.5.

Exports for the year 2007 are expected to grow by 25.2 per cent against import growth of 20 per cent and in 2008 by a further 20 per cent against a 21 per cent growth in imports. However, since the end of July, export forecasts for the third and final quarters of 2007 and the first half of 2008 may have shaded slightly against expectations that US economic growth may grind to a halt temporarily with knock-on effects in 2008 for the EU25. Nevertheless, it is unlikely that China's trade surplus will retreat from the US$216 billion high registered for 2006.

In terms of the ratio of the trade balance to GDP and based on Coface GDP predictions (see Table 2.5) and its July 2007 forecasts, the current account balance could rise to 10.8 per cent in 2007 and remain at that level through 2008. As also noted in Table 2.5, foreign currency reserves represented 14.8 months of imports at the end of 2006 and could climb above 16 by the end of 2008.

3

Inward and outward investment

Jonathan Reuvid

Until four or five years ago, inward investment to China comprised only of foreign direct investment (FDI). However, there is now an increasing element of portfolio investment as Western investors purchase shares in the initial public offerings (IPOs) and further share issues of the major state-owned enterprises (SOEs) and smaller privately owned Chinese companies that have floated on the Hong Kong, New York and London Stock Exchanges. These companies are usually floated at the same time (or previously) on one of the two domestic Chinese stock exchanges (Shanghai more than Shenzhen) with an issue of 'A' shares that can only be purchased by Chinese residents or registered Chinese companies. However, the restriction on foreign ownership of 'A' shares is expected to be lifted soon so that there will be a further inflow of foreign funds through this channel.

Over the same period, Chinese outward investment has also blossomed in three directions, as China flexes its muscles in deploying its US$1.3 trillion of foreign exchange reserves:

■ investment in oil and gas exploration, production and pipelines elsewhere in Asia, the Middle East and Africa;
■ the acquisition of Western manufacturing enterprises (eg, the personal computer business of IBM in the United States and MG Rover in the United Kingdom);

■ minority investments in financial services providers (eg, Blackstone and Barclays Bank).

This chapter offers a summary of both categories of inward investment and all three categories of outward investment.

Inward investment

Foreign direct investment

Since 1979, China's FDI soared, with regular annual increments, from barely US$57 million in 1980 to US$40,715 million in 2000 when the accumulated stock of FDI exceeded US$193 million.

The continuing progress of China's FDI from 2000 to 2005 is charted in Table 3.1 and compared with the FDI of selected trading partners.

Table 3.1 Foreign direct investment (FDI); China vs selected OECD countries (2000 to 2005)

	US	Japan	UK	Germany	France	Italy	China
2001	159,481	6,241	52,623	26,414	50,477	14,871	46,878
2002	74,452	9,239	24,029	53,520	49,035	14,545	52,743
2003	53,146	6,324	17,778	29,202	42,498	16,415	53,505
2004	122,401	7,816	56,214	(15,113)	31,371	16,815	60,630
2005	99,443	2,775	164,530	32,663	63,576	19,971	72,406

Source: http://stats.unctad.org/FDI

Except for 2003, the United States reaped more FDI than China with its share of world FDI fluctuating between 19.2 per cent (2001) and 9.5 per cent (2003). Over the same period China's share of world FDI, except for 2001 when it sank to 5.6 per cent, remained relatively constant between 7.9 and 9.6 per cent.

However, the United States and China are far from being the dominant destinations for FDI among the countries included in Table 3.1. The United Kingdom, France and Germany have all maintained levels of FDI comparable with China. The United Kingdom received more FDI than China in 2001, and again in 2005 when the United Kingdom gained windfall investment resulting from the consolidation of the assets of the two listed Shell oil companies into the Netherlands-based corporation. France's FDI surpassed that of China in 2001 as did Germany's FDI the following year.

For decades Japan has maintained a policy of protecting its major industries from foreign investment and this is reflected in its otherwise surprisingly low levels of

FDI. Nor is Italy in the same league as a destination for FDI compared with its three major population fellow Western European members of the EU. Poland, the largest of the new entrants to the EU in 2004 received US$12,873 million that year, but FDI declined to US$7,724 in 2005.

Within the United Nations' classification of 'developing countries', China has maintained an impressive share of total FDI received by this category, from 22 to 23 per cent between 2001 and 2005. India, as China's upcoming rival in economic development is receiving an increased inflow of FDI, which reached US$6,598 in 2005, the level that China achieved in 1992 when it became a leading global destination for direct investment.

China has not yet published statistics for FDI in 2006, but a reduction of 2.3 per cent in the first four months of 2007 over 2006 has been reported. Some of this fall may be the result of a surge of FDI this year into India, which is perceived, particularly by UK and US companies, as having comparable growth opportunities in a less difficult investment environment. With written and spoken English as the business language and a legal framework and system that is based on UK practice, the attractions of doing business in India are clear. Whether or not doing business in India is ultimately easier or less risky than China is debatable (see Roger Shashoua, 2007, *Dancing with the Bear*, GMB Publishing, London).

Another factor in play, which may impact FDI from January 2008 is the recent change in the corporate tax regime announced to take effect from that date. Hitherto, companies investing in China have enjoyed generous tax holidays and reduced levels of corporation tax, particularly in the designated coastal development zones. Now, as a part of China's WTO obligations, those concessions are withdrawn and a standard 25 per cent of corporation tax will be applied to the profits of all companies registered in China, whether domestically or foreign-owned. A new set of tax incentives is due for announcement relating to investment in specific hi-tech industries and R&D. Nevertheless, China enjoys a burgeoning inward flow of venture capital investment for start-ups, set to exceed US$1.2 billion in 2007 and growing at 50 to 60 per cent a year.

Introducing the tax changes on 8 March 2007, Finance Minister Jin Renqing reported that by the end of 2006, a total of 594,000 foreign-funded enterprises had been approved since the launch of China's special economic zones (SEZs) in 1980 with a value of US$691.9 billion.

Portfolio investment

The flotation and listing of Chinese companies, in which the state is the majority shareholder on overseas stock exchanges, is a 21st-century phenomenon and has provided a powerful new dimension to foreign investment in China. It has been argued that, for the Chinese government, the raising of funds in this way is primarily a device for relieving the state of the burden of continuing to finance its inefficient SOEs and to underpin the non-performing loans (NPLs) of its big four banks, mainly to the same unprofitable SOEs. There may be some force to this argument in respect of the shares listed on the Shanghai Stock Exchange to attract resident Chinese investors but hardly

Table 3.2 Leading Chinese company shares listed on the Hong Kong Stock Exchange

Company	Share price (HK$)	Price/ Earning Ratio	No. shares (000)	Market Capitalization HK$ '000
Bank of China	(HK)* 785,398	17.34	13.1	45,294
China Life Insurance*	27.60	36.9	317,213	8,755,079
China Mobile*	81.00	21.3	73,054	5,917,374
China Telecom	3.80	11.2	251,369	955,202
China Unicom*	11.40	33.1	18,337	209,042
CITIC Pacific	31.45	8.3	18,005	566,257
CNOOC*	7.53	10.4	317,784	2,392,913
COSCO Pacific	16.94	16.6	16,879	285,930
PetroChina	9.83	12.4	314,044	308,075
Sino Land	15.10	10.1	11,031	166,588
Sinopec	6.93	11.2	303,367	1,409,333
Total market value				HK$21,6551,821

Source: Financial Times closing prices: 17 August 2007
Notes: * Denotes shares listed in the Global FT500; exchange rate US$1=HK$7.8159

on the shares that have undergone the full process of an IPO on international stock exchanges.

It is impossible to identify the 'back door' investments made on international stock exchanges by resident Chinese investors, but the calculation in Table 3.2 of the market capitalization of the 11 largest China companies with primary listings on the Hong Kong Stock Exchange gives a clear indication of the scale of the overall value accruing.

Together, the shares in issue of these companies had a market value of HK$21.7 billion (US$2.7 billion) at the close on 17 August 2007. Six of these 11 companies are included in the *Financial Times* Global FT500 index. Not included in Table 3.2 is the Industrial and Commercial Bank of China (ICBC), China's largest bank, whose primary listing is in Shanghai. The ICBC became the world's largest ever IPO when the issue was completed in October 2006, raising US$5.1 billion in Shanghai and US$14 billion in Hong Kong. By the end of 2006, when its market capitalization reached US$25.1 billion, its market value stood ahead of Bank of America, albeit on a much higher price–earnings ratio. The combined share valuations of these 12 Chinese companies alone make a striking comparison with the stock of China's FDI at 2005 year-end of US$318 billion.

Another significant element in portfolio investment is the value of the funds raised by much smaller Chinese companies through IPOs in Hong Kong and on the

Alternative Investment Market (AIM) in London. Of the 1,637 companies listed on AIM, more than 60 are Chinese.

Outward investment

China's outward direct investment up to 2000 was meagre but started to grow in 2001 to US$2.2 billion and US$2.5 billion the following year. Having fallen back in 2003/04, outward FDI reached US$11.3 billion in 2005. By comparison, US outward FDI fell to US$9.1 billion in 2005 from US$244.1 billion in 2004, while UK outward investment rose each year since 2002 to US$101.1 billion in 2005. Chinese start-ups in the United Kingdom have been taking place for some years and in 2006, there were 62 new Chinese-owned companies registered out of a total of 1,431 new inward corporate investments.

Investment in energy resources

China sources from 80 to 90 per cent of its energy needs through domestic supplies from its coal reserves. In 2005, electricity consumption and production amounted to 2.5 trillion kWh, while oil consumption, of which 3,181 million tonnes/day were imported, was 6,534 million bbl/day. This dependence on coal is of major concern to the Chinese government and has been a key factor in the evolution of China's outward investment strategy. It is also of growing global concern to environmentalists.

The West–East pipelines

The US$18 billion gas pipeline venture between China National Offshore Oil Corporation (CNOOC) and Russia forms a basis for China's economic development policy for the impoverished Western provinces. Shanghai has been receiving supplies of gas through this pipeline since January 2004. A new 3,000-km oil pipeline from Kazakhstan is under development to transport crude oil from there, previously supplied by rail and road.

The Middle East

Until 2005, China had only one major overseas gas project with exploration rights over the Rub al Khali Basin of Saudi Arabia. Today China purchases liquefied natural gas (LNG) from Iran, which was named in January 2007 as the largest supplier of crude oil to China. While Angola is the second largest supplier of crude oil to China, Saudi Arabia now ranks third. In March 2007, the National Development & Reform Commission, China's central planning agency, listed nine markets for further oil and gas investment, of which five (Kuwait, Qatar, Oman, Morocco and Libya) are Arab League member states.

Africa

In the 18 months from January 2006 to June 2007, CNOOC and its sister company Sinopec made deep incursions into Africa. The development of oil sources has been, and continues to be, an integral part of China's trade drive in Africa, which includes economic aid in the form of soft loans for infrastructure projects repayable in oil exports.

In January 2006, CNOOC bought a US$2.3 billion stake in a Nigerian oil and gas field. This investment was followed in April by a further US$5.4 billion deal for drilling licences in Nigeria. In the same month, CNOOC signed a Kenyan offshore exploration deal and a Chinese and Japanese consortium were awarded an oil-related US$7 billion contract by Algeria to build a highway from Tunisia to Morocco. In May, Sinopec paid more than US$1.4 billion for a 40 per cent stake in an Angolan offshore block.

In 2006, China also launched its own aid offensive in Africa, which attracted considerable criticism from G-8 members because these agreements were without the political provisos and human rights undertakings on which Western aid to Africa is normally conditional. For the same reasons, these agreements were widely acceptable to the receiving countries. In June, China granted Senegal debt relief of US$20 million with pledges to build Africa's largest theatre for US$35 million. In November, at a China-African conference hosted in Beijing, China and the heads of government of African nations attending signed 16 agreements worth US$1.9 billion following pledges of US$5 billion of loans and credits to be doubled by 2009. In March 2007, China confirmed the true nature of its economic assistance by announcing that its US$5 billion China-Africa Development Fund will be used exclusively to support Chinese entrepreneurs and their projects on the continent. The long-term implications of China's growing investment and strong trade position in Africa are discussed in Chapter 7.

China's trade with Africa soared by 40 per cent in 2006 to US$55 billion, with imports and exports almost evenly balanced. About 60 per cent of Sudan's oil output is currently exported to China and there is particular pressure on China to use its trade leverage to help solve the genocidal tragedy in Darfur.

Chinese acquisitions of foreign companies

The deployment of a significant part of China's dollar reserves on the acquisition of significant foreign companies and other business assets in the West has been on the cards for some time. Successful acquisitions in Asia were made before 2004 and many smaller low-profile acquisitions had been made in the United States. The attempt in 2004 to acquire the domestic US petroleum company UNOCAL was aborted following unfavourable reaction on Capitol Hill. CNOOC pledged to sell off those assets relating to the US domestic market. The sticking point in Congress was that the acquirer, although listed, was majority-owned by the Chinese government, and UNOCAL was classified as a 'strategic asset'. In the face of an overwhelming vote against, CNOOC wisely withdrew.

Nevertheless, 2004 had ended on a high note with the outright sale by IBM of its global personal computer (PC) business to Lenovo, China's largest computer supplier, for US$1.65 billion. The deal multiplied Lenovo's sales fourfold and allowed it the use of the IBM's brand and its 'Think' trademark for five years. This time, any US opposition was muted. The enlarged company, listed in Hong Kong, has prospered and is headquartered in New York. The new range of Lenovo laptops are widely acclaimed technically and for their quality.

Another more controversial acquisition came in 2005 when Nanjing Automobile Company purchased the assets of the failed MG Rover business from the Receiver, while its rival, Shanghai Automotive Industry Corporation (SAIC), acquired the Rover brand from the former MG Rover owner, BMW. However, there was no political opposition in the United Kingdom's open investment environment although the equipment and machinery for all but the ageing MG sports car was transported to Nanjing in an impressive logistical exercise. The first 'Rowa' cars, effectively the old Rover 75 model, rolled off the Nanjing production line in 2007. The inside story of that achievement is related in Part 4.

The further acquisition by Chinese companies in the automotive and other sectors of substantial US and European businesses is likely in the next few years. However, continuing protectionist reactions are unlikely to abate, at least until the state dilutes its majority shareholdings in the listed companies that may be bidding. Meanwhile, some cash-rich Chinese companies, like China Mobile, have been focusing their overseas acquisition activity on other emerging markets such as Pakistan where China Mobile purchased an 89 per cent holding in Paktel, the telecommunications company, for US$284 million.

Minority investments in financial services providers

The first seven months of 2007 have seen important developments in China's strategy for investment overseas in the financial services sector. At the beginning of the year, China established a new sovereign investment agency, China Development Bank (CDB), subsequently capitalized in June with an issue of US$200 billion in bonds. Headed by a former vice-minister of finance, and ahead of the bond issue, the agency spent US$3 billion buying a 9.9 per cent stake in the IPO of Blackstone, the US private equity group. The Chinese shareholding was approved by the US Treasury Department, which affirmed that the deal did not merit a national security investigation. Approval was also helped by the fact that the deal did not breach the 10 per cent change of ownership threshold and the investor will not be exercising its voting rights.

In July, CDB combined with Temasek, Singapore's sovereign investment agency, to support the Barclays Bank revised bid for ABN AMRO by investing together up to €13.4 billion in new shares. CDB has taken a €2.2 billion initially with a further €7.6 billion to come if the ABN AMRO acquisition is completed. The investment represents the biggest investment to date by a Chinese company outside its own country.

The two deals are in counterpoint to the heavy minority stake investments made previously by US, British and other European banks in Chinese banks at the time of their flotation and more recently in China's financial services sector. Undoubtedly, they are the harbinger for further outward investment in the banking and financial services sector.

The long-term implications of these various elements of China's outward investment for the global economy are discussed in Chapter 7.

4

China and the WTO

Jonathan Reuvid

Overview

After 15 years of negotiation China joined the World Trade Organization (WTO) in December 2001, becoming the fifteenth country to accede to the WTO following its formation in 1995 as successor to the General Agreement on Tariffs and Trade of 1947 (GATT 47). From China's point of view, WTO membership has been an almost unqualified success. Since entry, the dramatic pace of import and export growth has accelerated, as illustrated in Chapter 2, and China is one of the few countries that has clearly benefited, in practice, from the lifting of formal and tariff and quota barriers. However, the impact of China on its trading partners post-WTO entry has been both uncomfortable and contentious as its dominance of the global low-cost manufacturing market has evolved. Trade imbalances were exacerbated by the ending in 2005 of the transition period of the Multi-Fibre Arrangement (MFA), a global quota system for textiles and garments that released a further flood of Chinese exports on North American and European markets. There followed a flush of much publicized emergency 'safeguard' quotas by the United States and EU to stem the tide but their scale and duration are limited, expiring for the most part in 2008.

The economic backlash against China's rising exports has taken the form until recently of 'anti-dumping' measures such as emergency import tariffs applied when goods from overseas are apparently being subsidized to win greater shares of world markets. These claims are generally rejected by the Chinese government taking action through the well-established WTO dispute procedures. They are rigorous and command respect but their execution is very slow so that anti-dumping actions provide an effective and troublesome breakwater against the tide. Meanwhile, China's efforts to gain 'market economy' status (MES) have been repeatedly rebuffed on the grounds of the state's continuing pervasive role in the economy. MES would impose on trading partners seeking to prove cases of dumping goods in their markets an obligation to compare prices with prices within China itself. Instead, they can compare China's export prices with carefully selected comparators from a similar economy, which almost always produces data to back the dumping allegation.

The odium that China attracts for its export surpluses with the United States and, to a lesser extent the EU, is not entirely fairly earned to the extent that China is the end of an Asian assembly line that supplies Chinese factories with semi-manufactures that are re-exported as finished goods to foreign markets, referred to by the OECD as 'triangular trade'(see again Table 2.4). In 2005, low value-added processing and assembly operations are calculated to have contributed 55 per cent of China's total exports of US\$762 billion, mainly from foreign-funded enterprises. The growing proportion of high-tech goods in the total export mix, reported by the China Council for the Promotion of International Trade (CCPIT) to have reached 30 per cent, also suggests that other developing Asian countries, such as Bangladesh for knitted garments, may take over from China as the primary source for imports of low-value consumer goods into North America and Europe as China marches up the value chain. That progression may not prevent the casting of China politically as the scapegoat in world trade imbalances.

Politically, accession to the WTO has had a positive influence on the reform of domestic institutions and policies. Compliance with WTO obligations has caused China to adopt disciplines that promote sound economic and regulatory policies and has supported the actions of its domestic reformers.

China's performance of its WTO obligations

Like all WTO entrants, China made commitments on entry to reduce or remove 'border measures' such as import tariffs and quotas. It also made commitments to reduce or eliminate anti-competitive measures in specific industries. Progress in all these areas was discussed in a November 2006 report of the working party of the Trade Committee of the Organization for Economic Co-operation and Development (OECD). The findings of the working party are summarized in this chapter. The report estimates that implementation by China of its commitments in goods and services sectors has increased its real income by almost 2 per cent. Eventual complete liberalization could yield a 3 per cent increase in real income. According to the OECD report, much of these gains are attributable to the improved efficiency with which China has started to use its resources.

Trade performance

Agricultural products

By the end of 2006, China's average bound tariff level for agricultural goods had fallen to 15.8 per cent against the commitment to an eventual reduction to 15 per cent.

As predicted, the products for which bound tariff levels were highest are cereals and their preparations at 23.7 per cent. Bound tariffs in the EU on agricultural products averaged 15.4 per cent and in the United States the average was 5.3 per cent.

Of course, import tariffs are not the only tools available to governments to disadvantage foreign competitors. On an international comparison, the level of direct support for domestic growers measured as a percentage of the value of gross farm receipts had fallen to 8.4 per cent in China by 2005 against 16 per cent in the case of the United States, 32.4 per cent for the EU and an OECD average of 28.9 per cent. In this respect, at least, China cannot be branded a protectionist in its treatment of agricultural products.

Industrial goods

China committed to a reduction in the average bound tariff level to 8.9 per cent, ranging from 0 to 47 per cent with the highest rates applied to photographic film, automobiles and related products. By end-2006 the average bound rate was 9.1 per cent, against a 3.9 per cent average for the EU and 3.3 per cent for the United States.

Services

Commitments on trade services resulting from WTO negotiations are focused on the opening up of market access to a broad range of service sectors through the elimination of existing limitations. By the beginning of 2004 all foreign services suppliers were permitted to engage in the retailing of all products and this led to the further expansion of retail giants such as Wal-Mart and Carrefour that were already established in China and the entry of other international players such as Tesco in groceries and B&Q in DIY. All firms have the right to import and export all goods except those that are still subject to state monopolies, such as fertilizers and oil.

By the end of 2006, foreign firms were allowed to distribute almost all goods throughout China. Foreign financial institutions in China were permitted to provide services in foreign currency business without client restrictions upon WTO accession; local currency services to Chinese clients by 2004, and in 2007 services to all Chinese clients.

Competition

As a result of the liberalization of service sectors since WTO access, critical sectors of the Chinese economy are now facing up to greatly increased competition. Telecoms, banking and insurance have been particularly affected. Many restrictions on foreign entry and ownership, as well as most forms of discrimination against foreign firms have been abandoned and China has promised to guarantee full access eventually through transparent and automatic licensing procedures. Only when the liberalization of the remaining sectors according to the schedule of the WTO agreement has been enacted will the full impact of competition in China be felt.

The current status of restrictions removed and remaining in the key sectors identified above is, as follows:

Telecoms

Most geographical restrictions were removed in 2002 and 2003. Foreign investment limits on the proportion of registered capital were raised to 49 per cent in value-added telecommunications (formerly 30 per cent) and in mobile voice and data (previously 25 per cent). Majority foreign ownership will not be allowed. Restrictions related to leased line or network provision and connections and private networks to the public switched telephone network (PSTN) remain. Nor is there any commitment to allow cross-border delivery of telecom services.

Banking

The limits on foreign equity participation coupled with limitations on the amount of foreign exchange funding that foreign banks can acquire from overseas through the imposition of a quota system induce a high level of restrictiveness. The percentage that an individual foreign financial institution can invest in the shares of a China-funded financial institution may not exceed 20 per cent. In practice, the maximum percentage of the sum of several financial institutions' investments in the shares of a China-funded financial institution is limited to 25 per cent.

In terms of its WTO commitments, the banking sector has been largely liberalized since 2001. Geographic limitations on the scope of business have been phased out. Local currency (renminbi) business with Chinese enterprises and individuals is now permitted. Since September 2004, new rules issued by the China Banking Regulatory Commission (CBRC) have lowered the market entry thresholds for foreign banks by repealing requirements such as the previous restriction on each foreign bank not to open more than one branch within one year or the ban on any foreign-funded financial institution to re-apply within one year of an application being rejected. Operating capital requirements for the Chinese branches of foreign-owned banks to provide local currency services to Chinese enterprises and individuals have been relaxed. Minimum capital requirements for wholly foreign-owned and Sino–foreign joint venture banks have also been lowered.

Insurance

The principal outstanding restriction on the insurance sector is that foreign equity holdings in life assurance joint ventures are restricted to 50 per cent and in non-life joint ventures to 51 per cent. The former restrictions on foreign life and non-life insurance companies to establish business in only five cities and restrictions on the scope of business have been lifted. As in banking, insurance licences are to be awarded solely on the basis of prudential regulations.

Distribution

Foreign majority ownership of Chinese-registered companies in the distribution sector is now permitted and there are no geographic or quantitative restrictions. The only restrictions remaining relate to cross-border trade and the delivery of a few products.

China has also committed to open permits for foreign-invested enterprises (FIEs) to distribute their products manufactured in China and to provide subordinate services. Foreign services suppliers are also authorized to provide the full range of related subordinate services, including after-sales services, for the products they distribute.

Compliance concerns

The WTO established a Transitional Review Mechanism (TRM) under Article 18 to monitor China's compliance with its Protocol of Accession on an annual basis for eight years with a final review in the tenth year. So far, the OECD report concludes, 'the TRM process has not proved effective as a monitoring and compliance enforcement tool as was envisioned in the protocol'. However, WTO members through the TRM process have identified problems in some areas, including industrial assistance programmes, standards, technical regulations and other non-tariff areas.

The WTO also completed its first Trade Policy Review of China in April 2006. Two particular areas of concern have been identified: specifically, market access for services and the enforcement of intellectual property rights (IPRs). The first concern is that China retains industrial policies that appear to limit market access by non-Chinese-origin goods or to provide significant government resources to support Chinese production and exports. This criticism, echoed by the 2006 United States Trade Representative (USTR) review, is directed particularly at preferences for SOEs, including state-owned banks. 'The promulgation of standards and other technical regulations that appear to favour locally produced products, and discriminatory enforcement of standards against non-Chinese products' are also highlighted in the USTR report.

Contrary to the favourable overall progress reported above in the services sector, the USTR report, which dates from the second half of 2006, also draws attention to barriers in the services sector in which Chinese regulators continue to frustrate efforts of foreign suppliers through the use of opaque regulatory processes, onerous licensing provisions and operating requirements.

Intellectual property rights (IPRs)

Problems with IPRs in China relate to enforcement by the regulatory authorities rather than the attitudes and actions of the government. Official attention to IPR issues is expanded in the current Five Year Plan and *China's Plan on IPR Protection and Action 2006* issued by the State Intellectual Property Office in March 2006. The action plan focuses on strengthening the IPR system in all four major areas: copyrights, trademarks, patents and international trade, including customs issues, and identifies nine types of action:

- legislative reform;
- law enforcement;
- institution building;

- advocacy (promotion);
- training and education;
- international exchange and cooperation;
- promotion of business 'self-discipline';
- improved service to rights holders;
- expanded research on IPR issues in China.

The government recognized that there was a cultural dimension in educating people to respect and honour intellectual property in schools and in Part 2 the impressive education programme now in place is described in detail.

The Chinese government attention that is being given to the IPR issue reflects three concerns:

- In order to maintain its drive to move up the value chain with hi-tech products and processes, China must be perceived by its foreign partners as a safe destination for technology transfer.
- China needs to protect its own IPR in global markets as its enhanced R&D investment bears fruit and must subscribe to a level playing field in IPR protection.
- The need for IPR enforcement in the domestic market becomes ever more acute as the tide of manufacturing activity moves westwards into the undeveloped regions of Western China and existing manufacturers in the higher-cost regions of Eastern China become more vulnerable themselves to piracy.

As with product quality issues, which remain of great concern internationally and to China, law enforcement by the standards and regulatory authorities heads the list of prescribed actions.

Threats to the WTO

The impasse in the Doha Round negotiations, after failures to agree any package in Doha, Hong Kong and Geneva casts a shadow over the long-term effectiveness of the WTO in promoting free trade. Discussions between the Group of Four key negotiating nations at the core of the Doha Round – India, Brazil, the United States and EU – collapsed again in June 2007. New proposals to cut manufacturing tariffs put forward a month later in the form of a draft agreement were deemed unacceptable by a group of developing countries. Expressions of optimism continue to be made by various players but may be little more than whistling in the wind.

Whether continued failure to agree will generate a growing mood of protectionism among WTO members remains to be seen. What is certain is the movement towards the strengthening of regional alliances and bilateral agreements on specific product and services sectors. In this respect, China's renewed alignment with the ASEAN group of countries, which reflects their interdependence in foreign trade is logical. In July 2007, the agreement signed in January opens up key service sectors and is a further step towards creating the world's potentially largest free trade zone. The agreement may also dull any sense of urgency on China's part in taking WTO liberalization further.

5

Hong Kong – Asia's business capital

Mark Michelson, Invest Hong Kong[1]

As a gateway for developing business in or with China, Hong Kong remains a popular choice. Equally, it continues to be Asia's most popular city for the regional offices or headquarters of foreign companies. Hong Kong consistently tops surveys on economic freedom, ease of business and as a location for foreign direct investment (FDI). This continued popularity has seen, in the past decade, a 50 per cent rise in the number of foreign companies basing their regional offices or headquarters in the city.

Since Hong Kong's change of sovereignty in 1997, the city has experienced its fair share of volatility. But this has done little to dull its appeal. On the contrary. Hong Kong's response to the Asian financial crisis of the late 1990s, the ensuing property market slump and the outbreak of SARS in 2003 has demonstrated to the world Hong Kong's resilience, adaptability and success at rising to the toughest challenges.

---

[1] Invest Hong Kong is the award-winning department of the Hong Kong SAR government responsible for assisting overseas companies to set up and develop their business in the city. Every year hundreds of companies, large and small, use its free services to help them choose the best location in Asia. Its goal is to help your company to prosper and grow in Asia – and especially China – from your base in Hong Kong. Invest Hong Kong partners with clients on a long-term basis and is available to help at any stage of your business development strategy; www.investhk.gov.hk.

For many Hong Kong watchers, its reversion to Chinese rule was considered its toughest challenge. And again, Hong Kong has overwhelmingly proved its doomsayers wrong. Since 1997, the graphs have been overwhelmingly up. GDP, trade, investment, the number of foreign companies, tourist numbers and, most impressively, its financial markets, have all benefited from its unique relationship with what Hong Kongers refer to as Mainland China. Hong Kong's macroeconomic indicators are summarized in Table 5.1 below.

Table 5.1   Hong Kong – macroeconomic indicators (US$ billions)

Indicators		2003	2004	2005	2006	2007	2008(f)	
Real GDP growth	(%)	3.2	8.6	7.5	6.9	5.6	5.3
Inflation	(%)	(1.9)	0.3	1.4	2.3	3.0	3.1
Public sector balance (% GDP)	(3.3)	1.7	1.0	2.7	2.7	3.0	
Exports		224.7	260.3	289.5	317.6	343.3	381.9
Imports		230.4	269.6	297.2	331.7	362.6	400.2
Trade balance		(5.9)	(9.3)	(7.6)	(1.4)	(2.0)	(1.8)
Current account balance (% GDP)	16.5	15.7	20.2	20.2	20.1	24.6	
Foreign debt (% GDP)		37.8	41.0	40.7	38.0	36.3	35.4
Debt service (% exports)		1.8	2.1	2.2	2.3	2.1	2.0
Foreign currency reserves (in months of imports)	4.8	4.2	3.7	3.4	3.2	3.0	

Source: Coface (http://www.trading-safely.com), 28 August 2007

The reason is clear. Hong Kong has achieved the delicate balancing act – with the support of China's central government – of maintaining the economic freedoms that fuelled its success in the second half of the 20th century, while reaping the new benefits bestowed on it from its position as China's newest city. Put simply, Hong Kong enjoys the best of both worlds:

> *The unique advantage Hong Kong provides to foreign investors is not to be underestimated: come and get a piece of the China action, but from a safe, stable and familiar base camp... On quality of life Hong Kong is tough to beat. But it's primarily a place for doing business – and on that front there is much to applaud. (fDi Magazine's 'Asian City of the Future 2005/06'award, in which Hong Kong topped the survey of 60 Asian cities)*

Hong Kong 10 years on

A question commonly asked by companies looking at Hong Kong is 'Has it changed much since the handover?' The simple answer is that a lot more has remained the same than has changed. The freedoms that both local Hong Kong and the international community hold so dear remain the same: the rule of law, civil rights and freedoms, the free – and very vocal – press; the free flow of capital, people and goods; and the multi-cultural, multi-religion and multi-national community.

For decades Hong Kong was the only commercially viable route into China for foreign business. This is no longer the case. Companies, subject to certain criteria (discussed in detail in Chapters 1 and 15), can now enter China directly. However, as the numbers demonstrate, this has done little to diminish Hong Kong's appeal for foreign companies. It seems that while Hong Kong's slice of the pie may be smaller, the pie itself is so much larger.

According to surveys conducted by international economic think tanks, as well as the main international chambers in Hong Kong, the city retains its appeal due to a combination of factors. These are often loosely clustered as 'enduring advantages', that is, those that have formed the backbone of Hong Kong's success for some time; and 'new trends', that is, advantages that have fuelled development in the past decade.

Enduring advantages

International business environment

With an awe-inspiring backdrop of rugged peaks and gleaming skyscrapers surrounding its iconic and always-busy harbour, Hong Kong is one of the most exciting and vibrant cities in the world. Its heart and mind is dedicated to business, with the soul of Hong Kong extending from the boardrooms and trading floors, to its glittering shopping malls, bustling street markets and 24-hour nightlife.

It's a city that works. Its enduring appeal is built on political stability, pro-business governance and free market principles. Low taxes, an independent legal system and sophisticated transport, technology and telecoms equip companies with the tools to succeed. It's a simple mix that has won the city the coveted title of 'world's freest economy' for over a decade and made it Asia's most popular city for international business:

Hong Kong – over a decade as the 'world's freest economy':

Asia's most popular city for international business.
A level playing field for all – no foreign ownership restrictions.
Low, simple and predictable tax regime.
No tax on offshore income, capital gains, sales, dividends or estate.
Rule of law and an independent, experienced judiciary.

It's a city that works. Its enduring appeal is built on political stability, pro-business governance and free market principles.

Strategic location

As the key city on China's southern coast, Hong Kong is ideally located at the heart of Asia's high-growth markets. Its convenient location and business environment make it an ideal centre from which to manage regional business.

Hong Kong lies within an hour's drive of the Pearl River Delta – the world's largest manufacturing region – and within a five-hour flight of half the world's population. Hong Kong-based companies have unrivalled access to the huge potential of the Chinese market. The city's business influence across China is extensive and deep.

Hong Kong provides almost half of the Mainland's inward investment, while the Mainland is the city's largest trading partner. Whether it's manufacturing, sourcing, or identifying new customers, Hong Kong's geographical position and network of contacts have given the city a proven competitive edge across China.

Hong Kong is at the heart of Asia's high-growth economies:

Within five hours of half the world's population.
A magnet for Asia's financial, business and trading community.
Asia's leading aviation and shipping hub.
A proven gateway to China's high-growth markets.
Adjacent to China's fast-growing Pearl River Delta region.

The city's business influence across China is extensive and deep. Hong Kong provides almost half of the Mainland's inward investment, while the Mainland is the city's largest trading partner.

Dynamic people

With a population of 7 million, Hong Kong is a busy and energetic international metropolis. A friendly and accessible city, Hong Kong thrives on its strong work ethic and can-do attitude. Hong Kong boasts a well-educated workforce, with almost half of all students attending universities at home or abroad. This local pool of experienced and entrepreneurial talent offers an essential mix of international market savvy with an appreciation of the business culture in the fast-growing Mainland cities, and across Asia. In offices and boardrooms, English is the usual language of business, while many in Hong Kong speak English, Cantonese and Mandarin, providing another vital link to business with Mainland China markets and consumers.

A ready pool of expertise, enthusiasm and talent:

Multi-lingual workforce – English is the language of business.
A highly trained, flexible and motivated population.
Experienced in travelling and working in Mainland China, and throughout the region.
Familiar with the latest international business practices.
Strong work ethic – industrial action extremely rare.

Hong Kong's local pool of talent offers an essential mix of international market savvy with an appreciation of the business culture in Mainland China.

Cosmopolitan lifestyle

Whether it's entertaining clients, or unwinding after a tough week at work, Hong Kong rarely disappoints. The city boasts an array of bars, restaurants and entertainment. From the most prestigious dining to a hurried bowl of the freshest noodles, Hong Kong has a style to match all tastes and budgets.

Away from the city, mountain tracks await intrepid or recreational hikers. Only 15 minutes from the central business district you'll find unspoilt views over turquoise seas and picture-perfect islands. Equally, sailing, golf, tennis and much more are available for enthusiasts or spectators.

Housing varies from contemporary high-rise apartments a stone's throw from the office, to country houses in peaceful villages. International schools, the highest quality of public or private health care and a crime rate that is the envy of cities worldwide create a comfortable living environment for families.

New trends

But to say that nothing's changed? For Hong Kong that would be impossible! Hong Kong's reunification with China has overwhelmingly brought new opportunities to Hong Kong. In recent years new trends have emerged that have supported Hong Kong's enduring advantages and helped fuel growth. These include:

Supporting China's corporate development

Hong Kong has emerged as a major player in the corporate development of Mainland China's new breed of entrepreneurs. Increasingly, China's privately owned-enterprises (or POEs) are leveraging the corporate experience, international exposure and capital-raising capabilities of Hong Kong to facilitate their expansion plans.

This new 'domestic' market has created strong opportunities in Hong Kong for both local and foreign companies looking to export such services to Mainland China. The financial, legal and business service sectors have been particular beneficiaries.

The result has been a compound annual growth rate (CAGR) of some 17 per cent in the past five years in service exports to Mainland China.

Rapid growth in leisure and business visitors

Hong Kong, with its small domestic economy, relies heavily on its export industries, or on the spending power of visitors to the city. Visitor numbers have risen sharply in the past four years, most notably fuelled by the rise in high-spending business and leisure travellers from Mainland China. In 2006, 25.3 million people came to Hong Kong, of whom over half (13.6 million) were from Mainland China. 2007 looks set to be another record-breaking year, with visitor numbers up a further 7 per cent in the first half-year. This influx has been of particular benefit to the tourism and retail sectors, with retail sales up 7 per cent to over US$28 billion in 2006 and restaurant receipts topping US$8 billion, a rise of almost 10 per cent year on year.

High concentration of high net worth individuals

Hong Kong's robust economy over the past four years has seen a sharp rise in the number of high net worth individuals (HNWIs) as well as an overall increase in living standards and spending patterns. Rising trade, low unemployment and a highly buoyant stock market have been the main drivers in this new-found wealth. The market capitalization of the Hong Kong Stock Exchange, for example, has risen some 240 per cent in the past five years, boosted by initial public offerings by Mainland companies, interest from global investors in investing in China-related stocks and, most recently, by the gradual opening of Hong Kong's stock markets to Mainland-based investors.

In short, Hong Kong's role has transformed in the past decade. In addition to its position as a stepping stone into China and as an Asia headquarters for foreign companies, it now plays a key role for Mainland Chinese companies interested in expanding outside China.

Which companies flourish in Hong Kong

Hong Kong is not right for everyone. It's a premium city that appeals to companies that require efficiency, convenience, an international environment, a service-oriented culture and access to discerning clients (both corporate and individual). Overwhelmingly, the foreign companies that are attracted to Hong Kong locate the following business processes in the city:

- *Asia headquarters* overseeing management, or expansion, of regional offices;
- *regional procurement and global distribution* functions;
- high-value and/or international corporate functions – such as legal, financial, HR, and sales and marketing functions – for companies interested in *managing risk when expanding business into China* (and other high-growth regional markets).

Hong Kong as your Asia headquarters

Hong Kong is the most popular city in Asia for regional headquarters – and for good reason. It combines a pro-business environment with the highest level of connectivity in the region. Hong Kong International Airport serves 140 cities worldwide, including almost 50 in Mainland China; its air cargo coverage has made it the busiest international express freight hub in the world; and 80 international shipping lines connect the city with 500 ports worldwide. Equally, the city tops the Economic Intelligence Unit's survey of e-readiness in Asia, ensuring that online connectivity with regional offices is fast and reliable. Hong Kong is particularly well suited for procurement offices (see below), trading offices and financial and professional service providers.

Hong Kong as a centre for procurement and distribution

Many of the world's leading retailers have major procurement offices in Hong Kong, which are responsible for sourcing from across the region, as well as global distribution. A combination of factors have led to Hong Kong holding such a key role in this supply chain management. These include:

■ *Proximity to the Pearl River Delta manufacturing region* of Southern China – an area that dominates the world supply of light consumer goods, such as textiles, fashion, toys, electronics, household appliances and household goods. Many of the factories in this area are owned or managed by Hong Kong-based companies.

■ *World-leading transportation infrastructure* – including the world's busiest (by volume) airport for air cargo shipments, as well as one of the world's most efficient sea and river container ports. The privately run ports use the latest in high-tech security and goods movement technologies to ensure a smooth flow of cargo to markets around the world.

■ *Free movement of goods and capital* – no restrictions or import/export tariffs on products shipped into or through Hong Kong (except alcohol, tobacco and various petroleum products), and no restrictions, or exchange controls, on the movement of capital.

■ *Stringent intellectual property rules* – this is an essential value-adding aspect that Hong Kong offers in a region where IP protection is still a challenge.

■ *Availability of experienced employees* – many foreign companies staff their sourcing offices almost exclusively using local talent who have strong in-China sourcing networks, as well as quality control, sales, marketing and after-care experience required by many international retailers.

Hong Kong as a platform for selling into China

The rapid expansion of Mainland China's economy, fuelled by its rise as a global manufacturing base, has created strong demand among companies and consumers for foreign products and services. It is estimated that China is home to more than 30 million middle-income families and this number is growing rapidly. Similarly, private-owned-enterprises (POEs) are the new growth engine for China and are fuelling demand for business expansion products and services. In particular, Mainland companies are using Hong Kong companies to help them tailor and brand their products and services for international markets, upgrade their management functions, and, most notably, to raise capital.

Hong Kong is now the world's third most important global financial market, after New York and London, and Mainland companies have raised over US$190 billion via initial public offerings and post-IPO fundraising.

6

The Chinese government structure and administration[1]

Jonathan Reuvid

The National People's Congress

The highest organization of state power in The People's Republic of China (PRC) is the National People's Congress (NPC). There are 3,000 delegates consisting of representatives from all 22 provinces, five autonomous regions, four municipalities (Beijing, Chongqing, Shanghai and Tianjin) and two Special Administrative Regions (Hong Kong and Macao), as well as from the People's Liberation Army. Delegates are elected from these bodies for five years by a process of quasi-democratic consultation.

The NPC meets once a year each October and, when not in session, its powers are exercised by a Standing Committee under whose direction there are a number of special committees. The NPC and its Standing Committee have the powers to:

---

[1] Most of the detailed facts on which this chapter is based have been drawn from the published work of Mr Li Yong, Deputy Secretary General of the China Association of International Trade (CAIT) whose contribution is gratefully acknowledged.

- amend the constitution;
- interpret laws;
- enact decrees;
- ratify treaties;
- appoint ambassadors;
- approve economic plans and reports on their implementation;
- approve the state budget and reports on its implementation;
- declare war and sign peace treaties.

Powers to appoint and remove the country's premier and vice-premiers who collectively comprise the State Council are also vested in the NPC and Standing Committee. The Standing Committee comprises of some 153 members, none of whom may hold office in state administration, judicial or procuratorial organs in order to maintain a separation of powers and objective supervision of the administrative organs.

President of the PRC and the administration

The head of state is the president of the PRC; he is also the supreme representative of China both domestically and externally. The president is appointed by and subordinate to the NPC, from which he receives instruction and his authority flows. The current president, Mr Hu Jintao, entering his second term of office in March 2008, is the sixth to have held office, since 1947 when the Republic was founded. Previous incumbents were Mao Zedong, Liu Shaoqi, Li Xiannian, Yang Shangkun and Jiang Zemin, Mr Hu's predecessor.

The central administration system in the PRC includes the central administrative organs that exercise leadership over local administrative organs at various levels. They are subsidiary to the NPC and report through the president.

The four principal organs of state administration reporting through the presidency to the NPC are:

- the State Council;
- the Supreme People's Court;
- the Supreme People's Procuratorate;
- the Central Military Commission.

Of these four, the State Council is the highest organ of administration, which operates through 28 ministries and state commissions listed below. Eight further national institutions are under the State Council's direct control. There are a number of other secondary organs and institutions directly under the State Council whose status changes from time to time.

The present incumbents of the five most senior positions in the PRC government structure are, as follows:

- National People's Congress (NPC) of the People's Republic of China – NPC Standing Committee;
  Chairman – Wu Bangguo;
- Presidency
  President – Hu Jintao
  Vice-President – Zeng Qinghong;
- State Council
  Premier – Wen Jiaboa;
- Central Military Commission
  Chairman – Hu Jintao.

No changes to these senior positions are anticipated at the next session of the NPC in March 2008.

The State Council is the highest executive body of state administration. It exercises unified leadership over local state administrative organs at various levels throughout the country, regulates the specific division of power and functions of the state administrative organs at the central level and at the provincial, autonomous regional and municipal levels.

Premier of the PRC

The premier is head of the State Council and is responsible to the NPC and its Standing Committee on behalf of the State Council. He is assisted by a vice-premier and state councillors. The premier is nominated by the president, the nomination is reviewed by the NPC and he is appointed and removed by the president. Other members of the State Council are nominated by the premier, reviewed by the NPC or its Standing Committee and appointed or removed by the president. The term of office for members of the State Council is five years and incumbents are not eligible for re-appointment after serving two terms.

The premier has final decision-making power and power of signature on all major issues in the work of the State Council and the power to make recommendations to the NPC and its Standing Committee on the appointment or removal of the vice-premiers, state councillors, ministers, the auditor general and secretary general.

Role of the Communist Party

The Communist Party of China is a parallel authority to the State Council run by a Central Committee. The politburo of this Central Committee is the PRC's most powerful political body. One of its primary functions is to advise the NPC and its Standing Committee on the appointment and removal of the premier and vice-premiers. The country's president is appointed by the above bodies combined.

The ministries and state commissions

The ministries and state commissions, with their websites are, as follows:[2]

National Development and Reform Commission	www.sdpc.gov.cn
Ministry of Finance	www.mof.gov.cn
People's Bank of China	www.pbc.gov.cn
Ministry of Foreign Affairs	www.fmprc.gov.cn
Ministry of National Defence	n.a.
State Commission of Science, Technology and Industry for National Defence	www.costind.gov.cn
Ministry of Education	www.moe.gov.cn
Ministry of Commerce	www.mofcom.gov.cn
Ministry of Science and Technology	www.most.gov.cn
Ministry of Culture	www.ccnt.gov.cn
Ministry of Health	www.moh.gov.cn
Ministry of Personnel	www.mop.gov.cn
Ministry of Labour and Social Security	www.molss.gov.cn
Ministry of Justice	www.legalinfo.gov.cn
State Ethnic Affairs Commission	www.seac.gov.cn
Ministry of Public Security	www.mps.gov.cn
Ministry of State Security	n.a.
Ministry of Supervision	www.mos.gov.cn
Ministry of Civil Affairs	www.mca.gov.cn
National Population and Planning Commission	www.chinapop.gov.cn
Ministry of Construction	www.cin.gov.cn
Ministry of Railways	www.china-mor.gov.cn
Ministry of Communications	www.moc.gov.cn
Ministry of Information Industry	www.mii.gov.cn
Ministry of Land and Resources	www.mlr.gov.cn
Ministry of Water Resources	www.mwr.cgov.cn
Ministry of Agriculture	www.agri.gov.cn
National Audit Office	www.audit.gov.cn

There are eight other key national institutions also under the direct control of the state:

General Administration of Customs	www.customs.gov.cn
State Administration of Taxation	www.chinatax.gov.cn
National Bureau of Statistics	www.stats.gov.cn
China Intellectual Property Office	www.sipo.gov.cn

---

[2] The various ministry, commission and institution websites are not uniformly accessible; they do not all offer English translations and some of their pages cannot be downloaded. Access is generally easier via www.google.com, which provides English translations of varying quality.

China Securities Regulatory Commission	www.csrc.gov.cn
China Banking Regulatory Commission	www.cbrc.gov.cn
China Insurance Regulatory Commission	www.circ.gov.cn
Xinhua News Agency	www.xinhua.org

Structure of a typical ministry

Ministries are usually organized under a management body consisting of the minister, several vice-ministers and assistant minister. There are various functional departments under each ministry, often supported by a research or information institution. Under the functional departments there are various departments that are usually the first point of contact for foreign businesspeople with the ministry.

In some cases, there are also industry associations that operate with relative independence but are affiliated organizationally with the nomination of key organization heads in the hands of the ministry. As a result of government reform to separate government functions from enterprise management, large SOEs and business corporations previously under ministries before 2005 are now independent of them.

Local government

There are local NPCs resembling the structure of the central NPC. The local People's Congresses exercise their powers and functions through their Standing Committees when the NPCs are not in session. Like the NPC, each local Standing Committee is composed of a chairman, vice-chairman and members.

Local governments are the administrative arms of local people's governments. Hitherto, local governments are established at five levels with top-down decision-making and bottom-up reporting. There are alternative hierarchical tracks under each provincial government, as follows:

- urban track:
  - city governments;
  - district/county governments;
- rural track:
  - municipal-level district governments;
  - county/county-level city governments;
  - township governments.

The 31 provinces, autonomous regions and municipalities all have provincial governments, of which the heads are ministerial-level officials. The provincial governments are bound by the State Council, which has the power to decide on the division of responsibilities between the central government and provincial administrative organs. The State Council can also annul the decisions and orders of provincial governments. The provincial governments hold similar authority over the lower levels of local government.

The structure of a provincial government

The provincial governments have a similar structure to the central government, with echelons corresponding to the ministries and commissions at the central level. For example, there are provincial bureaux of finance, bureaux of commerce, bureaux of education and development planning commissions that correspond to the Ministry of Finance, the Ministry of Commerce, the Ministry of Education and the State Development and Reform Commission.

The heads of the local bureaux and commissions are appointed by the provincial governments to which they are responsible while, at the same time, executing the policies made by both the central ministries and the provincial governments. There is therefore a strong 'dotted line' information and reporting relationship to the state counterpart in Beijing.

As we shall see in Part 3, foreign entrepreneurs seeking business partners in China who can build a good relationship with the research and administration institute of the relevant ministry in Beijing, are well placed to tap into the database of Chinese company information throughout its network in order to identify potential partners.

Lower-level governments

So far so good, but this is where the structure of Chinese government becomes more complicated. Chinese cities vary not only in size, but also in official ranking.

Some provincial capitals and cities of key economic importance have different administrative status and a certain degree of independence from the provinces in which they are located. There is a group of 'separately planned cities' that have independent administrative status and are chosen to enjoy quasi-provincial status in the national planning. In terms of 'dotted line' reporting routes, the government functions such as bureaux and commissions in those cities do not report to the corresponding provincial departments, but direct to those at central level.

Chief among those cities with 'separately planned' status are: Shenyang, Dalian, Changchun, Harbin, Jinan, Qingdao, Nanjing, Ningbo, Hangzhou, Xiamen, Wuhan, Guangzhou, Shenzhen, Xian and Chengdu. The heads of government of these cities are referred to as vice-ministerial officials.

There are also municipal-level districts, which are not districts in cities but an area that typically includes several counties. Most of the municipal-level cities/districts are under the jurisdiction of their provincial governments. However, the hierarchical ladder is no longer as rigid as it used to be. County-level cities can be promoted to municipal-level cities if they satisfy all of a series of closely drawn criteria.

Chinese whispers of change

There are hints in the recent pronouncements of President Hu Jintao that he will be proposing wide-ranging changes to the structure of government administration at the Communist Party Congress in October 2007, which sits every five years to prepare the agenda for the NPC the following spring. In recent months he has tolerated an unusually open debate about the country's political options, of which more in the next chapter.

Specifically, researchers in China have called for swingeing cuts in the bureaucracy, including the elimination of the townships at the bottom level and prefectures in the middle of the five tiers of government. Pilot exercises in this direction are being carried out in some places. In a recent shuffle of provincial and lower-level party leaderships, tens of thousands of posts at the level of deputy party secretary are said to have been culled.

There are also more controversial proposals on the table to slim the NPC to as little as 15 per cent of its present size and for election campaigns to be introduced for seats rather than filling them, without discussion, with party-approved appointees. However, the October congress will be Mr Hu's first as head of the party and these ideas may not be put forward for discussion. His main concern is likely to be the installation of his preferred successors in top jobs. These selections will provide important indicators of the extent and pace of further change.

7

China's place in the global economy

Jonathan Reuvid

We return now to the hypothesis at the core of the debate concerning China's future: that its economic miracle carries with it the seeds of its own destruction. The essence of the argument is that China's medium- and long-term prosperity is at risk and that the unrestrained dash for growth over the past 28 years and the continually increasing standard of living for the urban population are unsustainable. There are three strands to the argument:

■ First, that the structural defects of the Chinese economy and the weaknesses of its financial system and controls could cause the economy to implode.
■ Second, by the 'law of numbers', the improbability that by 2012 Chinese investment could triple again or that Chinese exports could grow to three-and-a-half times those of Germany, the world's current leading exporter – which is what an extrapolation of historic rates of growth implies.
■ Third, that the exploding trade surpluses with the United States (and the EU) and accumulating foreign exchange reserves are causing such imbalances in the global economy that protectionist measures against China are inevitable.

This chapter challenges each of these lines of reasoning. It is hoped that previous chapters of Part 1 of the book will help readers to form their own opinions on these issues and also on the more optimistic outlook that emerges. Finally, some of the political and emotional issues that China's phenomenal economic rise has generated are also addressed.

Structural defects and weaknesses of the economy

There are three main components to this argument, each of which is serious and could prove intractable unless the government takes decisive action soon.

The imbalance between East and West

For those visiting China, whose exposure is limited to the prosperous municipality and city environments of Eastern and Southern China or the vibrant urban communities of North Eastern China, the disparity in living standards between those locations and the undeveloped and rural areas of Western China, may not be apparent. We are struck by the unfamiliar dynamism of the local and, it is assumed, a national economy where the rate of growth is four or five times what we are accustomed to at home. In those parts of China, nothing seems impossible in the 'can do' atmosphere of an 'open market economy with Chinese characteristics'.

Others who spend time in the countryside or venture beyond Chongqing into Central China or even further westwards will gain a quite different impression. These are territories for which the door of economic development is barely ajar. Small wonder that the migration into the towns and cities continues, driven by need or ambition. It is said that some 130 million Chinese exist below international poverty lines, while 100 to 250 million surplus rural workers are in limbo between villages and cities, subsisting through part-time and low-paid jobs. And yet, 45 per cent of the population is still employed in agriculture, contributing only 11.9 per cent to GDP.

Allowing for those unemployed from the rationalization of SOEs and school and newly left college leavers, in addition to the migrant unemployed, one unpublished paper from the Kennedy School of Government, Harvard University in 2005 estimated that the real unemployment figure could be as high as 170 million, implying a need for China to create some 24 million new jobs a year in order to avoid rising unemployment levels. This need provides an underlying motive for government policies to maintain GDP growth by fuelling exports.

The gap between the depressed rural areas is growing wider. Since 2000, it has been calculated that eight of China's provinces and municipalities, accounting for 40 per cent of the population, have generated almost 75 per cent of national growth. According to Angang Hu, an expatriate Chinese academic (see *Great Transformations in China*, 2006, OUP, Oxford) the purchasing power parity (PPP) adjusted per capita income in Shanghai exceeded US$15,000 in 2006 compared with Guizhou in the rural west at US$1,247. The most recent UN *World Development Report* ranks China in terms of its Gini coefficient of equality behind the United States and the United Kingdom among developed countries and below India in the developing world.

The concern here is that, if left unchecked, the inequality between the rural and urban populations will generate serious civil unrest. The solution to this problem is twofold: first, a massive programme of public investment including infrastructure project spending on the scale of the mammoth US\$24 billion Three Gorges Dam, largely completed in 2006, which has revolutionized flood control and electrification in the area, albeit at the cost of displacing many millions of the population; and second, the deployment of government savings to improve education and social services and to stimulate consumer spending. As discussed below, a proportion of China's foreign exchange reserves could be deployed in that direction. Creating high employment centres of industry in Central and Western China would be the most effective tool for a longer-term remission to the West-to-East drift.

The funding for this gigantic development plan can only come from changes in the pattern of gross domestic investment, which is already the highest in the world at an estimated 40 per cent of GDP (eg, a further shift away from investment in SOEs), the application of a part of China's current account surpluses and, if necessary a redeployment of a part of the foreign currency reserves into the domestic economy. (We return to the foreign currency reserves issue in the context of the exchange rate shortly.) As the economies of the poorer regions burgeon and living standards rise, increasing domestic consumption will act as an accelerator. The undeveloped regions and associated unemployment issues are probably the greatest challenge to China's continued prosperity.

The inefficiency of state-owned enterprises (SOEs)

China's SOEs have been a major drag on the economy, representing inefficient consumption of capital with low productivity, an inefficient use of labour and a history of reinvesting all retained earnings in their own or associated low-profit businesses. They have also enjoyed the lion's share of bank finance and account for a high proportion of the non-performing loans (NPLs), which have plagued the Chinese banking system.

To the government's credit, it has grasped the nettle of restructuring state-owned industry. Between 1995 and 2005, the gross number of SOEs was halved from 300,000 to 150,000. The strategy has been 'to hold on to the big, while letting go of the small'. However, while the SOEs' share of GDP has fallen sharply, their share of value-added has fallen only slightly. Probably as little as 10 per cent of those discarded have filed for bankruptcy (although there is now an insolvency law in China). The remainder were restructured through mergers, leasing deals, management buyouts and reorganizations as 'shareholding companies', with the government often contriving to maintain the state's controlling interest.

Of course, the remaining SOEs still rely for their external finance on the banks in which non-state shareholdings are limited to 25 per cent. In the case of the 'big four' banks that are now listed public companies, the NPL issue was partly addressed before flotation by consolidating NPLs into packages that were sold off at discounts to foreign-invested financial institutions.

Unprofitable SOEs are hardly a problem that is unique to China. Loss-making nationalized industry has afflicted Western economies too from time to time. The ultimate solution is privatization, as in the case of the newer members of the EU, sometimes with the state retaining a substantial minority shareholding. In China's case, where SOEs have been restructured into joint stock companies and then floated through initial public offerings, enormous market capitalizations have been realized but the state retains a controlling interest. The benefits of listing are that the company is now set on a course where it has to deliver profits and distribute dividends to shareholders rather than ploughing them back into unnecessary, and often unprofitable, ventures or listed securities. In this way the state benefits from proceeds of the IPO and a revenue stream from its retained shareholding.

Another welcome change that would ensure that the government receives revenue from all profitable SOEs was announced at the end of May 2007 with a pilot programme for companies controlled by the state to pay dividends. The World Bank has estimated that a 4.8 per cent dividend payout from SOEs in 2002, when they were less profitable, would have paid the school fees for all Chinese children that year.

Weaknesses of the financial system

Compliance with WTO commitments has been an agent of change for the Chinese financial system and led directly to the 'opening up' of the financial sector, particularly banking and the insurance sector. Foreign-owned banks, under licence, can now service Chinese companies in both foreign and local RMB currency and joint venture (JV) insurance companies can underwrite both life and non-life business nationwide.

The state majority-owned banks, as a result of their flotations from 2004 onwards and the disciplines of international banking best practice have now improved management and more sophisticated systems. That is not to say that their lending practices are immaculate and they are still vulnerable to an overhang of NPLs made to SOEs. These problems may come home to roost, particularly when state shareholdings are diluted and their accounts become more transparent. However, any potential banking crisis on this account can be avoided by the government repeating the pre-flotation exercise of bundling NPLs into debt vehicles that it would take over, using foreign exchange reserves, for later disposal on financial markets.

Another improvement in financial management is the use today by the government, through the People's Bank of China, of all the classic central bank monetary tools, such as the requirement from time to time for banks to increase their reserve deposits in order to dampen domestic borrowing and investment. Formerly, the government used limited movements in interest rates as the only monetary tool and relied upon 'stop-go' government edicts to dampen or encourage investment in selected industries.

The government has introduced in 2007 a raft of measures to address the current asset bubble arising from overvalued RMB shares on the Shanghai and Shenzhen Stock Exchanges and to dampen speculation. Speculative property investment by foreign companies and individuals in anticipation of an appreciating renminbi (RMB) has also been addressed with the introduction of land development taxes and stamp duty.

Given the progress of the past six years, it is reasonable to suppose that China will resolve the remaining structural and technical problems in its banking and securities industries. Thanks to the rapidly increasing involvement of foreign financial institutions through FDI and setting up their own operations, the global nature of these sectors and the constant monitoring of the international financial press, transparency is significantly higher than in other sectors of the Chinese economy. Through its exposure and interaction with the Hong Kong Stock Exchange and financial regulators, the China Securities Regulations Commission (CSRC) has learnt fast and has introduced many of the same provisions and safeguards.

The statistical argument

The argument that the growth rates of China's GDP and foreign trade are statistically unsustainable is based on a sort of pre-Galilean assumption that the economic world is flat. If China's exports did grow to three-and-a-half times those of Germany, it does not follow that the global economy would sail over the edge into an abyss. For sure, there would have to be a quantum leap in the amount of shipping available and the capacity of ports to handle the freight, and there is already clear evidence of rising order books in the shipyards of Korea as well as China itself. However, it is entirely possible that the world could accommodate rising levels of Chinese exports and imports on this scale if we exercise some imagination as to how the patterns of world trade may change.

The analogy between the shift in global geo-economic patterns and the tectonic plates phenomenon of geology was first aired in my introduction to an edition of the *Coface Handbook of Country Risk* (Jonathan Reuvid, 2003, Kogan Page, London) several years ago. It applies particularly to foreign trade because the economic world is round rather than flat.

If we revisit Table 2.2 in Chapter 2, a range of possible shifts becomes apparent, if not in period 2007 to 2012 but certainly over the coming decades:

■ Increases in exports from China to South and Central America replacing exports from North America Japan and the EU balanced by imports of minerals and other agricultural and primary products. Capturing 20 per cent of these exports would gain US$31 billion at 2005 prices and volumes.
■ As China climbs the value-added ladder in electrical and electronic equipment and household goods, the evolution of the ASEAN free trade zone will help it to capture exports from Japan, as well as from the United States and EU into other Asian countries. Capturing just 10 per cent of that trade would add more than US$47 billion on the same basis.
■ Growing foreign trade with the emerging countries of Africa, where China is already in pole position through oil-related investment programmes will yield an increasing flow of exports from China throughout the range of its industrial and consumer products. By how much and how quickly these export markets will grow is very uncertain but those countries are likely to grow their imports in parallel with their exports to China. The addition of a further US$53 billion at 2005 prices by, say, 2020 does not seem too fanciful.

Adding these three elements together produces an additional export value of US$130 billion, representing about 17 per cent of 2005 trade.

The increasing foreign trade with China's oil- and gas-producing partners in the Middle East and Central Asia means further destinations for increased exports are likely. Continuing growth in existing trade with major markets at current prices with imports matching exports at the rates forecast for the short-term through to 2009 is not seriously challenged, by which time the new elements should start to build up.

Of course, China does not need the projected rates of increased exports indefinitely to maintain the continuing growth of GDP at the 10 per cent level. The employment-generating investment and rising consumption referred to above will add significantly to GDP as will the earnings from China's outward FDI if it reinvests a substantial part of its foreign exchange reserves in start-ups abroad and the acquisition of major international companies. Unless protectionism intervenes, it is entirely possible in the span of the next 10 to 20 years that Chinese-invested enterprises in North America and Europe will reap similar rich rewards to those earned by US and EU corporate investments in China. We should remember too the impact of Japanese investment in the 1970s and 1980s, notably in the United Kingdom and United States, as its leading manufacturers in automobiles and other consumer durables built new manufacturing facilities in their targeted export markets. This outward investment activity is also to be expected from maturing Chinese companies aiming to become global players.

Taken together, these trade and investment factors make the continued growth of the Chinese economy at current rates a plausible scenario rather than an outside bet. The consequences for those countries whose own foreign trade suffers in the process will, of course, be uncomfortable.

The return of protectionism

A slide into protectionism against Chinese imports, either unilaterally by the United States or in concert with the EU, in reaction to China's rampant trade surpluses is a possibility, although it is uncertain to whom such action would be of benefit. In a more general global context there is already a worrying shift towards regional and bilateral trade deals as progress on WTO negotiations has stalled.

The issue was explored with great clarity in one of Martin Wolf's regular articles ('The right way to respond to China's exploding surpluses') on the Chinese economy in the *Financial Times* on 30 May 2007. Comparing the present period of 'second globalization' with the 'first globalization' of 1870 to 1914 when the United States was the rising economic power and the United Kingdom was the largest exporter of capital, he points out that this time China has emerged as both the most dynamic economy and the largest source of global capital, mainly through its US dollar reserves, now topping US$1.3 trillion. Comparing the Chinese phenomenon with the rising economic performance of Japan in the 1970s and 1980s, Wolf also points out that China's 2006 current account surplus of 9.5 per cent of GDP was more than twice Japan's highest rate of 4.3 per cent in 1986. Adding on the balance of net FDI, China's balance of payments ratio in 2006 is increased to 12 per cent of GDP. A further dimension to the phenomenon is that China's gross domestic investment is calculated to be more than 40 per cent of GDP so that China is now rated as both the largest exporter of capital and as having the highest ratio of domestic investment to GDP.

However, the root cause of the United States' problem is that China's accumulation of foreign exchange reserves in recent years has matched almost exactly the sum of current account surpluses and net FDI inflows. There is no 'hot money' element in the outflows; the investment in foreign exchange reserves has been deliberate Chinese policy aimed at keeping the RMB exchange rate against the US dollar depressed.

Benefits of this policy, it is argued, are that it has helped to maintain low interest rates for the rest of the world, allowing more spending while at the same time stimulating China's rapid export growth as the means to sustain higher economic growth and employment.

In his article, Martin Wolf suggests that it is unlikely that the United States can continue to live with the present concentration of counterpart trade deficits, particularly as its economy slows down, and is likely to resort to protectionist action if it cannot persuade China to accelerate the revaluation of its currency. He also points out that massive accumulation of low-yielding foreign assets that are vulnerable to inevitable appreciation of the RMB against the dollar cannot continue to make sense to the Chinese government. Quoting a recent paper by Nicholas Lardy of the Peterson Institute for International Economics, Washington ('China: rebalancing economic growth', www.petersoninstitute.org), Wolf lists the consequent disadvantages of China's current development policy:

■ net exports close to 25 per cent of GDP;
■ low household consumption at 38 per cent of GDP in 2005;
■ growth over-dominated by the coastal regions;
■ low employment growth (only 1 per cent between 1993 and 2004);
■ energy consumption too high;
■ wasteful investment encouraged by low interest rates (before 2007);
■ savings too high at about 50 per cent of GDP.

These shortcomings have already been discussed either in previous chapters or earlier in this chapter. The classic remedies are all in the Chinese government's hands, namely:

■ Save less; in particular the government should spend more on social services and on supporting the undeveloped regions.
■ Allow the nominal exchange rate to rise faster.
■ Stimulate demand to grow faster than the rate of GDP and replace exports as the engine of growth.
■ Reinvest a major part of foreign exchange reserves in infrastructure and other capital projects in the underdeveloped regions.

The Chinese leadership is fully aware of all these problems and, except in the matter of redeploying its foreign exchange reserves, is already showing evidence of progress on each issue. Fortunately, the incumbent US Treasury Secretary, Hank Paulson, also understands the dilemmas for China and is in regular debate with his counterparts in Beijing. If the siren voices in Washington can be stilled, protectionist policies are avoidable.

The political dimension

American and European attitudes

The extraordinary rise of China has been viewed in Washington and the chancelleries of Europe with a mixture of apprehension and antagonism. In the case of the United States, whose economy has been more affected, the alarm is understandable. America is entering its long journey of discovery that its global economic hegemony has passed away and that its political and military dominance will inevitably be diluted by China's increasing role as a superpower on the world stage. Accommodating to these realities will be painful. There may be some advantages politically, for example the pivotal role of China in reaching agreement with North Korea to contain its nuclear aspirations, but reluctance to support America in other threatening areas of the world is becoming an important factor in foreign policy decision-making. Nor will a shift in the balance of military power in the Pacific region be welcome.

European attitudes are more ambivalent. Brussels will continue to struggle with the impact that Chinese imports are having on EU manufacturing, particularly its Southern European members, but China is regarded as less of a threat politically. For the United Kingdom, which has undergone its period of adjustment to reduced influence from previous generations, the opportunities for constructive economic engagement with China are more readily perceived.

When the giant stumbles...

In the introduction to this book I commented on the *schadenfreude* that often appears to accompany utterances in the United States and the United Kingdom when reacting to China's problems, or unfavourable comment that seeks to magnify the occurrence. It matters not whether the comment relates to returned orders from US toy companies on quality or health and safety grounds, environmental pollution that could affect athletes competing in the 2008 Beijing Olympic Games or human rights incidents; there is often an air of glee anytime that China falls short of the standards that we claim for ourselves. 'When the giant stumbles, the dwarves titter', and it is a reflection of our general anxiety about the growing influence of China on our lives that we should react in this way. China's performance in all these areas is imperfect and often far from admirable, but we need to separate fact from fiction and moderate our thinking where significant improvement through change is evident. Casting China in the role of ogre and ourselves as paragons is unhelpful.

The least bad form of government

Democracy has been described as 'the least bad form of government' but, in today's world, it is apparent that Western pluralistic democracy is not the most appropriate form of government, and certainly not the natural form, for all emerging states. If nowhere else, in our experience of regime change in Iraq, the imposition of our form of democracy has proved to be an uphill task and may not be ultimately what its citizens need. At the other extreme, parliamentary government in India, the world's most populous democracy has not led to efficient government and, until recently, did not generate dynamic economic growth; the development of infrastructure in India since 1947 compares poorly with China's since 1989. In Africa, the adoption of parliamentary democracy has not exorcised dictatorship in many states. Among the newer members of the EU, democracy is in some cases proving a tender plant and in Russia the preference for strong leadership has proved more important to the Russian people than support for democratic institutions.

And yet, in advocating pluralistic democracy for China commentators assume that the rule of law, social justice, respect for quality standards, fair and efficient administration and the banishment of corruption can only be achieved through adoption of a pluralistic form of elected government. Comparison between business conditions in India and China does not support these conclusions. The findings of an E10 Corporate Network Survey of January 2007 of 600 chief executives of multinational companies found that in China the top four concerns on their worry list were: shortage of qualified staff, bureaucracy and red tape, staff turnover and lack of legal certainty. Intellectual property theft and corruption ranked only seventh and eighth and inadequate physical infrastructure tenth. In India, corruption and inadequate infrastructure ranked higher together with bureaucracy and red tape.

'It's the economy, stupid' might have been written for Chinese leaders. Perhaps Bill Clinton was paraphrasing Deng Xiaoping when he coined the phrase. The focus on economic management for the past nearly 30 years has been amply vindicated. It is hard to believe that similar spectacular progress could have been achieved under another form of government. Talking to educated Chinese friends, both old and young in 1993, it was plain that, so long as their standard of living continued to rise and that there was no recurrence of a Tiananmen Square-type incident, the controls, censorship and restrictions of the government were an acceptable trade-off. In our terms, there is an almost Hobbesian social compact between the urban population and the state. Of course, this logic does not carry weight in the impoverished inland regions.

The leadership is keenly aware of the social pressures from the disaffected countryside and regions that are not yet sharing in China's prosperity. In the forthcoming Communist Party Congress, there may be further tentative moves towards the introduction of a more directly elected legislature, but whatever changes may be introduced it is certain that China will remain a single party state for the foreseeable future.

In my opinion, there is no great urgency for political change. China has a 'less bad form of government' that is addressing most of its pressing problems. And whatever form of semi-elected government finally emerges, we can be sure that, like China's open economy, it will be 'democracy with Chinese characteristics'.

Part 2

Basic business issues

8

Risk management in China – outsourcing and investment

Guy Facey, Withers LLP

Introduction – reasons for China outsourcing and investment

Why invest in China? China's phenomenal economic growth has been much written about. It has emerged as a global player in economic affairs and its seemingly insatiable demand for raw materials has had a worldwide impact on oil and commodity prices.

Fifty-five per cent of business leaders have plans to become involved in business in China in the next three years, and over a third of them intend to invest more in India. They are also looking at Brazil. Moreover, most of the CEOs interviewed said that their goal was to get access to new markets (not reducing costs). In relation to China, 48 per cent said that they were investing in China to cut labour costs but the majority responded that they were doing so to win new customers.[1] Private equity investors

---

[1] Articles in the *New York Times* and *International Herald Tribune* on 25 January 2006 reporting on a survey of 1,410 executives in 45 countries, conducted by PriceWaterhouseCoopers and released at the World Economic Forum in Davos, Switzerland.

are also increasing their stakes in the potential returns offered by China – last year predictions were that completed private equity deals would reach USUS$6 billion, up from US$3 billion in 2005 and US$1.75 billion in 2004.

In terms of global economic and political risk where does China lie in relation to investment in Asia? According to a posting on Aon's 2006 map,[2] China is rated as medium risk. The ratings are low, medium-low, medium, medium-high and high. (China was rated as medium together with India and Thailand (before the recent coup). Malaysia and South Korea were rated as medium-low, Japan as low risk and Indonesia, Cambodia and Vietnam as medium-high. Only North Korea, Burma/Myanmar and Nepal were classified as high risk.)

What is outsourcing? Outsourcing is often defined as the delegation of non-core operations or jobs from internal production within a business to an external entity that specializes in that operation. Outsourcing is a business decision that is often made to lower costs or focus on competencies. 'Outsourcing' became a popular buzzword in business and management in the mid-1990s.

Why outsource? Outsourcing offers an opportunity to reduce all the main costs: labour, materials, overheads and also lead times if you are moving closer to your customers. China may also be an opportunity to get closer to new markets. Global sourcing is therefore high on many companies' 'must do' lists, not only in the search for greater profits but also to remain competitive.

Risk and the lawyer in the Chinese environment

Risk management is a subject on which volumes have been written. This chapter is written by a lawyer. One would imagine that the lawyer's perspective on risk is narrower than the businessperson's. In some senses this is true. Law schools and professional ethics train the lawyer not to go beyond what the client asks of him or her. The businessperson should remember that when he or she hires a lawyer for a task the lawyer's perspective will frequently be circumscribed by how the businessperson defines the task. An advantage in the present context is that a lawyer's natural instinct is to negotiate and draft with a view to controlling risk. Part of the message of this chapter is to encourage businesspeople to broaden the scope of their lawyer's instructions to help address risk as broadly as possible.

Legal work tends to fall into various categories:

■ advising on how to structure deals, the best strategy with least risk;
■ drafting the contracts;
■ advising on problems mid-contract;
■ litigating to enforce contracts or on break-ups.

---

[2] A posting by the Riskape Blog to the Asia Logistics Wrap on Aon's 2006 map of global economic and political risk.

In the context of China, a useful starting point is the risk analysis used by lawyers in relation to problems disclosed to buyers in merger and acquisition (M&A) deals:

■ assess the risk; depending on its seriousness;
■ walk away from the deal;
■ exclude that risk from the deal;
■ renegotiate the price;
■ accept the risk but:
  – take an indemnity or warranty from another party;
  – insure against the risk.

The aspiration of this chapter is to illuminate the analysis of risk by talking about it from the point of view of a practising lawyer rather than a management guru. In some transactions the lawyer tends to be brought in (if he or she has a close relationship with his or her client as a trusted adviser) at the strategic planning stage, but frequently only at the contract drafting stage. Businesspeople are rightly wary of legal costs but sometimes a lawyer with experience can bring more to the table than just legal advice.

Types of risk

Outsourcing or investing in China implies going global, even if you are a small business and not a multinational. If your production is currently in one country, you will be extending your supply chain globally. These risks will have an impact on your costs, business development, even survival, so effective risk management is essential. This means looking at risk management in a very broad sense, more broadly, for example, than concentrating only on choosing the right partner and negotiating the best deal.

I have broken down the risks of outsourcing and investing in China into:

■ macroeconomic risk;
■ regulatory risk;
■ partner risk;
■ communications risk: language and culture;
■ supply chain risk.

There is also:

■ project-specific risk;
■ industry-specific risk, for example, China's export controls; 2004 foreign trade laws detailing restricted and prohibited commodities; and import quotas.

Macroeconomic risk

There are specific macroeconomic factors that apply to China. Consider the following:[3]

- If China continues to grow its raw materials demands, it will continue to push up oil and commodity prices.
- If China suffers a slowdown this will be good news for net oil importers such as the United States and the EU but bad news for other Asian economies and for net oil exporters.
- If China revalues its currency upwards it may allow other Asian economies to do the same; it will improve the United States' current account deficit and reduce the upward pressure on the exchange rate of sterling and the euro.

The risks of doing business in China were analysed in the Deloitte study (see footnote 3) as the following:

Financial and banking system

Chinese banks have large books of non-performing loans (NPLs), many of which have been transferred to asset management companies and there are corporate governance concerns. The Chinese government and the banking regulator, the Chinese Banking Regulatory Commission (CBRC), have implemented impressive banking regulations and governance rules and overseas training programmes and the banking sector is already partially opening up to foreign investment. However, liberalization and the transition to a free market economy have the potential for disruption and tensions (eg, rationalization of the NPLs resulting in redundancies in overstaffed Chinese state-owned enterprises).

Weak corporate disclosure standards

In May 2007 the government tripled the stamp duty on Chinese share purchases.[4] Speculation is rife for as long as the market keeps rising. However, corporate disclosure standards in the stock markets in China are weak and corporate governance generally needs to be improved. (Let's ignore the debate among economists about what markets did before insider trading laws and that rumours actually create efficient information flow – China needs to improve its release of information to the market in a modern manner.)

Currency revaluation

In addition to the results mentioned above, a renminbi revaluation would reduce the cost of China's raw material imports and increase local Chinese competition. This

---

[3] Much of the data in this section is derived from *China at a Crossroads: Seven Risks of Doing Business* (2004), a Deloitte Research Economic Study.
[4] *The Economist* (2007), 'A new tax hits the euphoric Chinese bourses', May.

would lower inflationary pressure in the Chinese economy and reduce the potential for it to overheat. It would reduce the price of exports to China allowing companies that sell there to be more competitive; and increase Chinese consumers' spending power possibly expanding the domestic Chinese market. It would reduce raw materials and components costs for companies producing in China. It would increase the price of goods exported from China, allowing other Asian economies to compete. Since the Deloittes study was published, China has revalued its currency upwards by about 6.6 per cent[5] against the US dollar in less than two years. However the revaluation has not affected the trade imbalance, nor has the trade imbalance had much of an effect on employment in the United States economy, which remains fairly full.[6] It can also be said that by subsidizing its exports China is merely subsidizing US consumption at the expense of its own workers.[7] However, international pressure remains.

Economy overheating

In 2004, inflation reached 5.3 per cent, although measuring inflation in China is not the same as in the West because the government controls many product prices. Low interest rates plus inflation mean that the true cost of borrowing is negative, encouraging Chinese firms to overinvest and overborrow with the consequent risk of failure. The implications for those who manufacture in China is that overheating distorts the key indicators of market changes (such as price increases reducing demand); inflates asset prices (especially for land) and creates shortages in materials and energy (the price of which is government-controlled). Overheating means there is a higher risk of a sharp slowdown; inflation and overheating remain a problem – in February the consumer price index (CPI) rose 3.9 per cent, in March 3.3 per cent and in May 3.4 per cent, against the government's target of 3 per cent.[8]

Risk of economy faltering and reform

The Chinese government is clearly trying to slow down the overheating. (On 18 May 2007, China raised the one-year borrowing rate to 6.57 per cent and the deposit rate to 3.06 per cent but this is still less than the inflation rate.)[9] Premier Wen Jiabao announced further measures on 13 June 2007 to prevent the economy from overheating but foreign observers believe that the measures are having only limited effect.[10] The National Bureau of Statistics forecast that the economy would grow by 8.5 per cent in 2006, down from 9.8 percent in 2005, but data shows China's economy continues to grow at a speed exceeding those figures (11 per cent in the first quarter of 2007)

---

[5] Or, according to some reports, 8.2 per cent since July 2005 (*Times Online*, 17 June 2007).
[6] Brian Wingfield, *Forbes Magazine Online* at Forbes.com on 5 March 2007.
[7] Carl Steidtmann, Chief Economist, Deloitte Research, 1 June 2007, Economist's Corner: 'Three cheers for globalization' (www.deloitte.com).
[8] According to reports from Beijing, mostly through the *China Daily*.
[9] *Bloomberg News*, Reuters, 15 June 2007.
[10] Associated Press, 20 April 2007.

and it is on track to continue with double-digit growth for the fifth consecutive year. However, the government is also taking measures to 'marketize' the economy. Two years ago in 2004 it was true that much investment had been inefficient and had wasted resources. This is improving, but if the economy falters this will erode political support for the further reforms that are necessary and will have a negative impact on other Asian economies (especially Japan) for which China has become the engine of growth. Some economists foresee the possibility of a tightening of monetary policy at any time or a reduction or cancellation of a 20 per cent tax on bank deposits to reduce flows of private savings from savings accounts to the stock markets.[11]

State-owned business (SOEs) and privatization

Whilst there has been a massive SOE sector, many of these have now been or are being privatized. There are still risks that SOEs have been able to expand quickly using cheap finance, thus creating huge manufacturing capacity and local competitors on the doorstep of the foreign manufacturers. However, this has not put foreign manufacturers off and local consumer demand is continuing to grow. The partial privatizations of SOEs by floating a percentage of their shares through initial public offerings (IPOs) has not fully addressed the problem and the restructuring of the Chinese economy will entail further structural stresses.

Trade conflict

There is potential for the EU and United States to behave in a protectionist manner when under political pressure at home. Punitive sanctions have been suggested in the United States. There may appear to be less aggression in the EU, but there has been heavy pressure, notably in the textiles and shoes sectors, to impose tariffs and/ or quotas. (It should be said that there has been lobbying in the opposite direction by major EU retailers and by some countries such as Sweden that see the quotas as protectionist.) This was seen in autumn 2005 in the 'bra wars' dispute, the effects of which are still continuing. Quotas were supposed to have been abolished with China's WTO accession but EU manufacturers still lobbied for their preservation. The temporary quotas negotiated in 2005 expire in December 2007.[12] In summary, there is still a risk of tariff barriers that could have a major impact on manufacturers in China.

Income disparities

Whilst the incomes of the emerging middle classes in Chinese cities have increased substantially, growth in the incomes of the agricultural classes has stagnated. The

---

[11] Chris Leung, Senior Economist, DBS Hong Kong and Frank Gong, Economist, JP Morgan Chase, Hong Kong, quoted in *Bloomberg News*, Reuters and reported in *International Herald Tribune Business*, 15 June 2007.

[12] Since then the EU has announced (9 October 2007) that it is ending the temporary quotas, but putting in place a joint surveillance system to track trade flows.

Chinese government is critically aware that to keep economic growth stable it must address the social tensions created by these disparities and is committed to shifting resources to the countryside to alleviate the disparity. This has been done by increasing its rural development budget and encouraging the expansion of credit by rural credit institutions.

Regulatory risk

These are the risks of the national or local government changing regulations, imposing taxes or duties or even nationalizing your assets. I have called this regulatory risk but other analyses might call it political risk.

Since the Chinese government is firmly committed to stable economic growth (with the emphasis on stable) and gradual (and this means in a controlled fashion) 'marketization' of its economy, regulatory risk is relatively low and conditions are favourable for outsourcing and investment projects. Nevertheless, the economy is still largely a controlled economy and there are strong political influences at work.

For foreign investors seeking to make acquisitions, one should bear in mind that the Chinese government is unlikely to permit, within a short time frame, foreign investors to take control of assets of national importance. China spent a year holding up an investment by the Carlyle Group in Xugong, the largest machinery manufacturing company in China, eventually (October 2006) negotiating the reduction of the investment to 50 per cent, with Xuzhou Construction Machinery Group, the parent of Xugong, taking the other 50 per cent. Originally, in October 2005, the Carlyle Group agreed to take 85 per cent in return for a US\$375 million equity injection. Forecasts for 2007 were that large acquisitions by foreign buyers would face delays because of the interpretation of new regulations but once they were clarified, acquisition activity would increase again.[13] Restrictions on foreign acquisitions are going to continue in certain industries that China regards as strategic.

Partner risk

Choosing the right strategic partner in a foreign market is possibly the most important choice to be made and China is no different. Although Chinese culture is very different from Western culture and arguably unique, Chinese businesspeople are pragmatic and focused on generating profit,[14] so they make excellent partners. One hears horror stories of backyard engineering, unauthorized subcontracting, poor quality or lack of understanding of material specifications; the partner who operated the factory at weekends selling the production privately at discounted prices; setting up clone operations copying the whole factory; and 'stealing' the foreign partner's technology. These stories when analysed usually lead to many questions about the behaviour of the foreign investor – why didn't he or she do his or her due diligence, monitor the

---

[13] PwC, Asia-Pacific M&A Bulletin year-end 2006.
[14] This really applies to private enterprise – Chinese businesspeople in state-owned enterprises may have other agendas such as preserving market share or employment rather than profit.

operations more closely; in short, spend more time on risk management? Perhaps more important, why didn't he or she spend more time and effort to get to know his or her Chinese partner, and in particular, maintain that effort on a continuous basis? Especially since one also hears from those who are successful, that the Chinese are absolutely trustworthy and excellent long-term business partners.

Communications risk: language and culture

The Chinese language is famously hard to learn. Even the Chinese government has, over many years, executed a project to simplify Chinese characters to mitigate illiteracy problems. Among the reasons the spoken language is hard is that it is tonal so that the meaning of the word changes with the tone used, and there is a large number of synonyms. The written language is impenetrable because each character has to be learned before it can be pronounced. The Chinese love plays on words and there are many amusing stories of foreigners using the wrong tone when attempting the language.

In addition, numbers are counted in units, tens, hundreds, thousands, ten thousands, and then hundreds of millions, so there are important translation risks once above ten thousand – one million is said as 'one hundred ten thousands' and one billion as 'ten one hundred millions'.

Added to this is a culture going back 5,000 years, of which the Chinese are rightfully proud, which is totally different from Western culture. Dealing with your Chinese counterpart is therefore a challenge that carries significant risks but is also an enriching experience.

Supply chain risk

When one considers that components sourced outside China have to be shipped there, used in manufacture together with other components sourced locally and then re-exported, one can see the tensions that may arise in the supply chain. Once the strategic partner and structure have been selected, the supply chain risk must become the key focus of the outsourcer's or investor's attention.

Here is a simplified (and I hope practical) breakdown of supply chain risks:

■ financial control risk: lack of working capital, poor accounting controls resulting in 'leakage', credit risk;
■ cost-saving illusory risk (although materials and local labour may be cheaper, what is the result when overall costs of shipping, customs duties, distance and delivery times are taken into account?);
■ knowledge management risk: protection of intellectual property;
■ commercial risk: enforcing compliance with contracts by counterparties;
■ quality risks;

■ operational or execution risk: inadequate equipment or raw materials;
■ long-term distortion of market.[15]

Risk management: checklist for outsourcing in China

I referred earlier to the sort of risk analysis used by lawyers in M&A transactions. This can be contrasted with other analyses, for example, the sort of analysis used in the health and safety environment:

■ Is it possible to eliminate the risk by changing the design or the work environment?
■ Is the risk tolerable? Is the statistical probability so small that one can live with the risk?
■ Is it possible to control the risk by some sort of control mechanism, either a physical barrier, work practice or process or administrative procedures?

Another interesting look at the process of risk management is this:[16]

1 Analyse internal requirements
  Understand risk tolerance
2 Analyse supply market
  Understand market risks
3 Determine approach and relationship type
  Risk, reduction, buffering
4 Identify and evaluate suppliers
  Risk assessment
5 Build and manage relationship
  Risk monitoring

Below is a suggested risk management checklist, with comments added from actual experience. It attempts to correlate the planning process with the risks already identified and to amplify the process in order to cover areas that are not strictly legal concerns:

---

[15] Some of these categories are based on the classifications used in Helen Alder, Senior Procurement Specialist, Chartered Institute of Purchasing and Supply (2004) 'Supply chain vulnerability', in *Managing Business Risk*, Kogan Page, London. Others are based on Markiles and Berg (1988) 'Manufacturing offshore is bad business', *Harvard Business Review*, Sept/Oct. Reviewed by Alan Braithwaite of Cranfield Business School (2006) 'The supply chain risks of global sourcing', in *Managing Business Risk*, 3rd edn, Kogan Page, London, who concluded that the same risks are valid today.
[16] Taken from George A. Zsidisin, Gary L. Ragatz and Steven A. Malnyk (2003) 'Effective Practices for Business Continuity Planning in Purchasing and Supply Management', White Paper.

- Internal planning (eg, drivers in existing business towards outsourcing):
  - Understand risk tolerance (risk controls come later).
- Market analysis:
  - understand market risks (*macroeconomic risks*) and industry-specific risks.
  - Do not ignore local competition, which is fierce.
- Due diligence on legal environment (*regulatory risks*):
  - One characteristic of China is the evolving interpretation of its laws by China's administrative bodies; this was seen (summer and autumn 2006) in the slowing down of foreign M&A activity in China as a result not of a change in the law but an altered interpretation of the rules on permissions for foreign acquisitions of Chinese businesses.
  - There is not much you can do about laws changing in the future, but the good news is that standards of legal process are rising rapidly. For example, there are now specialist intellectual property courts in the Shanghai region and we understand that if anything they tend to favour the foreign intellectual property owner, such is China's will to demonstrate that it is enforcing international standards.
- Due diligence on possible partners (*partner risks*):
  - This is now much more feasible than previously. A partner who is introduced to you may be better than one found at a trade fair. Relationships are *very* important in China.
  - Be aware that your local partner will have relationships with family associates and business partners, which you will only understand over a long period.
- Make strategic choices as to structure of outsourcing/investment:
  - Whether to go for a wholly owned company, an equity joint venture, collaborative joint venture with no equity play, or merely outsourcing to local manufacturers.
  - Build in risk controls at this stage.
- Register intellectual property at home and in China and take steps to protect trade secrets (*knowledge management risk*):
  - Register the Chinese version of your trade name. Even if you do not think it important, if you have any penetration of the local market it will be important to Chinese consumers who will use the Chinese and not the Western name.
  - It may be wise not to let the local manufacturer 'see' all of your technology; in addition to confidentiality agreements use the need-to-know basis of revealing know-how; one tried and tested strategy is using multiple sources for different parts of the product.
- Business plan preparation (*financial risk*).
- Address language and culture (*communications risk*):
  - Bearing in mind the importance of the relationship, your translator or interpreter is a key person.
  - Learn something about the Chinese language yourself. Small phrases will help the relationship more than you think.
  - If using an interpreter, speak in packages so that the interpreter has time to translate the sentence before you move on.
  - It will repay the effort to work on technical presentations with your interpreter in advance, before the meeting.

- If possible (this may be a luxury) have an English person with you who speaks Chinese who can listen to the interpreter.
- Remember that there are many dialects in China and that your interpreter may him- or herself have some difficulty in some regions.
- Some of our clients who are successful engineers outsourcing in China use drawings wherever possible – a universal language.

■ Research shipping, customs duties, shipping and logistics costs; take accounting of legal advice on customs duties and tax rates (*supply chain risk – cost saving illusory*):
- There is frequent reform of tax rates, for example, reducing the tax advantages in the special economic zones (SEZs), so research is essential.
- Some manufacturers have researched tax rates but ignored customs duties, to their cost.

■ Tactical choices (*supply chain risk*):
- Design of the organization: evaluate skill sets of those involved in the project.
- Choices of raw materials will have a major impact, where to source.
- If local, be clear on specification and quality expected.
- Consider multiple sourcing to reduce dependence on one supplier; build in flexibility and responsiveness to seasons, fashions, price; possibly an exit plan if all goes wrong.

■ Plan IT systems and procedures to protect your data (*supply chain risk*).

■ Set up quality assurance systems into your contracts and control procedures (*supply chain risk*):
- Avoid rejects: frequent visits for quality control are better, before the product leaves the factory.
- Consider having a local Chinese quality control manager (possibly full-time) to monitor quality. They are readily available, many based in Hong Kong, well educated and prepared to visit the mainland for audits.
- Build in ongoing measuring processes and continuous improvement of the products and management processes.

■ Segregation of duties (and perhaps more) (*supply chain risk*):
- Take practical steps such as segregating the signing rights on the bank account: avoid the stories involving fraud where a local manager has been given signing rights over amounts of money that represent more wealth than his or her family has seen for several generations.

■ Build in accounting controls (*supply chain risk*):
- Frequently told stories of the local manufacturer using the factory at night to overproduce and sell the overproduction on the local market without accounting for it; proper reporting may address this but it may not; frequent visits will reduce the risk.

■ Take employee factors into consideration: welfare, health and safety (*supply chain risk*).

■ Plan your contracts so that you minimize default (*supply chain risk*):
- Some of our clients do not believe in contracts and rely on managing the relationship alone; most commentators, including Chinese, recommend both.

   – It is no good writing the contract and then forgetting it. The Chinese regard the signing of the contract as the beginning of the relationship. Use the contract as the rulebook for the relationship.
   – Build the ongoing quality, logistics, revisions of price lists and payment procedures into your contract so that it is a reference point for the relationship. This will give the message that you respect your contract and you expect your partner to respect it.

Contract notes[17]

The following is not intended to be a contract checklist but highlights certain practical aspects of risk management through the contract process:

■ Consent required if the Chinese manufacturer wants to subcontract any manufacture.
■ Obligation on the Chinese manufacturer to maintain, repair, insure and recalibrate tooling.
■ Change of control clause if the ownership of the Chinese manufacturer changes – you have dealt with and trust your partner, not someone else.
■ Child labour – it is established practice in China for the Chinese manufacturer to be obliged to adhere to the International Labour Organization standards.
■ Obligation not to make custom products available to anyone else.
■ Chinese manufacturers have to answer for any non-compliance by any of their affiliates.
■ The usual clauses dealing with use of trademarks and confidentiality.
■ Quality procedures.
■ Logistics regarding delivery timing, ordering and, of course, payment process.

Conclusion

Whilst there are undoubtedly significant risks in outsourcing to China they are probably no more serious than in any other emerging market economy such as India or Latin America. Whilst China has particular characteristics that are unique, provided the risks are managed properly, it remains a good prospect for outsourcing and investment. Bear in mind its rapid growth rate, rising consumer demand among the new middle class, rapidly improving technology and the increasing skill levels of the workforce.

---

[17] Based on actual contracts between multinationals and Chinese factories.

9

The culture partnership

Joan Turley

Introduction

A seminal moment has been reached in our relationship with China, which we can view as an unprecedented opportunity or an inconvenient challenge. The facts of China's continuing economic ascendancy are inspirational with staggering GDP increases and ever-growing foreign trade surpluses. Even more interesting perhaps are some of the lesser-known sociocultural changes that are transforming the Chinese appetite for consuming.

Nowhere is this more prevalent than in attitudes to spending. Until recently, sacrosanct traditions of saving substantial proportions of one's earnings were the norm in China. This reflected not only a prudent and thrifty national disposition but also the intense commitment of the younger generation to provide for parents and grandparents economically in their mature years.

So sacred is this duty, in the eyes of most Chinese of all generations, that it is enshrined by legislation in Chinese family law. However, with the increase in earnings and prospects of many young Chinese, including increasing opportunities with high-paying multinationals and careers abroad, a new generation of consumer is emerging who can accommodate this sacred duty while permitting themselves some of the privileges of Western-style consuming.

The climate since Deng Xiaoping's comments on the duty of each citizen to create wealth has liberated an instinct to prosperity and expansive thinking endemic to the Chinese character and has galvanized a new urge to prosper and acquire. The opportunities in such a climate have never been greater for those who are willing to partner the Chinese in their new directions and aspirations, which are: to trade brilliantly; to innovate; to acquire knowledge in a range of fields, particularly the service sector; to relate well to global partners and to have the sophisticated skills to communicate effectively and proudly the unique properties of the brand that is China plc.

The simple truth, and one that has been poorly grasped, is that only those individuals, companies and entities who embrace the challenge of relating to China in a rounded and meaningful manner, and one that resonates with Chinese values and business practices, will become the preferred partners in the choice-filled contemporary climate of the new China.

The opportunities to partner China have existed for some time. Why then have we often chosen to sidestep the issue, preferring to analyse, observe, manage, deconstruct and contractualize this task of relating rather than proceeding with its accomplishment? The reality is that the terms of positive and constructive engagement with China have not been fully grasped. Where a partial or semi-adequate route has been provided it has rarely been accompanied by a dynamic toolkit, one that encourages the will to relate and provides the means to do so.

Ask a random selection of businesspeople, on a word association basis, to venture spontaneous appraisals of the prospect of trading with China and words ranging from problematical to minefield are proffered – views often sustained by Western analysts of China. Yet, since entry to the WTO, China's proof of commercial goodwill, flexibility and pragmatism has been undeniable.

Personal relationships are paramount

Moreover, when one probes further, it is not on the level of willingness to trade, incentives, ideas or positive models for business exchange that doubt exists. No indeed. The challenge is a relational one. Inherited stereotypes of inscrutability and unexamined differences in relationship models have often left us wary of trying to win Chinese hearts and minds. And yet, if we can learn to relate to China in a way that meaningfully communicates to the Chinese our commitment to partnership, professionalism and trustworthiness, we will gain potentially lasting business friendships and take our rightful place in one of the most dynamic economic stories of our time. Our starting point and chief means is the area of relationships. Why? Because it is China's, and to a degree unparalleled in even the most relationship-based business cultures of the West.

The term *mayo guan xi* (no relationship base) in a modern Chinese ballad, is sung by a famous Taiwanese balladeer as if lamenting the absence of food, air or water. Relationships are the means by which the Chinese apprehend and order their world, create security and a sense of safety, implement their decisions, resource their lives, achieve success, create and celebrate prosperity. They are at once goal, means and outcome.

In a world dominated by the importance of public reputation, where the *mianzi* (face) that an individual presents to the world is endowed with monumental importance, the associations both business and personal that individual makes are of the highest significance. As such, they are subject to great scrutiny and entered into with prudence and reserve.

So the challenge for all of us who wish to relate to China is to understand how reputation is built and maintained and even more crucially, how we can communicate to the Chinese that we are conscientious and reliable partners in the building and maintaining of such reputations. This acts not only as the basis for profitable and enduring business friendships but also as a guarantor for the meaningful, contractual recording of such relationships.

Understanding Chinese business relationships

The understanding then of Chinese business relationships for success is fundamental. The willingness to embrace and incorporate the 'rules' is equally crucial. With open-mindedness, those seeking to do business in China would do well to examine three areas:

- character;
- motives;
- conduct.

Unusual and rather Victorian sounding advice by today's Western business standards and yet, character repeatedly marks itself out as the determining factor in recent China success stories. This is because in China, you are the brand, not your company, its mission statements or marketing collateral, though prestigious names and proven track records open doors here as elsewhere in the world.

But it is the character and the presence of qualities that the Chinese respect within one's character that often prove the deciding factor in winning and keeping business in China. The generous and often lengthy process of hospitality that the Chinese bestow on business prospects and partners is a process where the character of those hoping to win business is encouraged to reveal itself and – in the case of successful candidates – prove itself to be unmistakably reliable as a partner in the business of public reputation and achievement. The most successful individual entrepreneurs I have observed in China are those whose business offer corresponds to China's needs but who, additionally, demonstrate a positive motive in the conduct of their business, a willingness to see China as prosperous and respected and to make their contribution to this goal.

After a history of encounters where many have come to take, China evaluates its potential business partners, allies and commercial associates thoroughly. Deluged with global interest proffering services, investment and business exchange, China is now looking at the motives of those who come to buy and sell and at their willingness to transfer skills, share knowledge and set fresh ideals that will raise China's brand positively within the world. It is in this way that prospective business partners give proof of true China-style business partnerships based on sound business conduct, character and motives.

Good practice in building relationships

So, what are the practical rules of engaging well in today's China? First, it is important to understand what type of business behaviour, communication styles and relationship exchange constitute good relationship practice and to adhere to them. In doing so one reflects a type of conduct, motives and objectives that play well with deeper Chinese values.

Context and tone are perhaps the two most overarching determinants of good interaction with the Chinese. In both, understanding how formality creates a safe context for the Chinese is essential. For example, no matter how much the Chinese provide Western alternatives for their first names, in a generous effort towards accessibility, formality remains an important context for the rituals of relationship-building in China. Formality and the even-paced evolution of business dialogue are crucial. Beyond that, steady communication of character and mutually beneficial intent alongside business goals and profit objectives go a long way to creating sustainable business relationships.

In fact, the equation is almost the reverse of what makes us feel comfortable here in the United Kingdom. We start with formal boundaries, we often move speedily to the use of first names, exchange business goals, set terms, do the deal – always mindful of demonstrating professionalism as we go along – and, subject to the success of our business outcomes, we then have a basis for the kind of business friendship and corporate gift-giving, which demonstrate progress in business outcomes and in the professional relationship itself.

In China, the deep mutual scrutiny of prospective business partners, followed by bonding and the establishing of trustworthiness is first carried out at length in the boardroom, the banqueting hall and the cabaret suite. When reliability of partnership in the all-important area of reputation and face is achieved, the real business can begin. One can then count on the newly established relationship to add order, texture and momentum to the business dialogue. The relationship will then carry a complex network of mutual obligations extending beyond boundaries of time, space and convenience. This acts as a statement of the value of the relationship that far outweighs the weight of obligation or significance afforded by any contract.

Relationships in China business settings are based on values of in-group interdependence, mutual advantage, favours and obligations, assistance and protection. These are collectivist inspired – we versus you and I – and are not attention or time constrained. To play well with such values, it is important to give proof of good intentions, pragmatic yet flexible character and astuteness. Furthermore, we must show our suitability for the role of acceptable and sustained partner in the building and maintaining of public face, professional reputation and effectiveness.

If you have grasped the breathtaking importance of relationship, the ritualized definition of business friendships and the daily, myriad ways that relationships are cultivated, stroked and maintained, then you have found the broad inside track to success in China. However, we must go far beyond the references to networks, covered in many of the survival manuals for Western businesses. To participate well in relationships with the Chinese, we need to invest in relationships as they do, seeing them as immense business collateral and being willing to do whatever it takes to enhance the relationship, knowing that if we do so, the business will follow.

If relationships are the all-pervading drivers then, not just of business but of life in China, it follows that the ability to signal an understanding of the defining influence of relationship on business dialogue as well as the rules and values underpinning the China model, will mark us out as serious and potentially preferred business partners.

Developing relationships into business

What then are the ways to cooperate in successful relationship and reputation-building and how do we communicate our trustworthiness and competence in respect of this important criterion for China success? The following three broad strategies have worked for many successful companies in achieving this goal:

■ communicating clearly, transparently and accessibly in English or, when appropriate, in Mandarin;
■ understanding the unique constitution of business teams and their leaders and Chinese variations on the decision-making process;
■ understanding how to signal respect for the traditions and protocol around the business process contributing to business reputation.

Much of the burden of demonstrating trustworthiness within the Chinese model of business relationships, and winning favour and ground in business dialogue, falls to the communication style we deploy. We can begin by understanding what communication represents for the Chinese and how language is viewed and deployed. What, if you like, language is for. It may be easier, in Western terms to say what it is not for: populating silences, as a show case for individual prowess or skills, communicating highly individual views or stance, dominating at public negotiations (where the leader is present) or engaging in confrontational debate.

Mandarin is essentially a language built for consensus and the Chinese carry this forward in their use of English. Language more commonly in China is used for the exploration of common goals, information-gathering, the verification of proofs of good faith, the subtle exchanges of common ground or experience, which builds mutual loyalty as a context for relating. When this is complete, language is used for the description of achievement and the celebration of success.

So communication must be handled with care. Language must be respectfully direct when responding to important questions yet indirect when publicly requesting outcomes or decisions from individuals in a team or team leaders. It must be warm but circumspect. The Chinese are highly adept at communicating the desire to bond with business partners while retaining the formal structures that help them feel secure as guardians of face. The asymmetric deference model that the Chinese prefer as a method of relating allows them to create business friendships in a way that is non-threatening.

Finally, language must be rich enough to hold the attention span of a race used to varied stimuli, but not heavy in figurative or idiomatic phrases that confuse and belittle serious dialogue in the eyes of the Chinese. Nothing is more disturbing at seminal business moments for Chinese interlocutors to hear than 'belt and braces' and 'ball-parks', as the face implications if they are unfamiliar with the idiom are extreme. Above all, language must not be so all-pervasive, that silence, and the reflection that it permits is curtailed, especially in a culture where reflection is a sign of business maturity.

Good communication styles for China are those that wholly demonstrate and uphold the value and reputation of Chinese partners and that mirror the respectful measured approach to communication that defines the Chinese business idiom. Next, the Chinese look to us for an understanding of the rituals and processes that underpin the way they prefer to do business and the criteria for success that they set.

We return obligatorily to relationships. At the core of the public face of business in China is respect for the person; from the often-cited formal seating arrangements, to the frequent mutual toasting of colleagues of the same team, to the celebration of achievement and relationship maturation. Through the exchange of gifts, the hierarchical layout of meetings and informed participation in banqueting protocol, multiple opportunities abound to demonstrate respectful awareness of the preferred business relationship model. This model prevails as strongly today as it has done in the past, albeit with strong private to public sector and regional/generational modifications. Nowhere is this more obvious than in the decision-making process.

In China, the decision-maker is first and foremost a leader of people whether he or she is in practical business terms a CEO or an MD. He or she, the leader, has the holistic responsibility for the development of all his or her team members and for charting a path through life for them. This, in turn, guarantees him or her a highly team-spirited group of executives for whom allegiance to the leader is both a matter of respect and face. Such a model brings about an even further insistence on the person-centred way in which decisions get taken and business gets done.

To achieve success in this climate we must lay aside our insistence on agenda, time- and outcome-driven business models, which even the most adroit intercultural negotiator can revert to in moments of pressure, and prove the adaptability of our relationship skills. If we do this, we will achieve much in respect of China. However, if we are prepared to go further, and signal a willingness to reach business goals having first explored compatibility of character, reputation-sharing and intention along the Chinese model, then we are looking at significant rewards and sustainable gains. China does not merely want to see the nature of our business collateral but the state of our intentions, manners and disposition.

We have a chance to excel in creating a model of partnership and trustworthiness that bridges business cultures in the most dynamic of ways, at this, the most exciting of times for China. A place in the continuing economic ascendancy of China is not lightly or easily won. But it rarely disappoints, in business or in any other terms, providing the appropriate handling of relationships has been the overarching guide and reference point by which we have built our partnership. Let us not disappoint.

Note: *Grateful acknowledgements to John Twitchim for his comments on good practice in building relationships*

10

Preparing for IP management in China – staying out of trouble

Joshua Whale and Luke Minford, Rouse & Co. International

It is still the case that a large number of companies take very few steps to protect their intellectual property in China. The majority of these companies appear to replace an IP protection strategy with a combination of hope, and a belief that nothing can be done. As a result, many do not even bother to register their rights, making it much more difficult to defend those rights later on.

China is no longer a legal wilderness where IP rights are unenforceable. IP theft is indeed a fact of doing business in China, but in most cases it is a manageable risk. There are concrete legal and practical steps that businesses can and should take to reduce IP losses. Many of these steps are surprisingly inexpensive.

In most cases, Western companies derive their competitive advantage in China from those areas most in danger of IP theft: technology, designs, brand, reputation and solutions to everyday industrial challenges. This chapter aims to provide a five-step practical guide for getting a company's IP 'China-resistant'. The sixth step, effective enforcement, is dealt with in Chapter 13.

Being IP aware – taking stock of IP

The first step in ensuring that a company's IP is China-ready is to know what you have. This can be a simple stock-take, or a formal 'IP audit'. At a minimum, the following would need to be clearly identified:

- what intellectual property you possess;
- the relative importance of these assets; and
- how they are currently protected at home and in China.

If companies do not take these steps they can be savaged by the grey areas that exist in a country like China.

Once the IP has been identified and prioritized, the company needs to decide how its IP is going to be strategically managed and protected. It is critical that this plan has the full support of senior management, and that it is communicated throughout the IP chain. This will help to ensure that employees and managers are taking IP into account in their decision-making. For example, employees responsible for product development and marketing can enhance the protection of intellectual property by understanding that the distinctiveness and consistency of use of design elements are essential elements of brand protection (in this case the most relevant rights are trademarks). Another area where this can be seen is when companies put in place systems for capturing innovation and preventing IP leakage.

Once the company is clear on what assets it possesses and their relative importance, and has ensured that all management and employees understand their relative value within the organization, then the company is in a position to implement a plan to protect those assets.

Getting into a good IP position for China – is your IP China-resistant?

China has a civil law system. This means that your rights are conferred by the state, rather than coming into existence by operation of common law. In most cases it is only when the state grants you a certificate, and not before, that you have an enforceable intellectual property right in China. China's overall market characteristics, including the size of the country and the population, the emphasis on low-cost manufacturing, and the civil law system, mean that rights-owners have to be that much more diligent in building a strong platform of rights recognized by the state. China has a reputation for being a counterfeit paradise, yet this should not overshadow the proactive steps that all rights-owners should take to register their rights.

The legal system in China is changing rapidly. Under this year's IPR action plan alone, China will draft, finalize or revise a total of 17 laws and regulations related to trademarks, copyrights and patents. As most of the key laws were amended in 2000–01 for WTO accession, this means that China is overhauling its entire IPR system in six-year cycles. This is in addition to the dozens of judicial interpretations and regulations issued by State Council bodies at all levels of government. At the same time, investment and activity from rights-owners means that companies are using the system more and more. The unprepared registration bodies have struggled to cope with the number of applications for patents and trademarks, and the high number of bad faith registrations has only made this worse. There is currently a three- to four-year backlog for trademark registrations, and invention patent applications are taking three to five years depending on their complexity. This makes early registration even more important. Although the delay may lessen the perceived usefulness of the right, filing an application first also precludes potential infringers from registering a company's brands and innovations in its stead.

While China's IP system has become increasingly useful, it is still in its adolescence. Possessing clear, officially registered rights is helpful when dealing with administrative officials or inexperienced judges, particularly outside the main centres. Registered rights also provide prima facie evidence of the right's existence and ownership, removing a major source of uncertainty when a company needs to enforce it. The certainty that comes with registered rights acts as leverage when negotiating with infringers, and transforms the right into an asset that can be sold, licensed or used as security.

Until registration is granted, a company may need to resort to other mechanisms to protect its rights. In the absence of a registered right, you will also need to prove that you own the right. Typically, evidentiary thresholds are strict. This makes it particularly important that companies take diligent steps to document the usage, reputation (eg, through media monitoring programmes) and consumer awareness of their brands. Carefully recording the invention and authorship processes is also vital for establishing copyright and patent rights.

The following sections set out the key characteristics for each type of registered right, as well as for trade secrets (which cannot be registered).

Trademarks

■ Trademarks can be renewed every 10 years. It currently takes three to four years to gain a trademark registration. However, under the draft Trademark Law, it appears that this pendency period will be reduced by eliminating substantive examination from the registration process.

■ The definition of a trademark is 'any visual sign that can serve to distinguish goods including any work, design, letter of the alphabet, numeral, 3D symbol and colour combination, or any combination of the above'. This means that distinctive 3D trademarks and colour combinations are registerable in China.

■ Most trademarks have localized Chinese versions as well as romanized Chinese *pinyin*. It is important to create and register these versions to prevent the market adopting names itself, over which a rights-owner has no control.

■ Ordinarily, a trademark's exclusive right is limited to products or services of the same classification. Being deemed a 'well-known trademark', however, prevents others from using a similar mark in *any* product class. In China, this additional protection can only be obtained by being tested in an actual dispute. This can be through:

- – an infringement action with the Administration of Industry and Commerce;
- – trademark infringement litigation in the courts;
- – opposition to registration of a similar trademark in a different product class (through the Trademark Office).

None of these mechanisms are binding, but all are highly persuasive in future actions.

Copyright

- ■ Duration is life of author plus 50 years.
- ■ Software is covered by the copyright law but has separate regulations.
- ■ A copyright can be registered with the National Copyright Administration (NCA). Consistent with the Berne Convention, registration is not a prerequisite for the right to exist, but generally speaking, recordal is strongly recommended as it provides prima facie evidence of subsistence and ownership. Because the recordal process does not involve substantive examination, it only takes one to four months to obtain a copyright recordal.
- ■ Having a recordal certificate can be a valuable tool for warning infringers and is often used as an attachment in a 'cease and desist' strategy. However, whether copyright actually subsists is a question for the courts or the NCA to determine.

Patents

- ■ Duration: 20 years for inventions, 10 for utility models and designs.
- ■ China is a Patent Cooperation Treaty (PCT) member. This means that if you file a PCT application anywhere in the world, you have 32 months from your filing or your chosen 'priority date' to file in China, during which you will have priority rights. If you have only filed a national patent, you have 12 months in which to file in China claiming priority.
- ■ Applying for patent rights:
  - – Invention patents take three to five years.
  - – Design patents and utility model applications take 10–14 months. They are faster and cheaper due to lack of substantive examination.
  - – Multiple rights can be applied for, to afford a level of protection while invention patent is pending.
- ■ It is wise to prepare clear evidence of ownership, in case of leakage before patent publication.
- ■ All patents require an annual fee.
- ■ Bad faith infringers can register the innovations of another. Cancellation is a slow process, and requires solid evidence of the priority right.

Trade secrets

Trade secrets are often extremely valuable assets, but can be very difficult to identify and protect within an organization. Because they are not registered, it is all the more important to take concrete steps to protect them.

Key elements of trade secret protection

The prerequisites for trade secret protection are similar to most countries, including the United Kingdom. There are four essential elements to successful trade secret protection in China:

1. A trade secret must be technical or operational information that is not publicly known.
2. The information must be of economic value to the owner.
3. The information must have 'practical applicability'.
4. The owner must have taken *reasonable steps to protect it.*

It is this last element that the courts and authorities have emphasized most when ruling in trade secret infringement proceedings. It is not enough for rights-owners to require IP protection measures in the contract and rely on their partners to execute them. It is vital that rights-owners actively supervise the implementation of those protection measures.

At the very least, employees and business partners need clear guidance on what they can and cannot divulge about the business. Employees should also be encouraged to adhere to those rules by signing confidentiality agreements when they are hired, and reminded with posters, training, e-mails and so forth.

Confidentiality and non-compete clauses

China's new Labour Contract Law allows companies to require confidentiality agreements, and confidentiality and non-compete clauses can remain in effect for up to two years after contract termination:

■ A prerequisite for a non-compete clause is that a reasonable amount of monthly compensation is paid during the period of the non-compete obligation. The definition of 'reasonable' varies between jurisdictions. This makes gaining good local legal advice on drafting such clauses essential.
■ Non-compete clauses are also limited to 'senior management, senior technical personnel, and other personnel who have specific obligations of confidence'. This means that if companies wish to retain a non-compete option, a confidentiality agreement is essential.
■ Employment contracts should include an explicit duty of good faith not to damage the employer's interests, and ban the copying or removal of specified materials both during and on termination of employment.

Production facility configuration

You should take the protection of unpublished IP into consideration when designing the layout of your production facilities, and restrict access to sensitive areas with swipe-cards or similar measures. Your IT systems should limit access to sensitive information, and track access and downloading of key files. You should also consider preparing key parts of each product in different parts of China, or abroad, so that no single facility contains all the necessary information to reproduce a complete product.

Due diligence – homework on your partners

There is very little publicly available information on companies and company directors in China. The only source at present is Administration of Industry and Commerce (AIC) company registration information, and this only provides basic details of the company's registered capital, legal representation and registered address. This means that the burden is on those doing business in China to take additional steps to check the status and reliability of their prospective partners, distributors, OEM producer companies and so forth. It is not an advisable strategy for companies to deal blindly with the lowest bidding factory, especially where valuable rights are involved.

Here are some of the key questions companies should ask when conducting due diligence on parties in China:

■ Is the party seeking to register another party's rights in bad faith? Local companies may also believe they are helping the relationship by proactively registering any rights that flow from that relationship in their own name. Companies can conduct a search of trademarks, patents and Customs recordals to ensure this is not occurring.

■ Is the party in this transaction located in an area that has a reputation for IP infringement? There are areas of China that are renowned counterfeiting hotspots, or that have a reputation for local government protectionism. While these areas may provide low-cost opportunities, they pose an extreme risk to IP and strict due diligence is advisable if IP is to form part of the transaction in that area.

■ What is the company's history? Do they have a habit of closing down and liquidating in order to avoid litigation? It is very easy to liquidate and set up new companies in China, and understanding that history can be crucial to your transaction.

■ What is the involvement of the state? Are there any directors or employees on the state payroll? Their political connections can be an advantage, but can just as easily become a disadvantage in a dispute. Partners with government ownership can also come under pressure to make decisions that serve political, rather than economic ends.

■ What is their litigation history? There are no centralized databases with this information, so it will come down to asking your partner, noting legal fees when auditing them and making general inquiries within the industry. You should also conduct an internet search, and companies can also search court records if they know which jurisdiction to focus on.

■ Does the party have their own IP strategy? Do they have their own plan for establishing and protecting their own IP rights, and what internal mechanisms do they have in place? What steps would they be willing to take to ensure your rights are protected?

- What is the party's ethical and environmental reputation? This is often a good indication of moral character.
- What is the party's financial health?

The following aspects of Chinese law should be considered during the due diligence process:

- Inventions 'made' in China must be filed in China first (Art. 20 Patent Law).
- Under China's technology transfer regulations, transfers of some technology require approval or are prohibited.
- Intellectual property developed by employees in their own time using company property might not be owned by the company.
- Inventions filed within one year of an employee termination that is similar to their work at a previous employer can be 'clawed back' by that employer.

Good contracts

Good contracts are indispensable in China. A portfolio of well-drafted contracts creates a parallel, private legal system that covers relationships with a company's joint-venture partners, employees, licensees, distributors, suppliers and service companies. This system should set out clear IP protection measures, dispute resolution systems, and penalty clauses for failing to comply. This system must take into account existing laws and regulations, but also try to anticipate legal changes resulting from China's intensive IP law reform programme.

Contracts must be clear and explicit. Common law systems create implied rights and obligations to bolster agreements. In China, if the right or obligation is not specified in the contract it does not exist. It is therefore paramount that the contract sets out exactly what is expected of each of the parties and which rights are transferred in painstaking detail.

Obtaining a high-quality translation that both parties recognize is equally important. Not only does this help avoid misunderstandings, but as a civil law country, China's courts expect a high degree of specificity. Examples of this include the following:

- Contracts should stipulate in as much detail as possible that a manufacturer may only produce the quantities agreed and set out clear requirements for dealing with factory seconds, moulds, films and designs.
- Licence agreements should clarify as far as possible what licensees can and cannot use the licence for, and what happens when the licence terminates. Licence agreements should state as clearly as possible how royalties are to be calculated, and the exact limits of the license right.
- Contracts should set out very clearly under what conditions parties can subcontract or sublicense with and without your consent.
- Contracts clarifying what happens to product improvements are also very important, as the default position is that the party making any improvement holds the rights to it.

■ Confidentiality and non-disclosure clauses with business partners and employees are essential. These should be clear and well developed, identifying all types of information covered and who that information can be shared with.

Official approval of contracts

Companies should also be aware that virtually every industry and product type has an administrative agency that regulates it. These agencies will often have to record, or even approve, products and contracts. This is another example of the need to get good local advice, as your contract risks invalidation if one of the applicable procedures is not followed. While courts are increasingly focusing on the intention of the parties, many venues still place a great deal of emphasis on the approval procedures.

Preventative measures

Apart from good preparatory analysis, getting your rights into a good position, conducting due diligence and crafting solid contracts, there are a number of practical steps companies can take to limit the chances of an infringement occurring:

■ The first and most obvious preventative measure is constant innovation. By constantly developing your products, you stay one step ahead of the counterfeiter. And this, more than anything, is the best way to beat infringers.

■ The education of your employees and consumers is another, often underrated, measure that can prevent infringement. Your employees will help you prevent IP infringement if they understand the importance of IP protection to the company, and to the prosperity of China as a whole.

■ Companies should consider becoming involved in the lobbying process. Companies should advocate constructively for the improvement and enforcement of laws and regulations in a way that demonstrates the benefits to consumers. China's IP action plan encourages rights-owners to involve themselves in the legislative process in order to help China improve its legislative framework.

■ Product security devices are one of the best ways to ward off counterfeiters. These include printed codes, holograms, microchips, self-destruction devices and copy-protected data.

■ Drawings or prototypes should not be left behind before the deal is finalized. Technical staff should not share designs and technology, even within the company's China business.

■ Consideration should also be given to splitting up production processes to separate the key designs and moulds, making it harder to reverse engineer the finished product. Production runs should not be exceeded, and all component inputs and finished units should be accounted for. Retaining control over a vital component is another method of controlling production overruns and products walking out the back door.

■ Compliance should be monitored while your contracts are in force, not only at the end of a contract or when difficulties arise. As much as possible, control should be retained over the distribution network, as fakes can easily infiltrate the legitimate supply chain. Exercising your contractual rights to ensure compliance is often something that is not done. If companies have the right to audit they should do so. Companies should also conduct regular checks and reviews of confidentiality agreements. This will help prevent trade secret theft, and avoid people thinking your IP is vulnerable.

These are just some of the preventative measures that should be considered as part of an overall IP strategy.

Conclusion

The steps that rights-owners need to take in order to make IP China-resistant are little different from those they would take in any other country. Identifying what IP you own, prioritizing that IP, and having a plan to commercialize effectively and protect it are common sense steps that should be taken in any country. However, if these steps are not properly taken, the pitfalls in China are greater than anywhere else in the world. The size of the country, the complexity of the market, the rate of its growth, the sheer size of the opportunity and the ability of the Chinese to copy, combine to elevate the risk to IP beyond anything that has been seen before. Taking steps to protect your IP is not rocket science. In fact, most of these steps are quite straightforward, yet they nonetheless require companies to be fully prepared to make the necessary investment.

The sixth and final step, discussed in Chapter 13 is the proper enforcement of your rights when they are breached.

11

Intellectual property education in China

Ruth Soetendorp, Business School,
Bournemouth University

Background

China has two good reasons to raise its levels of intellectual property awareness, competence and literacy. First, since becoming a member of the World Trade Organization (WTO) China needs to understand and respect the intellectual property rights (IPR) of others. Strong IPR protection helps in attracting foreign direct investment, technology transfer and IPR exploitation. Second, as it becomes a prime mover in global economic activity, China seeks protection of its own intellectual property.

China has a wealth of creativity and inventiveness from its long history as one of the earliest civilizations. The Chinese people's prolific innovation and artistic expression has flourished in a society that enjoys an attitude to IPR that is quite different from that of the Western world. Copying another's work, in China, is seen as a positive compliment or homage. Protecting ideas, as such, has not come naturally to the Chinese. They are more concerned with their relationship with their past, in which family plays an important role. This can be seen today in the mission statement of Guangdong Province IPR programme, which aims to teach the child, which will affect the family, which will influence society. Respect for parents resonates with respect for the words of ancient teachers. Confucius, the 6th-century-BCE sage taught

'I transmit rather than create'. It was contact with Western commerce at the turn of the 20th century that first introduced Western concepts of IPR to China. So it should not be surprising that proper protection (of IPR) in China is still in its early stage, and 'not yet mainstream and mature enough to warrant proper consideration and development by Chinese authorities and the public at large'. 'We started much later than developed nations', observes Judge Jiang Zhipei, Chief Justice of the Intellectual Property Tribunal of the Supreme People's Court 'but we are catching up quickly; faster than anyone could ever have expected'.[1]

Educating people in the ways of intellectual property has proved a challenge to most national governments. Looked at positively, innovators need to understand that IPR has its roots in the law. Without a basic understanding of how the law, national and international, operates, IPR is vulnerable and can disappear. A strong patent and trademark system is essential to grow national and international industry. But an understanding of the law alone will give little insight into how IPR should be managed to secure optimum financial value from its exploitation. From the negative perspective, consumers need to understand the dangers presented by markets flooded with counterfeit and 'rip-off' products. Imitation entertainment or fashion items pose an indirect threat through the revenue they raise for terrorism and crime. But imitation pharmaceuticals, cosmetics, batteries and auto spare parts pose a more direct threat, to life and well-being.

IPR law enforcement in China is under immense pressure. The generally unsympathetic public attitude of Chinese people to IPR enforcement makes the work of understaffed enforcement offices even more difficult. Where a factory producing counterfeit products is providing an economic solution to the poverty of a locality, even the enforcement officers will be hard pressed to find the enthusiasm to rush in and close it down.

Awareness of the IPR problems facing China is explained graphically by a middle school student:

> Having got used to freely using other's technological and scientific inventions, many Chinese enterprises have undergone severe sanctions after the entry to WTO. The leak of commercial and technological secrets happens frequently due to indifference to IPR. It is also a common phenomenon that people don't comprehend IPR and don't know how to protect it so that their IPR has always been infringed. It's even more common that people have infringed other's rights unconsciously.[2]

China is responding to the challenge of providing positive and negative aspects of IPR education, enabling its population to appreciate both the importance of respecting the IPR of others, and valuing IPR of their own. The first intellectual property teaching centre in China, was established in 1986 in what was then called People's University of

---

[1] http://www.chinaiprlaw.com/english/news/news5.htm.
[2] Liao Quiong, Class 5 Senior Grade 2, Nanhai No. 1 Middle School, WIPO/SIPO paper.

China in Beijing, now known as Renmin University. In November 1986, the Chinese Association for Intellectual Property Research at Tertiary Institutions was established at Huazhong University of Science and Technology in Wuhan. In 1993, the Intellectual Property School was established in Peking University.[3]

Most of the initiatives discussed in this chapter were described in papers presented during November 2005 to the World Intellectual Property Organization (WIPO) High Level Seminar on Intellectual Property Education in China, organized by WIPO and the State Intellectual Property Office of the People's Republic of China (SIPO), in Foshan, Guangdong Province. Guangdong Province, described in *People's Daily Online*[4] as 'a powerhouse', and particularly the city of Foshan, provide a case study of how IPR education can be approached in a comprehensive and systematic way in the school system, with exciting results.

IPR education in primary and middle schools

The Mayor of Foshan[5] described the steps they took, starting with a 'Foshan Intellectual Property Protection Steering Team' comprising the vice-mayor, with general directors of the municipal intellectual property bureau and education bureau. They recognized the problem faced by academics, internationally, looking to include IPR in the non-law curriculum. Because the legal articles of intellectual property are abstract and abstruse, even teachers, from non-law disciplines, have difficulty thoroughly understanding IPR laws and regulations. And of course, parents know little (and care less?) about IPR concepts.

The steering team's key finding was the importance of generating teenagers' awareness of the need to protect intellectual property: 'Teenagers are the true masters and constructors of the state in the future'. They sensed that the need to protect IPR would fit with teenagers' natural enthusiasm for invention and innovation, which in turn would lead to a society that strengthened and popularized IPR education. Their findings showed that if students could 'independently choose the partners, practice base and study contents which interest them' they would, through their research, produce results that would have more lasting impact. This echoes accepted understanding of the value of self-managed student learning.

Textbooks for primary, junior middle and senior middle school were devised in conjunction with the Intellectual Property Bureau of Guangdong Province. Twenty-one primary schools and several middle schools were selected to take part in the experimental IPR delivery. There was a complementary programme of teacher training, and a supplementary IPR education website was established. By 2005, entrance examinations to Foshan senior middle schools included IPR questions. Science courses integrate IPR case studies as part of a 'Comprehensive Practical

---

[3] Philip Griffiths, WIPO/SIPO paper.
[4] http://english.people.com.cn/200603/11/eng20060311_249789.html.
[5] Mayor of Foshan, WIPO/SIPO paper.

Activities' programme, which aims to achieve 'organic interaction of the student and his/her family, enterprise and community to raise a sense of social responsibility'.

The theme of Foshan's IPR education programme is 'teach one student, affect one family, influence the whole of society'. It was a moving experience observed as part of the WIPO/SIPO delegation to the Shimen Experimental Primary School. The top class of the school had prepared a presentation on trademarks for the visitors. Seated on primary school chairs, the visitors witnessed a sophisticated selection of small group scenarios in which the pupils role-played key trademark questions, including 'What is a trademark?', 'What is the function of a trademark?', 'What is the benefit of a trademark?'. The three Western IPR professors present agreed that not only were the children's presentations charming and engaging, the depth of knowledge displayed was impressive. One group brought branded packaging from their parents' factories or stores to explain the role played by the IPR in the family business.

From the Shimen School, the WIPO/SIPO delegation proceeded to a medium-sized engineering factory. The CEO explained how her son had made a visit to the factory, with a group of friends, as part of a school project to assess the company's level of patent activity. From discussion with her son and his friends, she had reviewed the company patent policy, and increased the number of patents applied for. In 2004 Foshan achieved 10,788 patent application filings, ranking second in Guangdong.

A pupil at Dali Experimental School in Nanhai, Foshan, took the knowledge he had acquired about trademarks and applied it to his father's chain stores. The chain store was called 'Guangtai' but the name had not yet been registered as a trademark. Persuaded by the son, the father had realized the benefit of trademark registration and proceeded to protect the family brand.

In addition to formal education projects, Foshan runs competitions to encourage innovation, art and design and trademark design. Competitions are widely recognized as good ventures to encourage young people's engagement with IPR. In September 2006, Philips[6] (read below about Philips' involvement in university and industry IPR education) and the Shanghai Intellectual Property Administration (SIPA – see more below) launched the three-year Philips Teenage Patent Award in Shanghai, from 2006–08. The award programme provides an opportunity to improve school students' engagement with innovation and patent applications. It is an 'important step towards China's target to be an innovative nation by 2020'.

People's Daily Online[7] recounts:

Other Chinese regions, such as Beijing, Shanghai, Tianjin and Jiangsu have also followed the precedent set in Guangdong. Jiangsu Province, which is also an economic powerhouse in East China has incorporated IPR protection into the educational plan of the province's primary and middle schools during the 2006–10 period. It has decided to train more than 100,000 IPR protection professionals during the same period.

---

[6] Konmklijke Philips Electronics NV, http://www.ip.philips.com/articles/backgrounders/ips_in_china20061004.html.
[7] http://english.people.com.cn/200603/11/eng20060311_249789.html.

Although Foshan recognizes that some achievements have been made through the 'child, family, society' chain of influence, it is only a part of the IPR education that needs to be carried out to influence the general public.

IPR education in the university

China's most reputable universities have undergraduate and postgraduate intellectual property programmes in faculties of law, politics, economics, social science, science and technology. International programmes of collaboration exist between Chinese universities and their counterparts in the United States and the European Union.

The Shanghai Intellectual Property Administration (SIPA) is an example of the way in which China is meeting the challenge of developing university-level IPR education opportunities. Eight universities in the Shanghai area each have an intellectual specialism, and collaborate within SIPA. For example, the Intellectual Property School of the East China University of Politics and Law was established in November 2003 with two teaching groups: IP law teaching group and IP management teaching group. The IP School cooperates closely with two research organizations: the IP Law Research Centre and the E-Commerce Law Institute of IP Research. The mission of the School is to cultivate elites with multidisciplinary knowledge: 'Establishing the IP programme for undergraduates satisfies society's need for new professionals in the knowledge economy and information era, in particular after China's accession to WTO'. The School offers an extensive curriculum consisting of four parts:

1. basic knowledge on economics and management;
2. science and technology, including science of science, industrial design, chemical engineering, electrical engineering and electronic technology;
3. fundamental knowledge of laws including civil law, criminal law, business law, civil and criminal procedural law, economic law and international law;
4. core courses on IPR including copyright, patents, trademarks, trade secrets, technology transfer, e-commerce and patent document searching.

The School has also set up IP training and is looking to cooperate with prestigious foreign institutes in collaborative education providing training programmes for enterprises. A comprehensive study of university IPR provision has been undertaken by Professor Phil Griffith of the Law Faculty, University of Technology, Sydney.

Collaborative industry IPR education partnerships

Many companies from the United States and Europe, seeking to trade successfully with China, have sought ways to collaborate to improve understanding of IPR, and increase respect for the legal demands imposed by national and international IPR laws and regulations. It is fair to say that for many of China's population, who are poorly educated and experiencing a very low standard of living, IPR is not very relevant. But for those whose standard of living looks set to improve by collaboration with a foreign investor, attitudes to IPR are ripe for change. Philips, the Netherlands consumer electronics group has taken that point and built a unique educational collaborative venture,[8] believing that its 'long term success worldwide depends largely on China's growth and Philips' success in China'. Philips declares itself committed to cooperation with China to create a sound IPR system in China.

Philips has set up three local IP Academy projects in China since 2004. The aim of an IP Academy is to share international IP expertise with Chinese students, thus increasing knowledge and awareness in China of IPR. Faculty of an IP Academy includes international experts from Philips with academics from the EU and United States. There is a scholarship programme, an IPR research programme and an exchange programme for Chinese and international academics. The three universities involved are Renmin and Tsinghua in Beijing and Fudan in Shanghai. About 650 law and science students follow Philips IPR courses. Topics covered include patents, copyright trademarks, design rights, trade secrets, international IPR treaties and the role of patent attorneys. The courses run on the basis of cooperation agreements with Philips and the universities. Philips is looking to add an advanced course, International Patent Application, to the portfolio of courses on offer.

In addition to the university courses, Philips collaborates in the organization of IPR seminars to increase IPR awareness amongst Chinese companies. Seminar topics consider IPR creation and protection, IPR and economic growth, and corporate IPR management. The seminars have received support from the Ministry of Economic Affairs of the Netherlands and the Shanghai Municipal Government.

The Philips course is well received, as described by a Chinese recent graduate[9] of Renmin University, who had previously done some postgraduate IPR courses at University of Technology, Sydney:

What I got from this course was not just traditional book lore, but also substantial two way communication between lecturers and students. In addition, any number of advanced seminars built around IP issues were also available to us. The IP Academy combined state of the art technological educational advances with the legal interpretation of Chinese IPR doctrines.

Despite her obvious enthusiasm for the course and the high quality of teaching, the student identifies some improvements that could be introduced:

Introduce comparative studies between international IP law and Chinese regulations, since we are making every effort to foster a mature atmosphere in respect of this promising market in global financial networks. Reflecting the interdisciplinary nature of IPR studies, economics and business strategy should also be included, rather than focusing solely on legal analysis.

---

[8] http://www.ip.philips.com/articles/backgrounders/ips_in_china20061004.html.
[9] Ms Miao Miao LLM, Law School, Renmin University of China WIPO/SIPO paper.

Future plans

As enthusiastic supporters since the inception of 26 April as World Intellectual Property Day, China supports the work of the World Intellectual Property Organization. At its meeting in Brazil in Spring 2007, WIPO launched a global network of academies dedicated to the teaching and research of IPR at the national level. It is designed to enhance international cooperation to strengthen delivery of IP education and increase access to IPR learning. Establishing the network, comprising representatives of various academies and research institutes, endorses the growing recognition by international policy-makers that IPR expertise has a crucial role to play in promoting national development strategies. The State Intellectual Property Office of China is one of the 10 states in the network, and expects to host its next meeting in 2008. Keen to continue increasing IPR awareness and competence, China has issued IPR education guidelines,[10] which anticipate increased activity at all levels, from primary school to judiciary training.

---

[10] http://english.ipr.gov.cn/ipr/en/info/Article.jsp?a_no=73788&col_no=925&dir=200704.

12

Due diligence and integration

Linda Lin and Ning Wright, KPMG China and HKSAR

Due diligence in China

Doing due diligence in China is very different from doing due diligence in the Western world, where information and data are generally of higher quality and the target management and their finance staff with whom you deal understand what the concept and term of 'due diligence' is about and can generally answer your questions or provide you with sufficient data for you to conduct further analysis. While things have certainly improved over the past few years, having a smooth and efficient due diligence process is often still not the case with Chinese target management.

The deal environment today

The deal environment has changed significantly in recent years. An increasing number of acquisitions are now subject to an auction process, and that is an increasing trend in China. This means a much more competitive market in which higher premiums are often being paid. As a result, many company executives may have that 'morning after' feeling when the deal closes. Instead of relief and celebration, they are often faced with pressing questions such as: What have I bought? How do I deliver the value paid for?

KPMG's recent global M&A survey set out to understand what acquirers are doing to enhance value from their acquisitions and what challenges they face in taking control of the target business.

The following six issues were considered the top post-deal challenges by companies and private equity houses who participated in the survey:

1. complex integration of two businesses;
2. dealing with different organizational culture;
3. people issues;
4. IT and reporting systems;
5. customer retention, especially the key accounts;
6. time and management efforts required.

And, in general, companies found that they did not start post-deal planning early enough. Capturing value from synergies and new strategies post-acquisition is often the difference between a successful deal and a missed opportunity. This is true around the world, but is particularly true in China given the due diligence challenges along with extreme competition for deals and high valuations.

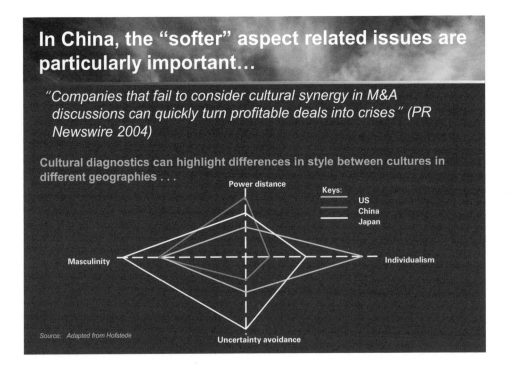

Figure 12.1   A cultural diagnostic

The 'softer' aspects of deal-making in China

When it comes to doing deals in China, the 'softer' aspect-related issues, such as cultural differences; building the right relationships and addressing people-related issues early on have been very important in the integration process. For example, looking at a cultural diagnostics can easily highlight the significant styles between cultures in different geographies and countries, as Figure 12.1 illustrates.

Based on the cultural diagnostics and analysis done by Hofstede (http://www.geert-hofstede.com/hofstede_china.shtml) and given its history and political background, China has a very high score on power distance and a low score on individualism, reflecting the country's acceptance of inequality of power distribution and the heritage of a collectivist society. Likewise, Japan has a high score on uncertainty avoidance, implying a society of strict rules, safety and security measures. In contrast, individualism tops the chart in the United States. Therefore, we know that differences in culture and people are critical as they need to be considered in the context of each practical integration step in order to deliver the overall objectives of an acquisition.

Before going into some actual case studies and project experience, let us highlight some of the common China issues that we often find during due diligence that may also raise integration concerns.

On the financial and accounting side

Very often, the Chinese target's financial records may not be up to international standards. In particular, when dealing with smaller-size privately owned and run companies, there may even be different sets of books for tax and management reporting purposes. Some companies, particularly in retail or manufacturing and distribution, may run into channel stuffing issues and/or managing earnings to meet bonus targets.

Certain payments or transactions (often with related parties) may be left off the books. Such omissions are not necessarily intentional but frequently reflect a lack of understanding of the definition as to what are considered related party transactions and what need to be accounted for on the books. The business may also be subject to certain contingent liabilities such as potential tax and underpaid statutory employee benefits exposures. Therefore, it is important to devise plans early on and take into account the potential additional costs of running the business post-transaction, and to reflect these in your valuation model.

On the regulatory side

In China, most of the time, contracts do exist and they are bound by a comprehensive set of laws and regulations. However, the actual application and enforcement of contracts are not as mature as we are used to in the Western world. Therefore, many times, in addition to having things in writing, the more important part of the agreement is to build the right relationships and have the right understanding between the contracting parties. As most people who read or learn about China discover, the word *guanxi* (relationship) just cannot be stressed enough; it is paramount to the overall success of your investment and business in China and something on which it is worth spending time and effort.

Aside from trying to quantify the potential historical tax exposures related to your Chinese target, you also need to think about issues such as deal structuring early on: how to enhance any eligible tax benefits and transfer pricing policies and strategies post-transaction.

With respect to ownership structure of the target company and group, in addition to the shareholders of the company, the operations of the business can often be influenced by other parties. Influence by other parties can mean other stakeholders such as the various government authorities and regulators. In addition to the various approval processes required in order to invest in your Chinese target, these people may continue to have a certain ongoing influence over the business and, again, it is very important to build and manage these relationships early on. If you don't have the capability or knowledge, find someone who does to assist you.

Once again, in China, *guanxi* is the key to everything, including becoming successful in your business and investment. Therefore, most of the prominent businesses are also intertwined with complicated personal relationships and a related party spider's web, which may translate into dependence on key customers, suppliers and business contacts. This is a very delicate element and yet the most difficult part for foreign investors to figure out; it is often missed or not followed up carefully during their discussion and negotiation with the target company.

Other issues

As most of the foreign investments into China are still on small-to-medium-size deals, these companies, often privately owned and run, are generally very entrepreneurial; they are business-focused and have probably been growing too fast. Therefore, they may not have the standards of internal controls and processes your company has and requires.

Also, the key financial personnel such as the financial controller, may be considered inexperienced and may not necessarily have the financial background, compared with Western standards, to meet your corporate reporting requirements. This makes compliance with your reporting standards post-transaction difficult and incurs extra costs for additional resources, training and time in putting in a system that will satisfy your standards.

With all the issues and complications mentioned, you can already imagine and predict that doing deals in China in general takes much longer than in the West. Likewise, integration would also generally take longer due to the various complications and different aspects involved. Figure 12.2 identifies the various steps in the integration process.

Therefore, identifying the issues and risks early on, making the necessary changes and closely monitoring the results are critical. But in order to do so, it is important to develop the right culture, meaning that the two companies from different cultures will need to accommodate and adapt to each other and find out what the optimal balance may be. While it is difficult to find two cultures that ultimately complement each other rather than create conflicts, there's a need to at least understand and figure out the right 'corporate' culture to make things work and the right people (ie, the right mix) so as to have the right team on the ground to help you drive towards success in China.

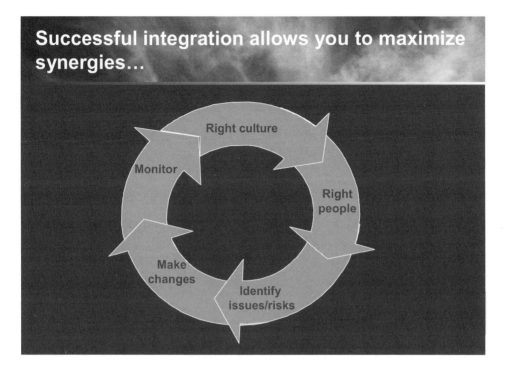

Figure 12.2   The integration process

Case Studies

Foreigners have a perception that China works under a law of its own. In reality, China has its own interpretation of rules and once understood, it can work very well. This point is illustrated by a joke common in China:

> *A tourist, just landed in Shanghai Airport, got into a taxi. The driver took off at such a speed that the tourist began to turn white. The driver turned round and said to the tourist that it was very safe driving around in Shanghai. His brother had been driving a taxi for 10 years and he hadn't had one single accident despite the fact that he never stopped at a red traffic light. Aghast, the tourist just wanted to get out of the taxi when the taxi approached a crossroads with traffic lights. Just as he dived down below the seat behind the driver, he noticed that the lights were green. To the tourist's surprise, the taxi driver slowed down to stop. Surprised, he asked the driver why he had stopped at a green light. The driver grinned and said you never knew when his brother was coming the other way!*

The three widely different case studies that follow will demonstrate to you how you can make a real success of investing in China.

Case study A – challenges of a complex group structure

KPMG China and HKSAR recently advised a European company on its acquisition of a privately-owned Chinese business with more than 1,000 branches across China. The sheer number of locations added to the complexity of the post-deal integration. The company faced a number of integration challenges in areas such as financial reporting, past tax practices and internal controls and system performance.

KPMG China and HKSAR worked with the company to understand the target's complex group structure, internal controls and management reporting system. We also helped identify significant financial, tax and operational risks and issues, which proved to be critical during deal negotiations and after the deal. We visited all key operation sites in order to understand what procedures and controls were in place at the branch level and accessed their consistency and integrity. We helped the company build a strong integrated internal control and governance framework, so that the target could apply the acquirer's policies consistently at all locations.

By being able to pinpoint the integration challenges at the due diligence stage, the company was able to mitigate many post-transaction complications. The integrated company has been able to operate more efficiently in a relatively short space of time after the acquisition.

Case study B – integrating two corporate cultures

KPMG China and HKSAR assisted a Chinese state-owned enterprise acquiring a business in Europe and subsequently integrated the acquisition as a subsidiary.

We initially assisted the company in performing due diligence which extended into post acquisition advisory, helping to develop a strategy for key staff retention. This strategy was particularly important as the two companies had very different corporate culture. Initially the European senior management wanted to resign because they could not align with the Chinese management style.

KPMG China and HKSAR evaluated the Chinese company's core business practices, covering financial reporting, capital appropriation and control processes. The Chinese company placed a lot of emphasis on centralized controls of all functions, whereas the European company has always adopted a local controlled framework.

Working together with the Chinese and European management teams, we assisted the Chinese company in developing new core business policies that provided them with oversight over the subsidiary and strengthened internal control processes which were acceptable to the existing management team. We also assisted in redesigning the compensation package of the European senior managers, creating a remuneration package acceptable to the Chinese company yet attractive enough to maintain consistency of management.

Case study C – providing a post-merger integration service

KPMG China and HKSAR assisted a foreign parts supplier to acquire a Chinese manufacturer. We were engaged to provide post-merger integration support, with the objective of stabilizing the business and implementing synergies to enhance profitability. We helped the company establish a post-merger management office to examine many areas of the acquired business, including culture, organizational structure, corporate governance and IT systems. The actions taken in key functions of the business are shown below in Figure 12.3.

The integration focused on improvements in the accounting, R&D and sales functions. The Chinese company was reliant on manual operations and controls, with many transactions and records not supported by evidence. Quality controls in the R&D function were limited and records poorly kept. We assisted the company in implementing a new governance structure and a new manufacturing cost accounting system. We also assisted the company in reducing R&D costs by identifying synergies and leveraging local universities in sales, a concept of cross-selling was introduced and improvements were made in credit risk management.

The acquirer's decision to design and implement a comprehensive post-merger integration plan (including operational improvements and strengthened controls) helped it achieve is post-acquisition profit targets.

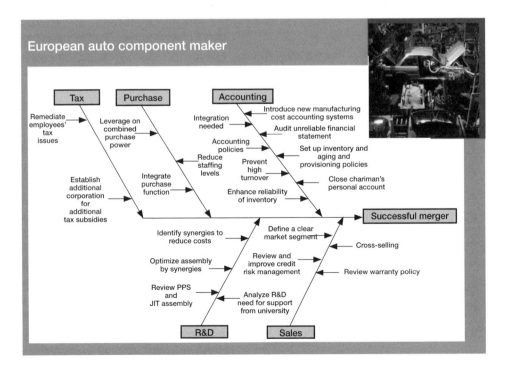

Figure 12.3   Action plans to achieve a successful merger outcome

If you consider the 'soft' issues and the post-integration challenges early on you will have a much better chance of getting ahead of the game, stabilizing your business and starting to increase your profitability. In turn, these outcomes will make your merger and acquisition work altogether more successful and rewarding.

13

Managing IP infringement: what to do when you get into difficulty

Joshua Whale and Luke Minford,
Rouse & Co. International

Introduction

Good preventative measures will reduce infringements while putting companies in a better position to respond to them when they occur. Unfortunately, prevention is unlikely to eliminate infringement entirely. It follows that the final step in safeguarding rights is a solid enforcement programme.

The main objective of an effective enforcement programme is deterrence: to persuade as many companies as possible that they are better off leaving you alone. How a company is perceived to respond to infringement is an important factor in determining whether or not someone chooses to infringe. If a company has a reputation for uncertain or meek responses to infringement, that company's IP is naturally perceived to be vulnerable to attack. If a company's response is swift, severe and well-organized, that company will cultivate a perception that it is both serious about defending its rights, and capable of doing so. This forces the infringer to recalculate their cost–benefit assessment.

So how does one cultivate such a perception? The first step is good organization: failing to take at least some of the preventative measures outlined in the previous chapter gives infringers an opportunity to infringe, and also encourages them to do so. Poor organization is usually apparent in slow decision-making and the lost opportunity to take swift action. It can also manifest in weak rights, where companies have failed to take basic steps to register or protect rights and so lack basic enforcement options.

Once effective protection mechanisms are in place, the rest is largely down to how a company responds to infringement. Companies doing business in China should assume that their IP will be infringed, budget accordingly and establish a market, investigation and enforcement strategy in advance. This chapter aims to provide practical advice on doing just that.

Strategy

Companies should work with their lawyers to develop a streamlined and clear strategy for finding, investigating and classifying infringements, and the swift enforcement of their rights. The majority of cases companies encounter are likely to have some similarities, thus allowing them to be dealt with by a standardized procedure. This will free up time and resources to concentrate on the more complex and important cases. Having a plan also helps companies to respond appropriately and swiftly to infringers. This not only stops them infringing sooner, but increases the chances of seizing vital evidence and freezing bank accounts. Most importantly, it reinforces the perception that a company is both efficient and serious about defending its rights.

To be effective, your strategy should include set timeframes for achieving each step, define responsibilities, include a market survey and investigation programme and a system for determining the appropriate enforcement response. Responses will depend on many factors. For example:

■ threat to public health and safety;
■ infringement size;
■ chances of getting damages out of the infringer;
■ whether the infringed right is registered;
■ likely damages;
■ usefulness as a test case;
■ whether the infringer values their reputation;
■ the potential harm to the market;
■ which jurisdiction the infringer could be sued in;
■ amenability to criminal prosecution and so forth.

An enforcement strategy would have different goals and levels of aggressiveness depending on the industry, the value and vulnerability attributed to the IP and budgetary limitations. For example, you would need to ask 'What are the desired outcomes?' – complete closure and a prison sentence, stopping the infringing and destroying remaining stock, compensation for damages or purchase of a licence?

A strategy would also need criteria for measuring success. These should include elements such as cost-effectiveness, the frequency, scale and overtness of infringements.

Gathering intelligence

Step 1: Surveys

China is a big country and finding infringers can sometimes seem impossibly daunting. However, the difficulty often depends on the industry and the type of infringement. The extent of your programme will naturally depend on your budget. However, it is also wise not to limit your awareness to China, as a great deal of infringing goods are manufactured in China purely for export:

- *Customs recordal:* It is recommended that companies record their trademarks, patents and copyrights in the centralized Customs database. This greatly increases the likelihood that Customs will catch infringing products in the process of being exported. Companies can also improve the likelihood of apprehending exporters with officer training sessions at individual Customs offices.
- *Internet monitoring:* Assign a junior staff member to search periodically the internet and online trading websites such as alibaba.com for infringing products.
- *Public and staff awareness:* Print consumer hotline phone numbers on packaging, and encourage employees to report sightings. If fakes are widespread, consider teaching customers how to identify them (but take care this does not harm consumer confidence).
- *Trade fairs:* Trade fairs are attractive to infringers as a cost-effective way to market their products. Likewise, they are a cost-effective opportunity for rights-owners to identify new infringers and monitor previous ones. With certificates of registered rights, enforcement options exist at major trade fairs, although they are generally limited to removing the items from display.
- *Market surveys:* More comprehensive programmes would actively go into the market to seek out infringing goods, starting with major urban wholesalers and mega-markets like that in the city of Yiwu, which is renowned for its trade in counterfeits.

Step 2: Investigations

Once a company has identified an infringer it would need to conduct a more in-depth investigation. This would mean sending an undercover investigator to the factory or premises to meet with sales reps or management, and to look around the factory. The investigator would try to determine which of the products are infringed, the stock and production status, company size, structure and businesses, and so on, as well as obtaining samples and photos. This information would then allow the company to decide which action is most appropriate, as well as supplying vital evidence.

There are hundreds of companies in China that offer intellectual property investigation services. Many have not been in existence for very long, so be careful about whom you select to carry out investigation work. It is worth doing your due diligence in advance of instructing this kind of work. The most important thing is that the information you receive is fresh, accurate and reliable.

The enforcement toolbox

Rights-holders have a range of progressively involved options at their disposal. From on-the-spot demands at trade fairs, through formal cease and desist (C&D) letters, mediation, administrative action, civil litigation and criminal prosecution.

In most cases, proceedings will begin with a formal cease and desist letter. If this fails to produce a satisfactory result, claimants can then proceed to mediation, an administrative action or civil litigation. Criminal cases tend to skip this step and go straight to administrative action, civil litigation, or occasionally, criminal prosecution.

Cease and desist letters

Apart from direct encounters at trade fairs, the 'cease and desist' or 'C&D' letter is the cheapest and simplest option in the enforcement toolbox. If successful, it can bring an end to the matter with a minimum of difficulty.

The objective of the letter is essentially to present the target with a simplified version of the case you might later bring in court. Rather than a mere demand, it should include all your evidence and make out a clear-cut, detailed case. You should also attach copies of your registration certificates and, where possible, any judgments or administrative decisions in your favour. This says to infringers: 'Look, we already have this much evidence against you, our rights are solid, we are organized and we have already beaten these guys: if you don't stop we will enforce our rights, and you *will* lose'. The company could then demand that the infringers agree to stop producing the goods and recall infringing stock to be surrendered or destroyed and verified. If you are particularly confident, you can ask them to cover legal fees or even pay damages.

Be aware that most C&D letters require active follow-up, including phone calls and even visits in order to obtain undertakings. Overall, the success of C&D letters also varies according to industry and location. C&D letters are not suitable for overtly criminal infringers, who are likely to use the warning to hide evidence and funds.

Where the infringer does not comply and negotiations fail, it is important to follow up the letter with further action.

Negotiation and mediation

China has a cultural inclination to mediated dispute resolution over conflict. Informal discussions, possibly with a mediator, could follow a C&D letter. However, formal mediation services are only a recent development, with most judges and officials taking on the role of informal mediation counsellor. Judges will actively encourage parties to settle their disputes, to the point where they may go to extreme lengths to get both sides talking. Administrative authorities, especially the Administration for Industry and Commerce, will also try to resolve a dispute in such a way that a formal punishment decision is not required, preferring instead the process of informal negotiation and settlement.

Formal proceedings

Where C&D letters and mediation fail or are not suitable, rights-holders can turn to instituting formal proceedings: administrative actions, civil litigation and criminal prosecution.

The enforcement environment in China has changed dramatically in the last five years. While administrative enforcement has been the preferred channel through which IP disputes are resolved (especially trademarks), it is no longer seen as a remedy severe enough to stop major infringers. Since China's accession to the WTO there has been a raft of changes made to the IP legislation. This has boosted confidence in civil procedure, and resulted in a rapid increase in the number of disputes proceeding to court. The result is that rights-owners are seeking a more balanced strategy that combines both the administrative enforcement tool with targeted litigation.

Administrative actions

Administrative actions are not criminal proceedings, but are swift official actions (known as 'raids') that generally result in small fines and the destruction of the infringing merchandise. Although still popular, many rights-owners now complain that despite hundreds of supposedly 'successful' raids, they still do not see any positive impact in terms of infringement levels. Because the authorities continue to issue trivial fines, many infringers are increasingly realizing that they have little to fear from them. Claims made to the AIC at least have a reputation for being fast, straightforward and cheap; the options for patent and copyright enforcement are slow, and the relevant authorities have fewer powers. Box 13.1 provides a list of the various authorities and the laws they enforce.

Box 13.1 Administrative authorities and the laws they enforce

Administration of Industry and Commerce (AIC)
Trademark Law and Anti-Unfair Competition Law, Company Registration etc

National Copyright Administration (NCA)
Copyright Law

State Intellectual Property Office (SIPO)
Patent Law

Customs General Administration (CGA)
Customs Law

Technology Supervision Bureau (TSB)
Product Quality Law and related product labelling rules

Administrative fines do not go to the victim, and in some areas, administrative authorities are also susceptible to local protectionism and corruption. Administrative cases must also be clear-cut: new administrative review procedures have unfortunately discouraged authorities from acting in borderline cases where they feel the threat of retaliation is real.

Alternative administrative enforcement actions

When mainstream IP laws are not available or effective, it may be possible to use less direct legal means. These include informing the relevant authorities of a target's breach of product labelling rules, failure to meet product quality or safety standards, failure to comply with business registration laws, or simply failure to pay their taxes. Such violations can also persuade otherwise reluctant authorities to conduct raids.

Civil litigation

Previously, litigation in China was primarily focused on more serious or complex cases needing judicial expertise. Increasingly, civil litigation is being used for mainstream enforcement. Growing numbers of less serious and straightforward cases are being filed that would historically be filed as administrative actions. There are a number of reasons for this, but chief among these is simply a greater deterrence value.

China's legal system is still young, but the quality of the judiciary has improved markedly. Damages awards are on the rise, and frustrating loopholes are gradually being closed. As a result, rights-owners have increasingly looked to civil remedies, rather than administrative action, as the best form of relief. This change in strategy has also been aided by the comprehensive round of legislative amendments that took place upon China's accession to the WTO. The impact of this change can be seen in the following ways:

- Decisions from the top-tier venues (Beijing, Shanghai, Guangzhou) are now considered of international standard.
- The levels of damages have been increasing (although still not at European/US levels).
- The problems of local protectionism/corruption come up far less frequently.
- The timeframes for cases involving foreign elements are decreasing (judgment is generally within 14 months of filing).

Advantages of civil litigation

- Civil cases are public record, whereas administrative actions are not. Many Chinese companies simply do not like the fact that they are *seen* to be infringing. It is considered a dirty activity, and ruins their chances of doing business with international investors.
- Infringers are often required to defend themselves in a venue that is not in their own backyard (forum shopping is possible). This causes them cost and discomfort and is often a major deterrent in itself. Administrative action is almost always taken where the defendant is located and can often lead to problems of local protectionism.

- Litigants retain control of the case, whereas complainants in administrative and criminal cases tend to have far less control, if any.
- Litigants can also walk away with damages and 'reasonable' expenses.
- Litigation can also be used to obtain a judgment recognizing the 'well-known trademark' status of an infringed brand, bringing broader protection for trademarks. While this is also possible through the administrative process, court recognition may bring greater weight in certain cases.

Drawbacks

However, there still exist many pitfalls to successful civil action in China.

- Introducing evidence in court is still very problematic, some judges interpret procedure very differently from others, and many courts are still not capable of handling complex IP cases. This result is that while a civil decision can bring great benefit and weight to an enforcement campaign, it is critical that the right cases are selected, and in the right areas.
- Civil actions are obviously slower and more expensive than administrative action. Cases do still take around 14 months from filing, and a reasonably straightforward piece of litigation argued by an international law firm will cost between US$40,000 and US$60,000.
- Interim injunctions are still very difficult to obtain. While pre-trial remedies of evidence and property preservation do exist, these are not as effective as an interim injunction and so place great limits on the pre-trial options available.
- Damages generally do not cover expenses, and actually getting the defendant to pay the award is problematic.
- There are no contempt of court mechanisms for holding lawyers and defendants to account for time-wasting and lying. As a result, defendants tend to bring plenty of petty counterclaims and obstructions.
- In patent cases, defendants can and often do challenge the validity of the patent, which will freeze proceedings for a year while the claim is assessed.

Damages

As in more developed jurisdictions, the claimant has the choice of three measures of damages: losses to the rights-owner, the infringer's ill-gotten gains and statutory damages. Statutory damages awards are frustratingly conservative, but to date, claimants are often left with little choice: lost profits are difficult to prove and China's embryonic rules of evidence discovery cannot compel defendants to produce their accounts.

Venue selection

There are major advantages to choosing cases that can be brought in Guangzhou, Shanghai or Beijing. Judges in these jurisdictions generally have far more experience dealing with IP cases and outside political influence or corruption is rarely a problem.

Venue options will depend on whether you can show that the infringing products are being sold in the venue that you are seeking relief in.

Criminal prosecution

The most severe threat to IP infringers is the criminal justice system. Courts can impose fines, and jail terms of up to seven years. In practice, sentences rarely exceed four years, although food and drug counterfeiters have been given the maximum sentence.

However, criminal prosecutions for IP crimes are rare. In 2006, the Public Security Bureau, which handles the investigation of criminal IP offences, brought 2,277 cases to trial, compared with 14,056 civil IP cases. Once brought to trial, however, conviction rates are high: of 3,624 defendants, only 116 were acquitted.

The small number of trials is simply because the PSB are under-resourced, and have other priorities. Getting a criminal prosecution can mean getting the relevant embassy involved. Complainants tend to have more success during a related government campaign or periods when public attention is drawn to problems in that area. Practically speaking, the burden is usually on rights-owners to investigate and satisfy that evidentiary thresholds will be met: essentially conducting the criminal investigation yourself, and passing the case to the PSB 'ready-made'.

As criminal cases are also difficult to control once they are handed over, your public relations department would also need time to prepare. Unless you have a straightforward, politically favourable case, and are certain that you want to bring the full force of the law on an infringer, it is advisable to pursue these cases in the civil courts.

Conclusion

China's legal landscape is one of the most rapidly shifting and evolving, and new strategies must evolve with it. Unfortunately, IP infringement remains a fact of doing business in China, and enforcing your rights is an inescapable cost of doing business here. However, options do exist to enforce rights effectively in China. The growth in the number of civil actions being filed, the fact that foreign rights owners are now much better equipped and prepared to take action, and the evolution of Chinese IP rights, have all led to a rapidly improved enforcement landscape.

14

Managing bank accounts and foreign exchange transactions in China

Amanda Gu, HSBC Holdings

Setting up accounts in China

Opening a bank account in China is not a simple matter because China's currency, the renminbi (RMB), is not yet fully convertible. A non-resident entity, for example a company not registered in China, cannot open an RMB account with a bank outside of China. At the same time, such a company is only permitted to open foreign currency (FCY) accounts in China, but not RMB accounts. However, as an exception, the designated merchants in Hong Kong are allowed to open RMB accounts with the designated banks in Hong Kong as a result of the PRC government encouraging the development of RMB business in Hong Kong. Another exception is that Qualified Foreign Institutional Investors (QFII) may open an RMB special account in local banks, subject to State Administration of Foreign Exchange (SAFE) approval, for their stock market investments in China.

Foreign currency accounts for offshore companies

To open an offshore FCY account, account-opening documents must be presented that fully satisfy regulatory requirements and confirm that the purpose of the account opening is justified by genuine business needs. The main types of non-resident FCY accounts include: temporary capital accounts, foreign direct investment accounts and some other accounts.

Temporary capital accounts

These are FCY accounts that may be used by offshore entities to hold capital and funds for the payment of expenses incurred before the subsequent establishment of an onshore foreign-invested enterprise (FIE). The account requires the approval of SAFE before being opened, and will be in the name of the foreign investor (shareholder). Once the FIE has been established, the funds in the temporary capital account can be transferred into the FIE's capital account. Where the funds in the temporary capital account need to be converted into RMB or transferred, SAFE approval is required for each transaction. A temporary capital account may also be opened for FIEs approved with business registration certificates before obtaining other documents necessary for capital account opening, such as tax certificates, certificate of enterprise code and so on. Such temporary capital accounts are in the name of the newly set up FIE. (The offshore account is available to non-residents only so the temporary capital account cannot be opened in the name of the newly set-up FIE.)

Foreign direct investment accounts

These are FCY accounts to be opened and used by non-resident entities to hold funds for payment related to their direct investment (including mergers and acquisitions) in China. The account requires the approval of SAFE before being opened. The funds therein shall be used for the designated purpose and SAFE approval is required for each transaction.

Other accounts

These are for the receipt of FCY funds only, and the FCY funds in this account cannot be converted into RMB. The funds must be paid either to suppliers in China in FCY, or paid to suppliers outside of China in FCY. Opening this type of account does not require SAFE approval.

Foreign currency accounts for onshore FIEs

An FIE registered in China would need FCY accounts and RMB accounts for conducting business in China. There are various regulatory requirements applicable to the opening and operation of FCY accounts. Different types of FCYs are opened for different purposes, and the operation of these accounts is subject to regulatory restrictions in relation to these specific purposes.

There are a number of foreign currency account types available to FIEs registered in China:

■ settlement accounts – for current account items;

- capital accounts – for capital account items, required for injecting or extracting equity;
- foreign debt special accounts – for foreign debt principal;
- foreign debt special loan repayment accounts – for foreign debt repayment, if required;
- foreign currency loan accounts (including loan accounts and repayment accounts) – for local foreign currency borrowings and repayment.

The opening of foreign currency accounts in China, except for settlement accounts and foreign currency loan accounts, requires before-approval from the local SAFE office.

For FIEs incorporated outside bonded areas, no before-approval for settlement accounts from SAFE is required while before-approval from SAFE is still a must for bonded area companies to open settlement accounts at the time of writing. However, from 1 October 2007, the approval will no longer be required.

Interest rates for deposits in US$, HK$, EUR or JPY (including current account and time deposits) below US$3 million or equivalent are regulated by the Central Bank, except for time deposits with two years or above for US$, HK$, EUR and JPY.

RMB accounts for local FIEs

There are four types of RMB accounts: the basic account, the general account, the special account and the temporary account. The main differences between the four types of accounts are:

- Cash can only be withdrawn from the basic account.
- Salary and bonus payments can only be effected from the basic account.
- Only one basic account can be opened by each company, in the same city as its place of registration, irrespective of how many banks are used.
- Multiple general accounts can be opened in any city.
- The special account and the temporary account can be opened for the purposes as designated in the relevant rules.

RMB services being provided by foreign-invested banks now include but are not limited to: RMB cheque accounts; statement savings accounts and time deposits; RMB lending and syndication; the issuance of RMB guarantees and RMB payment settlement. RMB entrusted loans, bank draft acceptance, bank draft discounting and RMB cash pooling are also available. The various types of accounts for onshore FIEs and their operation are summarized in Table 14.1.

RMB accounts can be provided by foreign-invested bank branches in China having RMB service licences. Foreign currency accounts can be provided by foreign-invested bank branches having foreign currency service licences. The restrictions outlined in Table 14.1 must be adhered to. It is possible to open cross-city foreign currency settlement accounts but capital accounts must be opened in the same city as the company's registered office.

Table 14.1 Account types for onshore FIEs (with official Chinese names indicated for easy reference)

	Account types	Inflows	Outflows	Outstanding Cap	Comments
FCY	Capital account 资本金账户	To receive capital injections and capital increases	Payments for current items and approved capital-items	The paid-in capital	In principle, only one account can be opened and only with a bank branch located in the same city as the company's registered address
	Settlement account 经常项目账户	Collections for current item foreign currency	As above	None	
	Foreign debt special account 外债专户	To receive loan proceeds from overseas	As specified in the loan agreement, but can not be used to repay RMB loans	Loan amount as approved by SAFE	Foreign debt registration certificate and SAFE approval for each loan required
	Foreign debt special loan repayment account 外债还本付息账户	Transferred from other foreign currency accounts, or exchanged from RMB	Repayment of the foreign currency loan principal and interest	Not more than the range of the next two repayments	It is not necessary in practice, as the foreign debt can be repaid directly through foreign debt special account
	Foreign currency loan account 外币贷款账户	To receive the loan proceeds from onshore foreign currency loans by banks or through entrusted loans	To repay the principal and interest of onshore foreign currency loans from banks or through entrusted loans	None	Exchange of loan proceeds to RMB not allowed

Account		Purpose	Payment	Limit	Notes
Temporary capital accounts 临时资本金账户		To temporarily receive funds related to direct investment in China before formal set up of onshore FIEs	Payment of expenses associated with direct investment in China	As approved by SAFE, up to one-tenth of total investment	One account only
RMB	Basic account 基本账户	To receive RMB collections etc	All kinds of RMB payments	None	One account only, PBoC's 'account opening approval' required
	General account 一般账户	As above	All kinds of RMB payments except for cash drawing and salary payment	None	RMB cash drawing not allowed
	Special account 专用账户	As above	RMB payments only for special purposes	None	
	Temporary account 临时账户	As above	RMB payments only for temporary institutions or activities	None	With a validity period less than two years; RMB drawing from temporary account for registered capital verification not allowed

Representative office accounts

Representative offices (except those of overseas airlines and law firms) are not permitted to engage in direct profit-making activities, that is, they are not permitted to issue invoices for sales, accept payment for goods, or contract for sales in the name of their home offices. Representative offices can hold both basic and general RMB accounts. Representative offices can hold FCY accounts for office expenses.

Borrowing in China

The various types of borrowing available in China are summarized in Table 14.2.

Table 14.2 Types of borrowing – sources of funding that are available to FIEs in China

Source of funding	In RMB	In FCY
Onshore bank loans	Restrictions on the interest rate. Foreign debt registration for cross-border guarantees upon realization	Restrictions on FCY convertibility to RMB. Foreign debt registration for cross-border guarantees upon realization
Cross-border borrowings		Subject to foreign debt registration within the 'borrowing gap' (as defined below) and SAFE approval is required
Inter-company	RMB entrusted loans	FCY entrusted loans for eligible MNCs
Chinese stock markets	A-shares (Shanghai and Shenzhen) listing (only available to eligible joint stock company)	B-shares (Shanghai and Shenzhen) listing (only available to eligible joint stock company)
Chinese bond markets	Issuance of corporate bonds by private sector companies is extremely difficult	
Foreign stock markets		Case-by-case approval basis H-share, N-share, S-share etc
Foreign bond markets		Issuance of foreign bonds by private sector companies is extremely difficult

Foreign currency borrowing

The borrowed funds must not be used to conduct stock transactions, and the borrowing term for a bank loan in principle shall not exceed 10 years. An FIE borrower needs to ensure that there is adequate headroom within its borrowing gap to undertake the required foreign debt registration when cross-border guarantees are realized. Regulations state what proportion of the total investment must be in the form of registered capital, as set out in Table 14.3 below.

Table 14.3 Proportions of registered capital to total capital required

Total Investment	Registered Capital	Percentage of Registered Capital: Total Investment
Up to US$3m (inclusive)	Being at least 7/10 of total investment	At least 70%
Between US$3m and US$ 4.2 m (inclusive)	Minimum being 2.1m	At least 50%
Between US $ 4.2m and US$ 10m (inclusive)	Being at least 1/2 of total investment	At least 50%
Between US$10m and US$ 12.5m (inclusive)	Minimum being US$5m	At least 40%
Between US$12.5m and US$30m (inclusive)	Being at least 2/5 of total investment	At least 40%
Between US$30m and US$ 36m (inclusive)	Minimum being US$12m	At least 33%
More than US$36m	Being at least 1/3 of total investment	At least 33%

The difference between the registered capital and total investment is sometimes referred to as the 'borrowing gap'. The foreign debt can be raised by FIEs within their borrowing gap. However, as a curb of the PRC government on the property sector, FIEs engaging in property development established on 1 June 2007 or thereafter are banned from borrowing funds from overseas lenders.

With the exception of export discounting, foreign currency loans including packing credits cannot be converted into RMB.

RMB borrowing

RMB lending facilities can only be offered by licensed branches of foreign banks or by banks that are locally incorporated. The lending base rate is fixed by the People's

Bank of China (PBoC), and banks are permitted to lend at not lower than 90 per cent of the base rate. As for home mortgage loans, the lending rate could be fixed as low as 85 per cent of the base rate.

Enterprises can also get RMB funding through entrusted loans. RMB loans of an FIE can be secured by guarantees from both PRC and non-PRC entities or individuals.

The sum of an FIE's cumulative medium- and long-term foreign debts, the outstanding balances of short-term foreign debts and the amount of the foreign guarantees should not exceed its 'borrowing gap' (ie, the surplus of the FIE's approved total investment over its registered capital). Upon realization of the foreign guarantee, the borrower should register the claim as foreign debt with SAFE within 15 days from the date of the realization of the guarantee provided that there is a sufficient borrowing gap.

FCY conversion/remittance

On 21 July 2005, China announced a 2.1 per cent one-off revaluation of the RMB against the US$ and the reform of the exchange rate mechanism. The RMB is no longer pegged to the US$, but managed with reference to a basket of currencies. Although the full detail of the basket was not disclosed at the time, on 10 August 2005, China indicated that US$, EUR, JPY, KRW were the main reference currencies in the basket; all these currencies are among China's top 15 trade partners.

China's currency remains broadly stable in the medium term. It is not expected that the Chinese government will deviate from gradual and stable appreciation. The process of resetting against the basket remains opaque and movement appears more closely aligned with major currencies than the basket as a whole. PBoC has iterated that the RMB would appreciate on average by 5 per cent a year although any further appreciation is likely to have a negative effect on Chinese growth and employment.

There are no restrictions on expatriates receiving FCY from overseas and remitting FCY funds from their FCY savings accounts. For PRC individuals, there are no restrictions on receiving FCY funds from overseas. For outward remittance, the daily limit for FCY remittance from FCY savings accounts to countries and territories outside Mainland China is US$50,000. For amounts exceeding this limit, customers need to provide relevant supporting documents to prove the authenticity of the transactions.

If a person wants to deposit FCY cash into FCY savings accounts, the daily limit for FCY cash deposit is US$10,000. For amounts exceeding this limit, customers need to provide relevant supporting documents to prove the source of the FCY cash.

For individuals, the conversion from FCY to RMB amount should not exceed US$50,000 per year. For amounts exceeding this limit, such individuals need to provide supporting documents or obtain approval from SAFE on a case by case basis.

According to foreign exchange regulations in Mainland China, expatriates can only convert RMB into FCY from their legal RMB incomes with relevant supporting documents as outlined below:

Salary in RMB

Supporting documents required (originals):

- written application for such purpose;
- passport/pass to Mainland for HK and Macau residents/pass to Mainland for Taiwan residents;
- employment contract showing salary paid in RMB;
- payroll slip;
- work permit in Mainland China;
- income tax clearance certificate.

Rental income in RMB for property in Mainland China

Supporting documents required (originals):

- written application for such purpose;
- tenancy agreement;
- leasing registration certificate;
- tax return;
- leasing invoice;
- ownership certificate;
- passport/pass to Mainland for HK and Macau residents/pass to Mainland for Taiwan residents.

Sales proceeds in RMB for property in Mainland China

People can remit the sales proceeds overseas upon approval from SAFE. SAFE must be approached to obtain approval by providing the following supporting documents:

- an application for RMB/FCY conversion;
- sales and purchase agreement;
- a tax return and a tax clearance certificate.

China Association of International Trade was founded in 1981 to promote research on international trade and China's open-door policies, and is now leading association in the field of international trade studies, training and consulting with institutional and personal members around the country.

Mission

CAIT aims to be a thought leader in the field of international trade theories. CAIT is committed to promoting academic exchanges and training in international tra research and practices within China and with the outside world through its associatic with domestic and international partners.
CAIT is dedicated to improving the well-being of the world trade community by enhancing the understanding between China and the rest of the world.

An affiliate of the Ministry of Commerce, P.R.China

中国国际贸易学会

China Association of International Trade

We bring minds together in research, training and consultin

Research: CAIT undertakes research projects from both government and non-government organizations in the field of international trade policies, theories and practices. CAIT also initiates research in its capacity as a national academic associat It holds, on annual basis, national research conference and announces "international research excellence awards" , which are regarded as one of the top research awards China. CAIT also sponsor/co-organises research seminars.

Training: CAIT offers a diverse range of training programs for international trade practitioners, including certification programs that develop skills in international business and move up international trade career ladder. CAIT now works with over 200 training centers throughout China to deliver the training programs.

Consulting: CAIT advises both domestic and international companies on their market entry strategies, partner selection and negotiations, cultural management, government relations, etc.

Contact us

Email: cait@yahoo.cn

China Association of International Trade
2, Dong Chang An Street
Beijing 100731, China

Tel: +86-10-65125843
Fax: +86-10-65128257
+86-10-65123234

Part 3

The investment environment

15

Identification of partners and JV negotiations

Jonathan Reuvid

Partner availability

WTO accession and the proliferation of privately owned enterprises, particularly in the more buoyant manufacturing industries, was followed by the widespread development of websites by Chinese companies and organizations in both the state-owned and private sectors. With the appearance of internet search engines providing B2B connections with Chinese companies in specific industries that offer their products worldwide (eg, www.gasgoo.com for automotive components), it would appear, at first sight, that the identification of suitable potential Chinese partners for trade and joint ventures (JVs) has become simpler.

While Chinese manufacturers no longer need the vehicle of a JV to export direct since the monopoly of imports and exports by state-owned agencies was removed, and have been able to build direct channels to export markets through the use of the internet, equity JVs (EJVs) with Western partners are still perceived as the most attractive route to global markets and to accessing foreign high-tech intellectual property and manufacturing capability. As Chapter 17 explains, corporate taxation incentives for foreign-invested enterprises will be withdrawn by the end of 2007, but there are residual benefits for shareholders in being involved in a JV, which is subject to a relatively clear JV law, less vulnerable to variable local interpretation than general company law. For Chinese managers in senior roles in JVs, even where the Chinese partner is an SOE at provincial level, there are the added benefits of profit-sharing and carried interest equity participation that are widely permissible.

Partner selection

As readers will already know, when it comes to choosing a JV partner there are more factors at play in the selection of optimal partners than technical capability, product quality and reliable service, which are the necessary and, perhaps, essential attributes for an acceptable supplier.

In China, the shortcut approaches that may seem tempting (in addition to follow-ups via internet information) are advice from those who have already entered JVs and the services that are on offer from various Western agencies, regional Sino-British associations linked to Chambers of Commerce or specialist consultants. Visiting delegations to and from China are another much used method for meeting Chinese companies in the same line of business, as is participation at industry trade shows in China. Any of these approaches may well find your company a partner but carry some of the risks described below. The following covers the disadvantages of each of these approaches:

Experience-based advisers and specialist consultants

Given the size of China, it is inevitable that the experience of others who have followed the path of JV development before you will be focused on particular locations and probably specific industries. If in the process such advisers have already built strong relationships with local provincial or city government, the specific departments that report to relevant Beijing ministries or commissions, then they may be able to provide through the networks to which they have access valuable introductions to suitable potential partners.

However, there are two issues that you should address before committing irrevocably to this route. First, you must be sure that the location in which your adviser operates is the one that suits you best. The only way to make sure is to apply certain general selection criteria first such as:

- preference for technically advanced partners in your industry (probably located on the Western seaboard or in a well-developed city where labour costs are relatively high and rising), versus location in a more remote or less developed area with lower labour and overhead costs where a greater input of management and technical training would be required;
- proximity to deepwater seaport with good freight and shipping services for exporting finished product and/or importing raw materials or components;
- sufficient local markets within easy reach to satisfy JV output for local consumption;
- convenience of travel and communications for visiting Western management;
- acceptable living environment for expatriate management.

Factors such as these, may eliminate the locations in which one or more of the specialist advisers who are offering their services operate. (For example, in the late 1980s one US multinational for whom I was consulting turned down an excellent JV partner in Tianjin, after we had established a relationship with the mayor through a visit to Boston, in favour of Shenzhen because the expatriate managers it had chosen for its venture found Tianjin unacceptable and wanted to live in and commute from Hong Kong.)

The second problem relates to assessment of potential Chinese partners, particularly those that are offshoots of SOEs or otherwise report to provincial-level authorities. The quality of the management of the company with whom you start to negotiate may be excellent, with dynamic well-educated senior managers in place, but the company may report to a superior organization that has a completely different outlook and would interfere with and impede the progress of the JV under discussion. This issue has been characterized elsewhere as the 'mother-in-law' problem and is particularly relevant to JVs where the Western investor is not the majority partner in the 'marriage'. Unless your adviser has an exceptionally good *guanxi* (relationship) at local levels of administration through their Chinese staff or connections, this factor may remain unexplored and might not surface even in the due diligence process.

An SOE is often able to extend 'favourite son' status to a JV in which it is involved so that land use rights or utilities, for example, are made available to the JV on a preferential basis, but these benefits could count for little if they treat the JV as an asset for their particular advantage and seek to impose their will on the general manager.

Sino-British associations and Chambers of Commerce

Similar limitations also apply to the proactive China departments of business schools and universities or local Chambers of Commerce that have established strong relationships over time with specific Chinese cities or provinces, sometimes on a 'twin city' basis. Assessment of 'mother-in-law' issues can be less of a problem if there has been an exchange of resident Chinese staff who know their home business environment well and have their own *guanxi* within the local government administration.

The China Britain Business Council (CBBC) with its multi-office service centres throughout the most commercially active regions of Western China is in a different category. It can offer its clients a choice of locations and of potential partners across the locations where its services are available. Resident Chinese management at each location can no doubt provide their own insight into the quality and attitudes of SOEs and local authorities in any proposed JV association.

In its early years in China, the CBBC was viewed with some apprehension by Chinese authorities by reason of its direct relationship with and funding support by the British government. There was an impression, which the hosting of Chinese trade and business delegations to the United Kingdom did little to dispel, that any dialogue with the CBBC should be treated as a political contact. However, through its work in China in bringing British and Chinese companies together, the CBBC has largely overcome this handicap and makes an important contribution as a facilitator to British industry's business with China.

Inward and outward trade delegations

Inward delegations from Chinese cities and provinces in the 1980s, often hosted by the CBBC (then called the Sino-British Business Council), played an important part in in establishing Chinese awareness of how Western business operated and of Western product and manufacturing standards. However, it was a less satisfactory way of identifying potential Chinese partners. To be sure, the delegate Chinese companies were all eager to establish business relationships with British companies, but often they were unsuitable business partners themselves.

Understandably, the Chinese delegations were largely composed of SOEs with severe business problems: typically, obsolete products and technology, inefficient manufacturing methods and in financial difficulties but having an insatiable appetite for FDI. Responding to these overtures, some British companies paid return visits to China and locked themselves into prolonged negotiations that led nowhere. In such trade missions, the delegates were picked by the Chinese organizers and British companies were therefore presented with a self-selected and unrepresentative sample of potential partners. Today, this kind of mission has become almost redundant since Chinese companies seeking Western partners can readily identify target shortlists from the internet and more conventional media references.

Formal outward missions to China suffer from similar defects. 'Flag-flying' delegations led by government ministers or captains of industry have their place but most readers are unlikely to be involved in such showpiece events. If you haven't visited China before as a businessperson and are included in such a mission, it will be a useful part of your learning curve but, unless you are a market leader in your industry and for the same reasons as above, do not expect to meet a range of suitable partners.

At best, even if you find a satisfactory partner by any of these means, there will always be nagging doubts: 'Was this the optimal partner available in this industry, province or municipality/city?' 'Should I have broadened the search to other regions or provinces of China?' In a country the size of China it may be impossible to allay all such concerns, but applying the general business approach to China that this book and many others advocate will remove some of the doubts and should achieve more satisfactory outcomes. The approach can be likened to peeling an artichoke: proceed from the general to the particular. Define the profile of the optimal partner that you are seeking in a total China context then proceed through a process of elimination, peeling off the outer leaves first; sample and discard those that are not to your taste and finally arrive at the heart of the 'artichoke', the succulent centre that provides the best solution.

Trade shows and expositions

Attending trade shows in China can be an exhausting exercise but specific industry exhibitions will give you a good feel for the range of companies in your field and the products that they offer. They suffer from the same defect as inward and outward trade missions: the companies exhibiting are a self-selected sample; however, you may well meet some potential partners with whom you feel that a follow-up factory visit would be worthwhile. If you intend to enter into discussions at a trade show, be sure to engage the services of a fluent Chinese speaker and to arm yourself with literature in Chinese about your own company and, of course, dual language business cards.

Exhibiting yourself at a trade show is not recommended for two reasons. First, participation is extremely expensive. Add to the hire of exhibition space, stand and equipment costs, transportation of products, travel and accommodation in Beijing, Shanghai or another business centre, the costs of your management time, the hire of one or more interpreters and a large amount of dual language literature (be sure to put out a limited quantity each day or it will all be taken in the first hour). Gone are the heady days of the 1980s when a company might hope to sell products off the stand and even the exhibits. (I can remember one automotive show in 1985 when BMW sold a 7-series saloon to the local vice-mayor and two motorcycles to the local police commissioner before there were any BMW service facilities in China.) Therefore, there will be no tangible offset to your expenditure. Second, among the flood of attendees, it is unlikely that you will receive visits on stand from many suitable partners for the same reason as before: visitors to any trade show are again a self-selected sample. Worthwhile partners have other means of contacting you direct.

If you have decided to search for a Chinese partner, a sensible first step will be to put one or more Chinese language information pages on your website. Potential Chinese partners can browse the internet in English without difficulty but the presence of pages in Chinese on your website is a powerful signal that you are a serious player.

An inside track to partner selection

Adopting the artichoke analogy, there is a way in which you may be able to harness the reporting structure of Chinese administration to help you proceed from the general to the particular in your partner search.

As explained in Chapter 6, there are 'dotted line' reporting relationships to the key ministries in Beijing from the relevant commissions in provincial, municipal and city government. These highly developed networks are an excellent source of information about all companies within a ministry's field throughout China. Establishing a strong personal relationship at the appropriate level of a ministry or, more probably a research organization or institute under the ministry's jurisdiction, may give you access to its database information or information that can be gathered on request from any of the local commissions reporting to the ministry. In this way, you can hope to:

■ identify the locations where companies serving your industry are concentrated;
■ identify potential partners that are industry/market leaders;
■ gain introductions to those companies that the research institute advises might be suitable partners.

The third step in this sequence is the most crucial. Depending upon your relationship with the research organization and its leadership, you will be given insight into the management quality and reporting structure of each individual company. This intelligence may help you to avoid potential 'mother-in-law' problems.

The Ministry of Commerce (MOFCOM), formerly MOFTEC, has access to information on all companies in all industries throughout China. It has two organizations under its jurisdiction and associated with it that provide consultancy services to foreign companies in this way.

The first of these is the long-established Centre for Market and Trade Development (CMTD), China's premier industrial market research organization and the MOFCOM research arm that specializes in providing consultancy services to foreign companies. The second, established in 1981, is the China Association of International Trade (CAIT), the first national research organization in the field of international trade. It acts as a think-tank for MOFCOM and is committed to studying issues that relate to China's trade and development policies. Under a directorate of top-level experts, ex-diplomats, government officials and scholars it maintains an open door to foreign entrepreneurs looking for help. One CAIT service of particular interest to those foreign companies engaged in technical and high-technology projects is the organization of seminars and workshops for key players from the institutes and senior levels of government departments whose support or approval is critical to the success of a project.

I have worked with CMTD or CAIT on all the joint venture projects where I have acted as a consultant since 1984 and have found their advice consistently reliable and their hands-on assistance invaluable.

Entering JV negotiations

The various steps in the JV negotiation process are summarized in Chapter 16. This can be a protracted and patience-stretching process even with the best of partners. Alternatively, joint venture negotiations can be relatively straightforward today since the approval routines have become streamlined, provided that they get off on the right foot.

The traditional route is to enter preliminary discussions with a selected partner with the intention of arriving at a formal memorandum of understanding (MOU) signed by all parties to the proposed JV. The MOU should contain a clear statement of intent to develop a joint venture to the mutual benefit of the parties. The Chinese partner then files the MOU together with a checklist of the major parameters for the JV, described as a 'pre-feasibility study' with the authority to which it reports. In theory, more detailed negotiations cannot be held until the reporting authority has given its preliminary approval in principle. For smaller projects and in locations where JV activity is high and the local authority is experienced, this requirement may be no more than an overnight formality. In some circumstances the MOU requirement may be waived.

There are perils in both the MOU and the pre-feasibility study that should be avoided. Signed MOUs in a JV context are not legally binding but are a commitment by both parties to continue discussions and to carry out a full feasibility study. Entering into negotiations with another party for the same project once an MOU has been signed is considered to be a breach of good faith, unless the MOU is first terminated by mutual consent. The efficiency of 'Chinese whispers' will ensure that you are probably found out if you do err in this respect, with the result that you will be judged 'insincere' and further negotiation may become impossible. For this reason, it is important to carry out as much commercial due diligence on the Chinese partner before signing an MOU. If in doubt, confine yourself to a simple minute, recording the discussions that have taken place and that will be resumed subject to the approval of the boards of both companies within a specified period of time.

The pre-feasibility study may be dangerous in a different way. Among the checklist data that has to be filed are some items that require quantification:

- amount and shares of registered capital to be subscribed by the partners in US dollars;
- planned production capacity (unit/volume of output) for manufacturing joint ventures;
- proportion of output to be sold in export markets;
- surface area of facility and of covered factory space;
- proportions of equipment to be imported or sourced within China.

Although these numbers are no more than a sighting shot and are the responsibility of the Chinese partner, the Western partner(s) are consulted. They may prove to be very far adrift unless a more detailed business plan has been prepared according to an international business model. In fact, the business plan and the JV agreement that it supports may turn out to be quite different and major deviations from the original submission can cause problems. Therefore, from experience, a rather different approach to early stage negotiations has evolved, which I have found useful and which Chinese partners seem to appreciate. It also has the advantage of side-stepping the formal protocol of the two sets of partners and their advisers confronting each other across a boardroom table at an early stage.

Mission statement and business plan

The first step is to put forward the idea of seeking to define the objectives of the JV, asking each party in turn to state the markets that it wants the JV to address, what it seeks out of the JV and what it expects to contribute towards the development, start-up and ongoing management of the JV.

If the Western partner puts its case first in a relaxed manner, inviting debate on each point, the result should be frank, free-ranging discussion with a mission statement as the outcome supported by 'roles and goals' to which both parties have contributed. The production of the mission statement is the result of a teamwork approach. Hopefully, most 'hang-ups' and alternative agendas will be exposed in the process and any obstacles and barriers to partnership revealed. The mission statement becomes the substance of the minute of the preliminary discussion. If no clear mission statement results, there will probably be no point in proceeding. However, no further time will be wasted.

The production of an outline business plan is the next step in this preliminary process, conducted again as a cooperative team effort. By now there should be the beginnings of a group dynamic to which all concerned will contribute openly. This may not be an entirely comfortable experience for Chinese managers used to a more authoritarian approach but is a good way of identifying at this early stage any promising potential general managers among the Chinese members of the team who demonstrate flexibility and leadership qualities.

The outline business plan will include items in the pre-feasibility study that the Chinese partner can quote later in their submission and much else as well. The focus of the business plan will be on capacity, projected sales for the opening years, facility and equipment requirements, development timescales, workforce build up, overhead costs, training and working capital requirements. These will determine the overall investment requirement and how it is to be provided. Competent Chinese partners will have the cost information required at their fingertips.

The revenue and expenditure or profit and loss part of the business plan will probably be more sketchy at this stage requiring detailed discussion about pricing, cost of sales and channels to market, as well as a manufacturing plan later. Hopefully, this outline plan will be sufficient to make the business case that there is a viable case for a profitable joint venture and to encourage all partners to proceed further.

However, nothing is ever certain in China and, as the following case study shows, even this careful approach may fail to reveal economic factors that can kill off a promising venture at the next stage of evaluation.

16

Broiler chicken project – a JV that couldn't fly

Jonathan Reuvid

At the beginning of 2004, a US investment banker and I were asked to carry out a search and make recommendations for a Chinese joint venture partner on behalf of a leading Middle East producer and distributor of frozen chicken and chicken parts. The preconditions for the project were that the Chinese partner should be an experienced and high-quality broiler chicken producer and processor, fully accredited internationally to *halal* standards of slaughtering and processing. It was also a requirement that the foreign partner should have majority ownership of the JV. To this we added our own brief, based on our own JV experience that the Chinese partner should be located in the northeast heartland of the provinces around Beijing and Tianjin, which is one of China's foremost chicken-producing regions.

Search and selection

We engaged the collaboration of my long-time Chinese associate, a consultant and senior member of the China Association of International Trade (CAIT) management team, to identify potential partners. Through the CAIT/MOFCOM (Ministry of Commerce) network database described in Chapter 15, he was able to recommend two possible partners, both subsidiaries of SOEs: one located in Shandong Province, some 500 km from Qingdao port and the other in Hebei Province to the east of Beijing and 120 km from Tianjin's container port. Both companies satisfied the selection criteria on paper and the three of us visited them together in March 2004.

The Shandong company, employing 12,000, was the larger of the two and was ranked among the top 50 national meat enterprises and the first 15 of China's national agricultural production companies. It already exported broiler chicken parts and whole birds in volume to the Gulf and Saudi Arabia, selling through brokers at what appeared to be competitive prices. Although plainly a high-quality producer, we gained the impression that it was not a low-cost operation and had a bureaucratic management organization. Its corporate brochure, strong on photographs of government leaders visiting the company and weak on details of product and production capability, labelled it as an 'old China' enterprise.

We were informed that the company already had one joint venture with a leading French broiler company, referred to in the brochure. Due diligence carried out after our visit revealed this JV was failing and confirmed that the reporting authority was 'difficult', with a record of unsuccessful JVs under its jurisdiction. For these reasons we rejected this company as a potential partner that we could recommend to our client.

If the Shandong company typified 'old China', the Hebei company was certainly an example of 'new China'. Founded in 1982 under the Beijing Municipal Government through its parent SOE, it was the first integrated broiler producer in China. In 1988, it had formed a JV with US and Japanese global market leaders to set up the largest chicken-grandparent-breeding farm in China, importing Roman 'grandparent' broilers from Germany. In 1999, the company won ISO9002 accreditation and the HACCP (Hazard Analysis Critical Control Points) qualification in 2001. The company now had six parent-breeding farms raising 30,000 'parent' broilers each year. Eggs from the parent farm were incubated and hatched by the company, with a growing cycle of 50 days and a mortality rate of less than 5 per cent. This operation had its own veterinary team and maintained the highest standards of hygiene.

The company managed its own feed mill, supplying both the parent farms and the outsourced broiler farms on its total land area of 45,000 acres. The broiler farms were operated under contract by local farmers, each receiving one batch of chicks and feed on free issue and then returning the grown chickens in exchange for a share of gross profit and the issue of a further batch of chicks and feed. Slaughtering was carried out by the *halal* method in an integrated operation from slaughterhouse to line processing including a freezing warehouse. Cooked parts and freeze packing were carried out in a separate unit. Both whole chicken and parts were vacuum-packed in bags then corrugated cardboard boxes and polythene outers before finally being loaded into freezer containers for shipment by road to Tianjin port.

In 2004, the company was producing 56,000 tonnes of chicken each year, equivalent to 26 million chickens at an unprocessed weight of 2.5 kg, with a workforce of 2,700. Domestic sales were made principally in the Beijing area through about 1,300 outlets accounting for 30 per cent of the local market and further afield to more than 20 provinces. Exports to Saudi Arabia and the Gulf were running at 500 tonnes a month. The delivered cost and freight (C&F) price to Gulf ports was marginally below current market prices but sales were made through a broker who added a margin. Unknown to our client who purchased chicken products from the same broker, the Hebei company was already a supplier.

The Hebei company expressed an immediate interest in developing a JV with our client whom it recognized as a world-class player in the same industry. This interest was confirmed immediately by the reporting authority that was already supporting the company's development of additional capacity for 80,000 chickens per day to meet anticipated demand during the Beijing 2008 Olympics for which the company had been selected as a supplier.

We were particularly impressed by the company's general manager who had received part of his business education in the United States and by the quality of the senior management team that he had selected. It was plain that he enjoyed a high degree of autonomy in the management of the company, unusual within the structure of an SOE organization. The company was profitable and was projecting a 25 per cent return on sales (ROS) for 2004.

Preliminary negotiations

During this first visit our client accepted our verbal report and recommendations that we should engage immediately in preliminary negotiations but directed that we should stop short of entering into a memorandum of understanding (MOU). We sat down with the management of the prospective partner and discussed the project in the sequence suggested in Chapter 15. We began by agreeing a mission statement for the JV around the proposition that the JV should have a completely separate facility for the purpose of producing broiler chickens and parts, excluding feet and wings, for export to our client company with possibly some import from them of feet and wings for sale in the Chinese domestic market. The only function that would not be repeated in the new facility was the grandparenting. The JV would source the parent stock from the Chinese partner. The capacity of the JV, it was agreed, should be 150,000 chickens per day and the operation would be sited in another part of Hebei Province southwest of Beijing where land use rights were cheaper than in the present location. It was agreed that our client should have an 80 per cent majority equity interest in the JV but that the Chinese partner with the remaining 20 per cent shareholding would also provide the management. Provision would be made for the management to have a carried share interest in the JV company to be provided from our client's equity interest.

We then proceeded to write the capital investment part of the business plan based on actual cost data that the Chinese company was able to produce. Subject to further review, we arrived at a total investment cost of US$47.5 million, including provision for working capital, of which US$30 million would be equity with the balance of US$17.5 million to be funded locally as loan capital. We were unable to write an operating account with an income statement because all the cost elements were not immediately available. However, we were confident that at our next meeting we would be able to produce a complete business plan that showed a satisfactory profit within the first three years. There was sufficient detail at this point for the Chinese company to submit the necessary pre-feasibility study.

Instead of writing a minute of our discussion we decided that this business plan outline would be a sufficient statement of the initial agreement that we had reached and, on our return to the United States and United Kingdom, we completed the written report to our client, and copied those parts relating to this Chinese company and our recommendations to the general manager with whom we had developed the plan in Beijing. At this point we felt that we had found an excellent partner and that there was the framework for a successful joint venture. However, we did sign reciprocal confidentiality letters.

Second visit

Two months later we returned to Beijing with our client's international management team whose director had recently carried out similar appraisals of the opportunities for new broiler chicken businesses in Brazil, Ukraine and elsewhere. Before proceeding with detailed JV negotiations with the Chinese company that we had selected, his mission was to compare the economic benefits and risks between the various locations and make his recommendation to his parent board.

The plant visit by our clients was a success. With minor quibbles related to the outsourced chicken-rearing under contract and the feed mill, they expressed themselves satisfied that product quality, the processing methods and health and safety provision were up to best international standard.

We then sat down with the complete Chinese management team to write the operating account part of the business plan, having examined and verified our previous work on the capital account. And this is where we found a major stumbling block. In chicken broiler production the cost of breeding and rearing the chicken is typically 60 per cent of total operating cost and the cost of feed is 70 per cent of the rearing cost, that is, the grain accounts for 42 per cent of total cost. To our surprise we found that the price of grain produced in China was significantly higher than the world market price. The reason was that the Chinese government had fixed local grain prices at the world price plus freight cost in order to support farmers. The price differential was further widened by the requirement that the broiler chicken company had to pay VAT on its purchases and that the farmers to whom the rearing of the chicks was subcontracted were relieved of VAT so that there was no offset for the company.

Nor were there any other elements in the cost structure where China was cheaper than the other developing countries that our clients had surveyed. Agricultural labour costs in Brazil and Ukraine were as low and the land use and construction costs that we had thought were particularly low compared unfavourably with our client's existing facilities in Egypt. Accordingly, the project foundered on the overall price comparison amid expressions of regret by all parties. We were particularly disappointed for the Hebei general manager and his team; their company is a first-class operation and they had generously opened the books on all the cost elements of their business.

Conclusions

The first lesson learnt from this abortive project was that we should have briefed ourselves more thoroughly on the cost structure of our client's broiler production business. With that information, we would have investigated the impact of the dominant cost of feed at the outset.

Our negotiation strategy and tactics had served their purpose well and it was some consolation that no time had been wasted in lengthy formal JV negotiations in advance of developing a business plan. Under more conventional procedures, we could easily have wasted several months or more of valuable management time.

A final and more satisfying conclusion is that visitors to the Beijing Olympics 2008 may be sure of enjoying chicken dishes and snacks of the highest quality throughout their stay.

17

Company, foreign investment and joint venture law

Jonathan Reuvid

This chapter is not intended to be a definitive description of Chinese law in the areas of foreign investment and joint ventures. Nor does the chapter that follows offer professional advice on the current practice of accountancy or audit requirements in China. In these areas, entrepreneurs investing in China are recommended to take professional advice from one of the international law firms and one of the major international accountancy firms in practice in Beijing or Shanghai before making any binding commitment. Instead, these chapters are written to provide a layperson's perspective of the legal and accountancy playing fields. Readers should study this chapter in conjunction with Chapter 8 on risk management by Guy Facey, a lawyer practising in China, who takes a similar line.

A digest of Chinese company law

Recognizing that a developed legal system would be necessary to support economic reform, the National People's Congress (NPC) revived China's legal system through radical amendments to the Constitution from 1982 and developed a body of commercial law. However, the law remained fragmented until the 1993 Company Law that unified regulations dealing with corporate government came into effect in 1994. Company law has been amended twice and the Revised Version of the PRC Company Law (2005) became effective from 1 January 2006. Although PRC company law takes many concepts from Western company law, and is to some degree modelled on other legal systems, it is derived from general codes rather than the judicial precedents on which common law systems are based.

Joint venture law

Until 1994, the only integrated laws on which foreign investors could rely were the key regulations relevant to Chinese–foreign joint ventures, in particular the Law of the People's Republic of China on Equity Joint Ventures Using Chinese and Foreign Investment (amended and effective from 4 April 1990, as the 'Equity Joint Venture Law'). The Equity Joint Venture Law set out the structure for the formulation of joint venture agreements and contracts and provided wording for many of the standard clauses. The English language version was in quite simple layperson's language, but allowed for some ambiguity, and it was uncertain whether it captured nuances in the meaning of the Chinese original. There were certainly differences in interpretation between some local authorities and central government, at that time the Ministry of Foreign Trade and Economic Cooperation (MOFTEC), now MOFCOM (Ministry of Commerce). However, in the more advanced business centres, the problem of construing the law correctly was addressed by issuing additional commentary on the law for both equity and cooperative joint ventures. In the municipality of Tianjin, for example, the Commission for Foreign Trade and Economic Cooperation (COFTEC) had developed a limited edition dual language 'blue book', which offered an expanded version of the Equity Joint Venture Law including relatively unambiguous standard contract clauses. I continued to find this handbook invaluable in JV negotiations, in other jurisdictions as well, through to 1995.

There have been a number of revisions to cooperative and equity JV law and the rules for its implementation since 1995, of which the most significant are PRC Sino-Foreign CJV Law (Revised, October 2000); PRC Sino-Foreign EJV Law (2nd Revision, March 2001); Detailed Rules for the Implementation of the Law of PRC on Sino-Foreign EJVs (3rd Revision, July 2001); PRC Law on Wholly Foreign-owned Enterprises (Revised, October 2000). The basic framework for equity JVs is discussed later in this chapter.

The new PRC insolvency law

Although bankrupt SOEs have been restructured and siphoned off in increasing number since 2000 and there has been an explosion in the registration of privately owned enterprises over the same period, there was no insolvency legislation to cover failed businesses until the new law was promulgated in August 2006. The new legislation that became effective on 1 June 2007 applies to all 'enterprise persons existing under Chinese law' and includes SOEs, FIEs and private domestic companies. The only exclusions are companies incorporated under foreign law, partnerships, sole traders and other unincorporated businesses.

Under the new law the double conditions of cash flow insolvency and balance sheet insolvency must be satisfied for creditors to take advantage. The legislation also applies where a debtor 'obviously lacks capability to pay' but there is no clear definition of how this alternative test interacts with the double conditions. Moreover, there is no equivalent to the 'statutory demand' procedures with which Western companies are familiar as a method for proving cash flow insolvency.

Subject to these limitations, the provisions for court proceeding, the appointment, authority and responsibilities of an administrator, including payment priorities and creditors' meetings are similar to English law. The new Chinese law also provides for a reorganization procedure similar to 'Chapter 11' in the United States, 'administration' in England and 'provisional liquidation' in Hong Kong. Finally, the law includes provision for conciliation procedures and a conciliation plan to be approved by two-thirds of the value of unsecured claims and the court.

Unified tax law

A new Enterprise Income Tax Law (EIT) comes into effect from 1 January 2008 and is described separately in Chapter 19.

Property law

Another long-awaited piece of legislation, the new Property Law, came into effect on 1 October 2007. The law encompasses the property relationships of state-owned property, collectively owned property and private property. 'Property' is defined under the law to include both land and other forms of property.

Although the Property Law encourages the development of the private sectors by reinforcing land protections for private property, it re-confirms the dominance of public ownership of property under China's socialist market economy. There is still no freehold tenure of land in China. However, as well as consolidating existing laws such as the Land Administration Law, the General Principles of Civil Law and the Security Law, the new law provides for the automatic renewal of residential land use rights upon expiry. Socially, this is a major step forward for residential property owners and will ensure that financing remains available for their property when its land use term nears expiry.

Under the Property Law, non-residential use right terms are not granted automatic renewal but the ownership of non-residential buildings can be governed by contract. This is a significant improvement on previous regulations for foreign partners in FIEs; they stated that buildings revert to the ownership of the state without compensation upon expiry of the relevant land use term.

Other provisions of the new Property Law are of benefit to certain foreign partners in FIEs. Easements are now recognized under Chinese law that will be of particular importance to those infrastructure projects, such as pipeline construction, where the project owner does not hold land use rights. More generally, the new chapter on security provides for mortgages over future equipment, raw materials and semi-finished product. The pledging of receivables and unit funds is also expressly permitted under the Property Law and will widen previously limited debt financing opportunities.

Land use tax

From 1 January 2007 land use tax rates per square metre were tripled to between RMB0.90 and RMB30, according to the classification of the land. FIEs and foreign enterprises are expressly liable to the land use tax. Beijing was the first to implement the rules from 27 April 2007.

Anti-Unfair Competition Law

While the protection of intellectual property remains a preoccupation of all foreign companies doing business in China, the Supreme People's Court has recently clarified its interpretation of the various provisions of the Anti-Unfair Competition Law. The interpretation assists those seeking greater protection against the misuse of trade secrets, but considerable discretion is left to the People's Courts.

Commercial franchising

With effect from 1 May 2007, the commercial franchising regime has been updated with new rules covering franchiser qualification, information disclosure and contract filing with MOFCOM. There are also new measures regarding financial leasing that took effect on 1 March 2007 and financial supervision ratios that the China Banking and Regulatory Commission (CBRC) is authorized to adjust as necessary.

Enforcement

The process of enforcement is subject to considerable delays and is one of the weakest links in the Chinese judicial system with the individual judge overseeing an enforcement action having wide discretionary powers.

Two sets of rules came into force on 1 January 2007 that are intended to improve the transparency and efficiency of the enforcement of judgments, arbitration awards and other legal instruments in the People's Courts. The rules are grouped under the two headings of rules on improving the transparency of enforcement cases and rules on the time limits for processing claims for enforcements. The impact of these rules is as yet uncertain.

Foreign-invested enterprises (FIEs)

Foreign-invested activities take the form of:

- equity joint ventures (EJVs);
- wholly foreign-owned entities (WFOEs);
- cooperative joint ventures (CJVs);
- representative offices;
- compensation trade; and
- other specific agreements between foreign and Chinese companies.

The first three of these categories are described as foreign-invested enterprises (FIEs). They share common characteristics and are subject to the same or similar PRC legal requirements. FIEs and other foreign businesses are regulated and governed by the PRC Ministry of Commerce (MOFCOM) and the State Administration for Industry and Commerce (SAIC) and their local branches. The approvals for FIEs in most industries are delegated to local Commissions on Foreign Trade and Economic Cooperation (COFTECs) according to the scale of investments, but all FIEs, whether approved by MOFCOM itself or local COFTECS are registered centrally with MOFCOM in Beijing.

Limitations of FIE operations

Specific types of foreign investment projects that fall into the categories of 'encouraged', 'restricted' and 'prohibited' were listed in the *Foreign Investment Industrial Guidelines Catalogue,* implemented on 1 April 2002, to which amendments have been made subsequently as the markets of various industries are further opened up under China's WTO commitments. These arrangements are detailed in the annex of the catalogue. As an example, the maximum permissible foreign equity ratio of mobile voice and data service ventures had increased from 35 per cent to 49 per cent by 11 December 2004. Such ventures can now be WFOEs from 11 December 2006.

FDI projects not listed in the catalogue are generally considered to be 'permitted' and do not require special approval. Up to WTO entry, FIEs in China were prohibited or restricted from engaging in full-scale trading and distribution activities. Since July 2004, trading rights are granted automatically to domestic and foreign enterprises that are registered with the relevant AIC office upon completion of a routine filing process. There are no minimum capital requirements to be met.

EJVs and CJVs are entitled to full distribution rights, provided that they comply with the provisions set out in the Administrative Measures on Foreign Investment in the Commercial Sector (the 'Commercial Measures') effective June 2004. These rights were extended to WFOEs from 11 December 2004. Therefore, FIEs may now import products for sale purposes in China or provide services for products that they do not manufacture.

Capitalization rules

There is no longer formal requirement that the aggregate foreign investment in an EJV or CJV must be not less than 25 per cent of the registered capital. However, for joint ventures to enjoy preferential treatment such as the reduction of or exemption from import duties, the aggregate foreign investment must be 15 per cent or more. 'Registered capital' is the total amount of capital contributed by the parties and registered as investment with the Chinese authorities, whereas 'total investment' is the sum of registered capital and the company's actual or potential external borrowings (within China or from abroad).

In this context, FIEs must maintain certain debt to equity ratios depending upon the total amount of investment (ie, debt plus equity) as detailed in Table 17.1.

Table 17.1 Equity to debt ratios

Total investment	Minimum Registered Capital
Below US$3 million	70% of total
US$3–10 million	50% of total
US$10–30 million	40% of total
Above US$30 million	33% of total

The minimum registered capital required for establishing a limited liability company used to be RMB500,000. It was reduced to RMB30,000 across all industries in the new Company Law, effective 1 January 2006.

Subject to verification procedures and certain limitations, the parties to an FIE may make their contributions to registered capital in cash, tangible or intangible property (eg, technology, equipment and IPR), land and buildings. The new Company Law relaxed previous limitations by allowing shareholders to contribute up to 70 per cent of the registered capital in intangible assets. Valuation of the in-kind contribution made by a foreign party to an EJV is subject to an asset valuation by the local commodity inspection bureau.

An EJV is an independent separate legal entity with limited liability companies that are not joint stock companies (ie, the registered capital is not divided into share units and therefore share certificates are not issued). However, there are now rules for the establishment of a joint stock company that can be formed through private placements with a minimum of two investors. Joint stock companies are, of course, necessary for company independent public offerings (IPOs) on either the Shanghai or international stock markets on which the listed shares are traded. The new Company Law also relaxed the minimum registered capital requirement for joint stock companies from RMB10 million to RMB5 million.

Unless special approval has been granted by the relevant examination and approval authority the foreign party to an FIE must commit to making its capital contributions to the registered capital of the FIE within a fixed period of time from the issuance date of its business licence. The timing for payment in full depends upon the size of the FIE's registered capital, varying from one year where the registered capital is less than US$500,000, through one-and-a-half years for registered capital from US$500,000 to US$1 million to two years for registered capital from US$1 million to US$3 million and three years for FIEs with registered capital from US$3 million to US$10 million.

Timing for subscription to FIEs with registered capital over US$10 million is determined by the relevant authorities. Typically, there will be a lump sum of perhaps 15 per cent payable within six months from the date on which the business licence is issued followed by instalments.

The term of an EJV is typically between 15 and 30 years and may be renewed with the agreement of the parties subject to the approval of the original approval authorities. One factor in agreeing the original term may be the duration of the land use rights passed to the JV by the Chinese party. During the term the parties may not withdraw their contributions to the registered capital or transfer or assign their equity interests without the prior agreement of the authorities. Transfers of equity interests are subject to the pre-emptive rights of the other investor(s) and their consent. Upon termination and liquidation of an EJV, the assets are distributed in proportion to the parties' equity stakes.

Approval authority

As noted above, the ultimate approval authority for all FDI in China is MOFCOM, which delegates its authority to its local branches in provinces and municipalities known as COFTECs or COFERTs (Commissions on Foreign Economic Relations and Trade, renamed in some provinces as 'commerce bureaus' to be consistent with the 2004 change of ministry name). The limits of authority are defined in Table 17.2.

Table 17.2 Approval authorities for FDI in China

Investment amount	Approval authority
Up to US$100 million	Local branches of the State Development and Reform Commission (SDRC) for application Reports. Local branches of MOFCOM for JV contracts and Article of Association.
US$100–500 million	SDRC and MOFCOM approval required. For 'restricted projects' the threshold is from US$50 million.
Above US$500 million	SDTC, MOFCOM and the State Council. For 'restricted projects' the threshold is from US$100 million.

At the local level, as well as the approval authorities, the department-in-charge that supervises the Chinese party and ultimately the FIE and other relevant departments such as the Labour Bureau and local planning commission may also play roles in the approval process.

At both provincial and central levels there may be other authorities with an interest in a project that have not been consulted initially but can still 'throw a spanner in the works' even after formal approval has been signalled. Perhaps the most famous example is that of British American Tobacco (BAT), which announced in July 2004 that the State Council had granted approval for a US$1.5 billion cigarette manufacturing facility after many years of negotiation. Within 24 hours the State Tobacco Monopoly Administration (STMA) that controls the industry, followed by the State Development and Reform Commission (SDRC), denied that they had approved the BAT project. Similar instances on a less dramatic scale have been reported in the field of media companies, content distributors and cable/satellite/terrestrial/mobile operators where powerful provincial government authorities have assumed the right to a rather 'wider' interpretation of the rules and have intervened to frustrate projects for which central government approval was forthcoming.

The structure of JVs

Documents

The key documents in any EJV are the joint venture contract and articles of association (see Table 17.2). The contract is effectively a partnership agreement setting out the capital contributions and the relative detailed responsibilities of the parties. The latter document is roughly similar to the memorandum and articles of association that are standard under English company law although provisions for the operation of the management of the company are more detailed in the Chinese version. Many of the articles are a repetition of clauses in the contract.

The joint venture contract may be supported by supplementary agreements of which the most common are:

∎ lease from the Chinese party to the JV in cases where the Chinese party has the land use rights and leases the land or an existing facility with buildings to the JV;
∎ export sales agreement between the JV and the foreign party;
∎ technology, patent or copyright licence from the foreign party to the JV;
∎ training agreement between the foreign party and the JV, covering training outside China and subsequent on-site training in China; and
∎ consultancy agreement between the foreign party and the JV to cover the continuing provision of foreign experts and/or management support.

EJV board and management authority

The board of directors is the supreme authority of an EJV and the chairperson of the board is the company's legal representative. The general manager manages the day-to-day operations of the company and is appointed by the board of directors. Members of the board are generally appointed in proportion to each party's contribution to the joint venture with the majority shareholder appointing the chairperson and having the right to nominate the general manager.

Board decisions are usually arrived at on a simple majority basis, except for the following decisions where the unanimous consent of all directors attending a meeting is required under PRC law:

∎ amendments to the articles of association;
∎ any increase and any transfer of registered capital and adjustment of each party's capital contribution ratio;

- any merger or consolidation of the JV company with any other economic organization;
- any separation of significant assets (by way of transfer, assignment, sale, lease or other means of disposition) of the JV company; or
- the termination, dissolution or liquidation of the JV company.

Approval procedures

The documents to be submitted to the examination and approval authority (in Chinese) are the joint venture contract and articles of association supported by a detailed feasibility study. From the foreign party's point of view, it is important that the feasibility study should be fully congruent with the business plan that the parties have developed in the course of their negotiations to avoid subsequent misunderstandings.

The approval authority may request amendments to the documents if any terms are found to be contrary to Chinese law or policy. They must approve or reject the application within three months of its receipt. In practice, for smaller non-contentious projects the approval time is generally much shorter.

Following approval the EJV contract becomes effective and the parties then have 30 days to file the approval and documentation with the SAIC or its local branch, which will issue the EJV's business licence usually within a further 30 days. Issuance of the licence establishes the EJV as a formal legal entity and the EJV must then register, again within 30 days, with the relevant authorities responsible for taxation administration, finance, customs and foreign exchange.

Cooperative joint ventures

A Chinese–foreign CJV may be formed by at least one Chinese and one foreign cooperator for the purpose of generating profit. A CJV is characterized by its flexibility and can be an unincorporated joint venture or an independent separate legal entity with limited liability. The joint venture parties are free to fix their contributions, including forms of assistance or service to the CJV instead of capital contributions, between themselves. The CJV contract may provide for the profits and losses to be shared between the parties according to a formula that may or may not reflect their respective contributions to the registered capital.

Unlike an EJV, pre-emptive rights in a CJV are not obligatory but are subject to contractual agreement between the parties. However, any transfer of equity interests will require the consent of the approval authority in addition to the other party. The rules for establishing a CJV are much the same as those governing the process for establishing an EJV.

Wholly foreign-owned entities

A WFOE is an independent legal entity with limited liability in which the equity interest is wholly owned by its foreign investor(s). Formerly, a WFOE was allowed as an investment vehicle only if it either utilized advanced technology or exported at least 50 per cent of its products. This caveat has been relaxed and the sole criterion is that a WFOE 'benefits the development of the Chinese national economy'.

Procedures for the establishment of a WFOE are similar to those for an EJV except that the investor may be required to submit first a project proposal for approval to the local government at or above county level where the business is to be established.

Representative offices

A representative office may be a useful lower cost alternative as a first step that allows a foreign company to explore the China market, introduce its products and services and search for investment opportunities. Approvals are generally easy to obtain and capital outlays are generally low. However, the annual budget for a modest single representative office in Beijing or Shanghai, the most popular locations, is unlikely to be less than £200,000.

The permissible scope of representative office activities is limited and does not include:

■ entering into commercial contracts in the name of the parent company;
■ buying property or importing production equipment;
■ collecting or making payment in connection with sales or purchases;
■ providing services to any company other than the parent;
■ directly engaging in revenue generating activity generally.

The role of lawyers in joint venture negotiations

You will probably need the advice of a Western law firm to check that the FIE in which you are about to engage is within the framework of Chinese law and that the contractual documents (JV contract and articles of association, etc) that you intend to sign do not carry unacceptable risks. However, except for high-value projects involving negotiations with the authorities at central government level, there are few advantages in bringing lawyers to the negotiating table. There are three reasons for this view:

■ First, there are no Chinese equivalents to Western-type lawyers. The Chinese entity will take advice when in doubt from its local reporting authority and the presence of a Western lawyer will introduce an unhelpful level of formality to 'face to face' discussions. The relaxed relationships that you have built during the earlier stages of discussion (see Chapter 15) may be impaired.
■ Second, just as the Chinese party may wish to consult its advisers outside the negotiating chamber on points of difficulty, so it is useful for the Western party to be able to ask for a recess to consult its advisers. In JV negotiations, when an impasse is reached, it is quite acceptable for either party to say 'Let's come back to this point tomorrow and move on to something else today'.

■ Third, it may be counterproductive to focus on the small-print minutiae of each clause. Contracts and articles of association that are written in unambiguous business language are the best that you should strive to achieve. You will have no control over the Chinese language version submitted to the approval authorities nor any input unless you are fluent in Chinese. And in foreign–Chinese joint ventures the Chinese language version will prevail in cases of disputed interpretation.

Remember, above all, the Chinese perception of contracts. They are not written in stone but are a snapshot of what the parties agreed at the time. As the venture evolves the parties will probably want to make changes and to exercise flexibility according to the demands of the business. Whether the business succeeds or fails will depend on the depth and warmth of the relationships between the partners. As with all human activity in China, personal relationships are paramount.

18

Audit and accountancy

Jonathan Reuvid

This short chapter provides a layperson's cursory view only of the accounting and auditing requirement and practices for foreign-invested enterprises (FIEs) in the PRC. In addition, it offers practical suggestions for foreign investors as to how they should organize the accountancy and audit aspects of the equity joint ventures (EJVs), cooperative joint ventures (CJVs) and wholly foreign-owned entities (WFOEs) in which they participate.

Development of accounting regulations

The most important wave of reform in accounting regulations was introduced in 2001 following formulation of the first comprehensive set of regulations in 1992. Overall, accounting standards are now developing clearly towards International Financial Reporting Standards (IFRS). A detailed comparison of PRC Accounting Standards with IFRS and US General Accepted Accounting Principles (US GAAP) may be found in Reuvid and Yong (2005) *Doing Business with China*, 5th edn, GMB Publishing, London.

Before 1992, the accounting rules and regulations, known as fund accounting, were in force. Their primary purpose was to establish an information and reporting system to maintain administrative control over assets of the state in SOEs and as a reporting system for the implementation of economic policies. The fund accounting system was appropriate for resource allocation in China's planned command economy but not at all for the new wave of FIEs that followed the transition to China's open door policy from 1989.

The programme to restructure SOEs into joint stock limited companies for eventual flotation was undertaken in the 1990s and a third set of accounting regulations specifically for joint stock limited companies was introduced and then revised in 1998. These were replaced by the Accounting System for Business Enterprises (ASBE) issued in early 2001, which was also made mandatory for all FIEs in 1992. The Ministry of Finance (MOF) is responsible for formulating, promulgating and administering accounting regulations. Neither the Accounting Society of China (ASC) nor the Chinese Institute of Certified Public Accountants (CICPA) have any jurisdiction or discretion in interpreting ASBE.

ASBE allows companies a greater degree of judgement than formerly in formulating their accounting policies to suit their specific circumstances. For example, companies may determine the amount of provision set against asset impairment and can set their own fixed asset depreciation policy to reflect their economic consumption by the company.

ABSE largely adopts the core principles of IFRS, including accuracy, completeness, prudence, timeliness, materiality, accrual basis, matching, substance over form and going concern. Major features of ABSE that may differ somewhat from IFRS are:

■ Companies must take the calendar year from 1 January to 31 December as their financial year.
■ Transactions should be recorded in RMB except where a company's transactions are predominately in foreign currencies when a foreign currency may be used. However, the foreign currency books of accounts must be translated to RMB in the preparation of financial statements.
■ The historical cost convention must be used with assets recorded initially at actual cost adjusted subsequently for any impairment. Revaluations are not generally permitted.
■ Since PRC accounting regulations are legally enforceable, substance over form may be followed only if the regulations are not breached.
■ The concept of fair market value applied to fixed and intangible assets is only used where there is an active market.

Although some footnote disclosures may be less comprehensive than elsewhere, Chinese standards are rigorous in areas such as the preparation of cash flow statement, comments on the fairness of transactions between related parties and disclosure of the corporate identities of related parties. Overall, ABSE permits management to exercise experience-based judgement within a defined accounting system.

Auditing requirements and standards

As in most countries, limited liability companies are required to have their accounts audited annually by independent external auditors charged with stating an objective opinion on the fair presentation of the financial statements. In China, auditors also work to a second agenda: to ascertain the accuracy and legality of the financial records of a business (ie, whether transactions comply with relevant state laws and regulations).

The general auditing standards introduced by the MOF since 1988, and throughout the 1990s, form the basis of auditing standards in China and have brought them very close to those of International Standards on Auditing (ISA).

The audit report

The audit report normally consists of three paragraphs:

- *an introductory paragraph* identifying the financial statements being audited and setting out the responsibilities of the management and the auditors;
- *a scope paragraph* setting out the principal audit work and procedures carried out;
- *an opinion paragraph* stating whether the accounts have been prepared in accordance with the relevant accounting regulations and expressing any qualification.

Sometimes, other government agencies may ask for certified public accountants to express an opinion on additional items. If these additional requirements have not been agreed by the MOF or the CICPA or fall outside the normal competence expected of certified public accountants, they may be retracted.

Managing your accounting and audit issues

EJV accounting systems and the role of chief financial officer

As David Steeds notes in Chapter 29 on the independent director in China, the status of the finance department and chief financial officer (CFO) in a Chinese company are devalued, a relic of the old managed economy in which accountants were no more than 'bean-counting' bookkeepers. The concept of the CFO working alongside the general manager (CEO) in a joint venture to control the company financially and to develop and implement business plans is foreign to most Chinese JV partners.

For the foreign investors in WFOEs or equity joint ventures (EJVs) where they are majority partners it is essential that a CFO installed is an English-speaker and understands IFRS. On a relationship level, this is a key appointment that must be approved by the foreign investor, even when a minority JV partner. The appointee must be someone whom the general manager will accept as part of his or her management team and whose judgement he or she respects. There are growing numbers of young Chinese certified public accountants but they do not come cheap and for smaller EJVs it may be more appropriate to take a less qualified youngster with a good personality approved by the general manager who can be trained either at the foreign party's home office or by sending a qualified foreign accountant on a temporary training assignment to China. In the case of manufacturing joint ventures where the preparation phase before the plant becomes operational is extended, bringing back the appointee to the foreign partner's place of business in Europe or the United States will be more cost-effective and will immerse him or her thoroughly in international business practices.

Training should be focused on providing a management accounting system to the foreign partner's standards and on providing a set of additional entries in the financial accounting system to adjust the Chinese accounting statements to International Accounting Standards (IAS). For WFOEs and all majority-held EJVs, consolidation of the Chinese company's accounts into the foreign company's group accounts becomes an issue and should be tackled in regular quarterly and monthly reporting as well as year-end audited accounts. Foreign companies that are minority equity holders in an EJV may take a more relaxed view of the financial accounting but will not be comfortable without a management accounting system that is akin to their own.

Auditing issues

The top global accounting practices all have highly experienced offices in China, mainly in Beijing and Shanghai, with some European or US partners but largely with Chinese audit managers. Many of these are first-generation expatriate Chinese who have returned to China after qualification in the United States, Hong Kong, Singapore or Europe. Therefore, professional advice to the best international standard is readily available.

Not surprisingly, the Western accountancy firms dominate the company flotation field, both in Shanghai and international markets from Hong Kong to London and New York. They perform the separate roles of auditors and reporting accountants. Increasingly, however, the accountancy work on initial public offerings (IPOs) in China is shared with Chinese firms of certified public accountants who have forged alliances or local partnerships with the resident Western practices. This distinction is important to foreign companies starting up their joint ventures in China because the cost differential between the Western accountancy firms and the Chinese firms is very significant. Typically, the day rates of audit managers in reputable Chinese firms are one-third or less than those of the Western practices. If you take into account the travel and accommodation costs of an audit manager flying in from Beijing or Shanghai to, say, Dalian or Qingdao the difference in cost is greater still against the fees of a local Chinese auditor.

For multinational companies or foreign companies with WFOEs or controlling interests in large EJVs where they have invested highly, the reassurance of global audited accounts may be necessary to satisfy shareholders and the financial communities in which they are located. That argument is strengthened if there is an expectation of an early IPO for their FIE. However, for the foreign partners in smaller EJVs cost will be of more immediate concern and the appointment of Chinese auditors is a perfectly acceptable alternative. The quality of the EJV's incumbent trained CFO may be the deciding factor.

19

Taxation

John Lee, KPMG Shanghai and Hong Kong SAR[1]

New tax regime

In March 2007, China took an important step towards harmonizing its tax regime for foreign and domestic companies. The government's State Council is now working through the details surrounding the implementation of this new system.

Introducing a level playing field

China has long relied on taxation as a tool to attract and incentivize foreign investment, particularly in its manufacturing industries. If imitation is the sincerest form of flattery, then China's tax regime has undoubtedly been a success; its tax models have been emulated by countries around the world from Southeast Asia to the emerging economies of Eastern Europe.

Now the Chinese authorities are changing tack. The preferential tax rates and tax holidays that have been offered to foreign-invested enterprises (FIEs) are being stripped away in favour of a more uniform income tax regime. The authorities are levelling the playing field between foreign and domestic companies and opting for more targeted and sophisticated tax incentives in their place.

---

[1] KPMG in China and Hong Kong SAR has published a guide to the new EIT Law and also issues regular alerts on PRC taxation. For more details visit the KPMG website: www.kpmg.com.cn.

Introduction of the EIT Law

The new Enterprise Income Tax Law (EIT Law) was promulgated by the National People's Congress on 16 March 2007 and will be effective from 1 January 2008. According to the new law, EIT applies to all enterprises, including FIEs, foreign enterprises and domestic enterprises.

Incentives

The EIT Law contains tax incentives that are targeted at enterprises engaged in certain designated industries rather than on the basis of their geographical location. It offers tax incentives ranging from reduction in taxable income, bonus and accelerated deductions, to tax exemption or reduction for designated industries such as energy- and resource-saving, environmental protection and high-tech development.

Transitional measures

As certain tax incentives applicable to FIEs before the introduction of the EIT Law have been revoked, transitional grandfathering relief has been introduced for qualifying FIEs. Transitional measures also apply to certain areas in the PRC that previously offered a lower tax rate. For example, under the transitional measures, the current EIT rate of 15 per cent in special economic zones will be gradually phased up to the 25 per cent EIT rate over a five-year period.

Application of the new tax regime

The new EIT Law reflects the level of economic development that China has now achieved. The authorities want to provide more support to growing domestic enterprises, which had previously faced a corporate income tax rate as high as 33 per cent. The government also wants to focus on developing more sophisticated and energy-efficient industries that will support the next stage of growth and wealth creation in the country.

The EIT Law should be considered as more of a broad framework for the application of the new tax regime. However, successful implementation of the general provisions in the law would require detailed implementation rules, which would further define and supplement the general EIT Law provisions. The issuance of these detailed implementation rules falls under the authority of the State Council, an executive body empowered (specifically under the EIT Law in the present case) to promulgate tax regulations and provisions.

While a number of areas need clarification through further provisions and implementation rules, it is clear that the law will have significant ramifications for foreign companies investing in China. Inevitably, these tax reforms will increase the income tax burden on many foreign-invested enterprises. This will be especially true for companies currently receiving tax incentives.

Foreign investors that intend to invest in China will need to consider the impact these changes will have on future investments, mergers or acquisitions. Foreign companies already operating in China have also started reviewing their tax strategies to prepare for what will be one of the largest regulatory changes to hit foreign companies in recent years. Box 19.1 highlights the main changes to China's tax regime.

Box 19.1 Key changes to China's tax regime

Income tax liability will be governed by the residency status of taxpayers. The law introduces the concepts of 'resident enterprise' and 'non-resident enterprise' to distinguish between taxpayers.

The existing system of granting five-year tax holidays (consisting of a two-year exemption followed by a three-year 50 per cent reduction of the applicable tax rate) to foreign-invested production enterprises will be revoked. Companies that are already in, or are about to embark on their tax holiday, will be offered a transition period.

The new law sets out a general tax rate of 25 per cent. A special reduced rate of 20 per cent will be available for enterprises deemed to be 'small-scale' with low profits, and a third, further reduced rate will be offered to 'encourage' high-tech enterprises. Detailed criteria for companies to secure the reduced rates have yet to be released.

Companies that are currently subject to a reduced income tax rate under the existing law (for example, those companies in special economic zones) will be eligible for a five-year transition period, during which the tax rate will gradually increase to the unified rate of 25 per cent.

A number of new tax incentives will be available in certain circumstances. For example, companies involved in qualifying energy and water saving projects will be able to apply for tax relief. In addition, income from environmental protection projects and technology transfers that meet the prescribed criteria will receive a tax exemption or reduction.

Tax relief previously offered to export-oriented enterprises has been repealed, as the lower tax rate offered to such enterprises was considered to be in violation of WTO principles.

The standard withholding tax rate for dividends, interest, royalties, capital gains or other income derived by a non-resident enterprise from sources in China will be fixed at 20 per cent. However, the new law does provide the possibility for exemptions or reductions by the State Council.

Every UK company with an international outlook now needs to develop a China strategy.

The **China-Britain Business Council (CBBC)** is the UK's leading independent source of China business information, advice, consultancy and services for UK industry.

As an independent, business-led organisation, we support British companies of all sizes by providing **Business Services, Practical In-Market Assistance** and **Industry Initiatives.**

Our membership scheme offers enhanced benefits including discounte⌐ prices for services, special member-only events and information – essential for those realising the time is right to get actively involved in the China market.

Part 4

Joint venture management

20

Managing joint ventures

Jonathan Reuvid

Having completed the arduous tasks of identifying potential joint venture partners, selecting a preferred partner, negotiating the joint venture and undergoing the approval and registration procedures, the foreign investor may feel like heaving a sigh of relief. However, unless he or she has addressed the organizational issues and particularly the selection of a general manager during the negotiation process, any relief will be short-lived.

Chinese EJV (equity joint venture) contracts provide for the formation of a preparation group or committee as soon as the joint venture has been approved, whose mandate covers site preparation and construction, the selection and ordering of equipment, its installation and commissioning, the supply of utilities, programmes for management and staff training (including travel and accommodation arrangements if Chinese staff are to be trained at the foreign partner's home facility) and all other work necessary to develop the joint venture before commencement of operations. In principle, the preparation group's job is complete and it is disbanded when the joint venture facility is fully operational and can be handed over to the general manager.

The preparation group consists of the chairperson and deputy chairperson (Chinese and foreign respectively if the Chinese party is the majority equity partner and the reverse if the foreign party is in the majority), the general manager and various experts and managers from the two parties. It follows that the selection of the general manager should be made, if possible, before the approval of the authorities is received.

There are limited alternatives for organizing the management of a normal EJV although there are more expensive options for very large joint ventures with high levels of equity investment. These alternatives are discussed below. Although the two big company approaches will be beyond the pocket of most joint ventures, there are elements in each approach that can be deployed to advantage in smaller enterprises.

The big company approach

Very different approaches were adopted by Volkswagen (VW) in Shanghai and Fiat in Nanjing for their 50/50 joint ventures in China. For its 1985 JV with Shanghai Automotive Industry Corporation, which established the joint venture as the dominant automobile market leader in the 1990s, VW chose to introduce a parallel organization with joint general managers, one Chinese and one foreign, and jointly responsible managers at all senior and middle management levels downwards. This may sound cumbersome but it ensured that VW technical and quality assurance standards, management systems and production processes were securely installed in the joint venture and maintained at VW international standards. Although the VW share of the larger Chinese automotive market has been reduced below 25 per cent today, as a result of the arrival of newer entrants and the growth of local Chinese manufacturers, this joint venture remains the most profitable automotive manufacturer in China.

By contrast, in its joint venture with Nanjing-based Yuejin Automobile Group Corporation for the manufacture of the Iveco Daily light commercial vehicle, Fiat opted to develop as close to a 100 per cent Chinese management team as possible. Chinese managers and staff travelled to Turin, in groups of 200 at a time for six months to be trained and to work on the production line at the Iveco plant. On their return, they were supported by a limited number of Fiat expatriates who acted as mentors to the Chinese managers during the start-up period and early operational phase of the Nanjing factory. By 1997, there were only two Fiat managers remaining in the plant, a consultant mentor to the general manager and sales manager, and a hands-on production manager to assist the Chinese factory manager. One interesting outcome of this programme was that the managers communicated to each other in Italian.

Appointing the general manager

EJVs with minority foreign equity partners

Where the Chinese partner is the majority investor in an EJV, the contract provides for the nomination of the general manager by the Chinese party that also appoints the chairperson. This convention also applies to 50/50 EJVs. It is unlikely that the Chinese chairperson will submit his or her nomination to the board of directors for appointment without consulting the foreign partner, but the selection of the appointee is high on the list of priorities.

Forming judgements on the capabilities of nominated Chinese general managers is difficult for foreign partners even if they have fluency in Chinese. In most Chinese EJVs the day-to-day decision-making is wholly delegated to the general manager, including the power of signature on behalf of the company and the company 'chop' (a stamp used with an ink pad (see Chapter 24 for the dangers of 'chop' misuse). The general manager needs to be someone of high integrity who will at all times act in the best interests of the EJV rather than in the better interests of either equity partner.

It is hoped that the strongest candidate for general manager will emerge during the long process of JV negotiations. The Chinese negotiating team will probably be headed by an English-speaking senior middle manager who is entrusted with the negotiating task. The decision-maker may take a back seat in the negotiations or not even participate at all. However, if the foreign partner has managed to create a relaxed and open relationship between the parties during earlier discussions (see Chapter 15), other members of the Chinese team may play an active part in the negotiations. In this way, it may be possible to identify other general manager candidates as well as the chief negotiator.

In the event that the Chinese side's chief negotiator is clearly incompatible, I favour the rather risky step of making it clear that it is difficult to do business with him or her. If this point is made subtly and without discourtesy in the early stages, the most senior Chinese manager present will pick up the foreign partner's unease and very likely a different chief negotiator will be appointed for subsequent sessions. If the Chinese partner insists on nominating an unsuitable general manager, you should hold out for as long as you can and ask for alternatives but ultimately you may have to accept a weak candidate.

EJVs with majority foreign partners

Conversely, where the foreign partner holds the majority equity interest, it has the right to appoint the chairperson and nominate the general manager. It is tempting to appoint an expatriate general manager for at least the first few years but there are disadvantages. A Chinese general manager is better placed to develop a management team with close relationships and good relations with the workforce, suppliers, customers, the local reporting authorities and tax office, the company's bankers and the bureaus responsible for the provision of electricity, water and other essential services. In an environment where land use rights, local taxes and utilities costs may be 'flexible', a Chinese manager is likely to achieve better results for the company.

If no suitable Chinese candidate emerges, you may finally decide to install experienced expatriate managers as general manager and, perhaps, for one or two of the other senior positions on a more temporary basis. You might consider adopting the Fiat-type mentoring approach if you find Chinese candidates for these positions who require training and are weak on experience. Hesitate before recruiting an expatriate general manager externally as this will introduce an additional element of unwelcome risk.

Wholly foreign-owned enterprises (WFOEs)

The case for appointing an expatriate general manager is clearly stronger here, particularly if your aim is to replicate your home base operation in China despite the disadvantages highlighted in the case of EJVs of non-Chinese appointments. However, given the differences in the cultural, social and business dynamics of Chinese companies, it is doubtful whether a 'carbon copy' operation is ever achievable, or even desirable. If budgets allow, you might consider adopting the VW parallel management approach for the senior positions in the opening years that can be relaxed into the Fiat mentoring model subsequently.

Other key management appointments

Standard EJV contracts provide for the general manager and the deputy general manager to be appointed by the board, leaving the general manager responsible for the selection and appointment of other senior management positions. The foreign investor should insist during negotiations, even in EJVs where it is the minority partner, that the board retains responsibility for the approval and appointment of the chief financial officer (CFO) and the quality assurance (QA) manager in the case of manufacturing and some services joint ventures.

CFO

The importance of this position has been emphasized in Chapter 18 and is referred to again in Chapter 29. Given the status to which chief accountants are relegated in most Chinese companies, it is unlikely that a candidate for the CFO position will surface in the course of negotiations or even in the joint preparation of the business plan. Probably the best course of action is to ask the general manager-elect, in whose management team the CFO will be a senior member, to put forward for your appraisal and approval, English-speaking candidates with whom he or she feels that he or she can work harmoniously. The appointed CFO should certainly participate in any training programmes held in your home operation and should be encouraged to establish a 'dotted line' reporting relationship with your CFO or chief accountant.

QA manager

Since the adoption of ISO 9000 and other international quality standards in the late 1980s and the development of a nationwide network of quality certification bureaus China has focused on quality assurance. Some Chinese enterprises have adhered to the old total quality management (TCM), which focused only on the quality control of the final product and ignored QA from the delivery of raw materials and components at the factory gate right through the production process to finished goods. QA managers from that environment should be avoided. However, there are a number of experienced QA managers in Chinese manufacturing fully conversant with international standards who can be recruited. During the period of the preparatory group, the QA manager should be tasked with the translation of the foreign partner's QA manual and management systems into Chinese for immediate installation and application in the joint venture. As in Western companies, the QA manager should on no account report to the production manager but should have independent status as a senior member of the management team.

Deputy general manager

In a Chinese EJV, the deputy or assistant general manager has formal responsibility to stand in for the general manager when he or she is absent from the plant but his or her role is mainly administrative. He or she will carry out the detailed paperwork for dealing with the authorities and local service providers and performs many of the tasks that would normally be assigned to the company secretary in a British company. He or she will be a confidant of the general manager, hopefully alongside the CFO, and his or her selection can be left to the general manager.

Other appointments

Again, recruitment of the technical manger, production manager, sales manager, distribution manager and personnel manager can all be left to the general manager. The first three of these should be included in the overseas management training programme. It is important for them and the other members of the management team pinpointed above to have exposure to an international business environment before taking up their duties.

There is no shortage of competent, young and well-qualified engineers in the manufacturing centres of China, many of whom can be attracted to working for a joint venture. Those that have been employed in the technical centres of large companies tend to be strong academically but weak on experience. The technical manager whom your general manager recruits should be balanced by a production manager who is long on experience.

Sales managers may have an unexpected background. In the 1980s and early 1990s it was not uncommon for the company driver to be promoted to this position. The logic was simple; the driver was the only person in the company who was authorized to drive and who knew where potential customers were located.

EJV board meetings

For foreign businesspeople appointed to the boards of EJVs for the first time, the first Chinese board meeting is a 'whole new experience'. Unless carefully stage-managed, board meetings can last a week or more, not least because every member attending expects to discourse at length on every item whether or not he or she has any experience of the matter in hand or any useful comment to make. This is particularly true of the 'non-executive' directors appointed by the Chinese partner who may be semi-retired and have been given the directorship as a sinecure. The problem is compounded in joint ventures where the Chinese company is the majority equity partner and the appointed chairperson has no experience of running board meetings.

An effective solution is to arrange with the chairperson for a pre-board meeting to be held, at which all items on the agenda and other important company matters are discussed fully between the chairperson, general manager, vice-chairperson and other foreign directors, with other members of the management team in attendance for specific items where they are involved. If the relationship between the chairperson and general manager with the foreign vice-chairperson is cordial, this procedure will be welcomed. The aim is to achieve consensus on all items of the board meeting agenda and then to hold the actual board meeting for one day only, with a second allocated to production and approval of the minutes. The process can be assisted if the foreign partner directors schedule their flights home for the day following.

There is an obligation in the JV contract to hold at least one and normally two board meetings each year, of which one should be held in China and the second may be held abroad. The latter is a benefit much valued by Chinese directors.

Day-to-day management

Complete books have been written on day-to-day management experiences in foreign–Chinese joint ventures, as many focusing on problems and failures as on successes. In this part and the next part of the book we focus on the case study experiences of a handful of UK-invested FIEs over diverse industry sectors. They are intended to provide useful examples and some guidance of what companies investing in China today can expect.

We begin with the case study of an unusual joint venture that has proved successful although not entirely in the direction that the partners had originally expected.

Case study – Jinan Fuqiang Power Company

The opportunity

In early 1995, a UK Midlands-based engineering company engaged in the re-manufacture of automotive engines was invited to replace the US partner in an approved joint venture to re-manufacture engines in China. China National Heavy Duty Truck Company (CNHTC) located in Jinan, Shandong Province had been chosen by the State Council, to which it reported at that time, to establish an EJV to introduce engine re-manufacturing techniques and skills to China by engaging with a foreign company experienced in this field. The US company engine re-manufacturer that CNHTC had chosen, owned by Chinese expatriates, had failed to make its equity contribution after approval of the joint venture.

Faced with this embarrassing situation, CNHTC had sought the advice of the Centre for Trade and Development (CMTD), the market research consultancy arm of MOFTEC (now MOFCOM, the Ministry of Commerce) referred to in Chapter 16, who had in turn enlisted my help. I identified and approached the UK engine re-manufacturer, which confirmed its interest and asked me to open negotiations on its behalf. It was quickly apparent that the UK engineering company did not have the financial resources to take over the position of the US company and provide further investment and a UK-managed offshore investment group was brought in as a second foreign partner. Preliminary negotiations proceeded rapidly and on a first one-day visit to Jinan we drafted a formal memorandum of agreement that was signed by all three parties in the days following. The basic elements for a pre-feasibility study were agreed at a distance and a proposal was submitted to the relevant authorities shortly thereafter.

Negotiation
Three months later after receiving preliminary approval, and confirmation of withdrawal from the US partner, the joint venture negotiations took place in Beijing with the assistance of CMTD on the basis of a draft joint venture contract and articles of association prepared by CNHTC. Over a period of two weeks that included a visit to Jinan to inspect the CNHTC facilities and the site offered for the location of the JV, the detailed negotiations were concluded and the draft contract and articles of association signed for submission to MOFTEC and the other approval authorities. At the same time, a mission statement and a detailed business plan was also developed jointly and signed off. The basis of the JV was that CNHTC retained the 51 per cent equity interest that it had been allocated in the original JV, and the two foreign partners would share the remaining 49 per cent in agreed proportions. The contract provided for a registered capital of US$2.05 million

The preparatory group and training programme
One bonus from the two weeks together was that the chief negotiator on behalf of CNHTC, a young engineer from its technical centre who had replaced the original unsatisfactory head of the negotiating team, emerged as a clear candidate to be general manager. Although he did not speak English at that time, intelligence and maturity were evident and immaculate translation by the CMTD general manager enabled us to assess his quality. From that point onwards, there was no question who should be appointed general manager of the new joint venture, which was named Jinan Fuqiang Power Company.

The approval and registration procedures were carried out over the four months following the Beijing meeting and the preparatory group started work from January 2006. In the interval, the financial condition of the British engineering company had deteriorated, mainly because of its declining business with the ailing MG Rover Group, and the investment group decided to step in and buy the UK company outright. This ensured that the joint venture could proceed without financial difficulty. CNHTC and the authorities agreed readily to the consolidation of the foreign shareholdings.

During 1997, the preparatory group under the leadership of the now appointed general manager carried out the considerable job of taking over a largely derelict group of buildings on the site in central Jinan rented from CNHTC and adjacent to its technical centre, and transforming them into a modern facility with an office block rebuilt from workers' former accommodation and to a high standard of decoration. The building and installation works were carried out on time and, amazingly, within the budget approved by the board. Under the guidance of the UK technical director, the factory layout was prepared and equipment ordered. Standard high-quality machine tools were procured within China and the purpose-built machines and equipment were ordered through the UK partner from a range of European and US suppliers. Towards the end of 1997, while the equipment was on order, the Chinese training group headed by the general manager with the production and QA manager and a team of machine-setters came to the United Kingdom for training. They quickly showed that they were the equal of the UK factory employees on the production line, working on older equipment, in some cases of inferior design. The first full board meeting of Jinan Fuqiang had been held in the United

Kingdom during the previous summer. So far everything had proceeded according to plan.

While the training group were in the United Kingdom, the deputy general manager supervised the remaining preparation work for receipt of the equipment that began to arrive in Jinan as the group returned in time for the 1998 Chinese New Year. During the summer all the equipment was installed and commissioned.

Sales development

The chairperson, who was the vice-president sales of CNHTC, and the British deputy chairperson started to focus on sales development and toured the leading foreign–Chinese joint ventures in Beijing, Shanghai and Nanjing to explore the opportunities for taking on their engine warranty work, and, in the future, servicing their sales outlets with re-manufactured engines as a Chinese used car and truck market developed. The results were disappointing, particularly with Shanghai Volkswagen where the German management expressed strong interest initially but were deflected by their Chinese partner and the labour union who insisted that their joint venture should set up its own engine re-manufacturing unit. This setback was mitigated by confirmation of demand for the re-manufactured engines of CNHTC heavy trucks from its customers, particularly owner-drivers engaged in construction projects such as the Three Gorges Dam. CNHTC was also ready to assign its engine warranty work to the joint venture.

The start-up

By the autumn of 1998 the factory was in production and a management problem soon emerged. The equipment installed was of balanced capacity enabling a wide range of engines to be treated and for production to run on double shift as sales expanded. However, a flaw appeared in the form of a gap in the production planning function necessary to coordinate the efficient flow of work through the various manufacturing processes. The training programme had not addressed this issue fully and the computer that had been ordered for this function was inadequate. The problem was solved over the next six months with the installation of well-proven computer software and systems designed for this function. A related problem of finding a sufficient inventory of 'core' in China (old engine blocks no longer in service) was also solved by offering trade-in terms.

A change of emphasis

By the spring of 1999 the factory was operating well but at a lower level of activity than hoped. It had been written into the JV contract that the UK engineering company would send a proportion of its engine core and components to Jinan for re-manufacturing there and re-export to the United Kingdom although no pricing was specified. However, the UK factory was leaner by now and its operating costs were reduced so that the Jinan prices, after allowing for freight costs in both directions, made the export trade unprofitable. CNHTC understood this dilemma and the JV did not try to hold its UK partner to the commitment. Instead, the Chinese management set about generating machining work on the components of new engines from the nearest CNHTC engine plant to make up the balance.

Changes of strategy

Over the next two years, although relations remained cordial, the interest of the investment group partner in building a business in China dwindled. Having explored the possibility of developing a component-sourcing business through a company that it could control under the umbrella of Jinan Fuqiang Power Company the investment group found that approvals from the authorities would be difficult and decided to re-focus its interest globally on South Africa. CNHTC had gained approval to offer its partner the opportunity to subscribe further in order to bring its share of the registered capital up to 50 per cent but the offer was not taken up. The investment group decided that it was content to leave the running of the joint venture in the capable hands of the Chinese management and to become a passive investor.

The JV continued to make steady progress and in 2003 registered RMB2 million net income after writing off RMB2.85 million of organization expenses against sales of RMB11.3 million. The general manager decided to cultivate a relationship with the technical arm of the People's Liberation Army (PLA), which needed to upgrade its own engine re-manufacturing capability. This relationship was fruitful and has enhanced Jinan Fuqiang's reputation throughout China for technical excellence. The company has been named as a model manufacturing operation by the China National Development and Reform Commission.

The joint venture has been relocated into a new, bigger factory close by the main CNHTC engine plant from which its machining and component manufacturing orders have multiplied. Its sales are reported to have topped RMB200 million in 2006.

21

Airport construction in China

Peter Budd, Arup

Background

Few would disagree with the assessment that China has taken its place on the world stage as a major political and economic force. Since it first seriously opened its domestic market to foreign involvement back in the early 1980s, China has quickly demonstrated an eagerness to increase its influence. Membership of the World Trade Organization (WTO), which occurred in 2001, has heralded changes not only in China's own domestic marketplace, but also in the global economic marketplace. China is now the third-largest trading country in the world, and by 2010 expects to increase imports and exports to over US$2.3 trillion, an average growth rate of 10 per cent a year. Given the importance of trade to China's future, the role of aviation in sustaining economic growth and securing its position in the world is a significant one.

China's aviation market is sizeable. According to the Civil Aviation Authority of China (CAAC), the government body with overall responsibility for the aviation sector, the country had 147 civil airports by the end of 2006 (26 of them capable of handling large planes such as the Boeing 747). This infrastructure meets China's basic economic and social development needs, with 61 per cent of the population and 82 per cent of all economic activity within 1.5 hours' drive from a civilian airport. However, this assessment hides an important fact: China's airport infrastructure is struggling to meet the needs created by the country's rapid economic development.

In 2006, the last year for which official figures are available, 1.73 million flights were served by China's airports, with 160 million passengers and 3.4 million tons of cargo. Beijing Capital International Airport grew to be the ninth largest airport in the world, with 48.75 million passengers, and Pudong Airport reached number six in the world for cargo turnover, with 2.16 million tons. The country has seven airports which regularly have annual passenger numbers of over 10 million.

Further statistics from the CAAC are instructive: between 1995 and 2005, passenger throughput increased at an average of 12.3 per cent annually, with cargo throughput increasing at just over 13 per cent. (Over the same period of time, China's GDP increased at an average of 8.8 per cent, and this growth is accelerating.) Over the next five years, the average growth rate of Chinese air transport is projected to be 15 per cent year-on-year.

Infrastructure growth

To meet this growth, China's airport infrastructure will need to grow accordingly. From 147 civil airports at the end of 2006, there will be 186 civil airports by 2010, according to CAAC, including three international hub airports and eight regional hubs. All of this equates to an investment in airport construction of around US$18 billion over the next five years. The Chinese government's development strategy for this industry sector focuses on three main enabling opportunities:

■ Maintaining economic growth:
  – China's GDP is expected to increase to US$60 trillion by 2020, with an annual average growth rate of 7.18 per cent. The ambition is to be the world's third-largest economy within this timeframe.
  – Per capita GDP reached US$1,755 in 2006, and is expected to grow to more than US$5,000 by 2020, based on population figures of 1.4 billion people.
■ Growth in tourism:
  – By 2006, there were just under 125 million visitors to China, with 34.5 million Chinese making trips abroad.
  – According to the National Tourism Bureau and the Ministry of Foreign Affairs, the number of Chinese people making trips abroad will reach 47 million by 2010 and rise to 100 million by 2020, an annual average growth rate of 8 per cent.
■ Increases in the development of international trade:
  – China is the world's third-largest trading country.
  – In 2006, total imports and exports reached US$1.76 trillion, at a record-high 24 per cent growth rate.
  – By 2010, the total import and export figures for Mainland China will exceed US$2.3 trillion.

All of this points to a high rate of growth over the next few decades. By 2010, 540 million passengers are expected to use China's airports, along with 12.8 million tons of cargo. But for this to happen, China needs to overcome a series of challenges.

The first of these is the geographic distribution of its airport infrastructure, which is heavily biased towards the Eastern half of the country where China's main economic powerhouse cities reside. Growth in airport capacity in these Eastern geographic areas would be limited by the natural capacity of its air space.

The second challenge is related to the economic sustainability of China's existing airport infrastructure. According to the CAAC, most of those airports that earned a profit were the large-sized airports. Around 75 per cent of all airports lost money, and 91 per cent of all airports whose passenger numbers were less than 1 million per year lost money. All those airports with less than half a million passengers lost money.

The third major challenge is the ability of China's existing airport infrastructure to expand in a timely manner to meet the country's rapidly expanding demand. Beijing Capital International Airport is undergoing expansion, with the creation of Terminal 3 (see below), which will open in time for the Beijing 2008 Olympic Games. But these major upgrade projects are time-consuming.

The fourth major challenge relates to the operation of existing airports in these more demanding times. Systems and processes are needed in order to guarantee that the airports expand capacity in a safe and sustainable manner. International hub airports are developing rapidly in Beijing, Shanghai, Guandong and Kunming, and domestic capacity is also expanding dramatically.

Arup in China

Arup is helping China to address these issues. The company has had a presence in the country for over 30 years, and almost a quarter of its worldwide total of 9,000 staff are based there, including 1,900 people in Hong Kong and Macau. The firm's early work in the region was run from the Hong Kong office, but offices on Mainland China have grown to include Shenzhen, Shanghai, Beijing and Guangzhou.

Success in China rarely occurs overnight. Instead, it is dependent on demonstrating a long-term commitment to the Chinese market, a commitment that is expected to involve a two-way transfer of knowledge and experience. Arup has spent a lot of time and resources investing in local talent and expertise, and up to 90 per cent of the company's staff in China are recruited from the local population. This approach has allowed us to build and maintain long-term relationships with local business and government officials, relationships that are so important to success in the country.

But there is another important success factor at play. Arup's success is also based upon the Chinese appreciation of the firm's global reach, its knowledge base and extensive experience on many of the world's most iconic projects.

Arup's work in China's aviation industry can be characterized by an overview of three different airport projects, each very different in scope, but each demonstrating the importance of the aviation industry to China's ongoing economic success.

Shenzhen Baoan International Airport

The Shenzhen Baoan International Airport (designed by the Arup–Llewelyn-Davies team) was the first major airport that Arup developed in China. As an airport, it was the first modern international transportation hub that combines air, road and sea transportation in a single airport in China. The project covers design of the airport terminal, piers, terminal connector and elevator forecourt.

The upgrade of Shenzhen's airport to an international facility was driven by the phenomenal economic growth of Shenzhen as the gateway city to China's first special economic zone. This included a new domestic terminal able to handle 7.2 million passengers by 2000, which doubled in size by 2005.

The airport is situated on a coastal plain at the east bank of the Pearl River Delta area, 32 km away from the city. With an extensive airfield area and good air space conditions, the airport is operational 24 hours, as befits a large international airport dealing with both passengers and cargo.

Passenger movements are simple and direct, and this clarity is helped by the grand space of the departures concourse, which lies beneath an undulating roof formed of long-span steel trusses. The roof is modular and repetitive for ease of construction, and was inspired by the airflow across an aeroplane wing in a wind tunnel.

Shenzhen Baoan International Airport is close to the major roads linking Shenzhen with Hong Kong, Zhuhai and Guangzhou. The airport authorities also own Fuyong Ferry Terminal, which accommodates 1,000-ton cargo and passenger ships to and from Hong Kong. Shenzhen Baoan International Airport is the only international airport in China available for operation by aircraft to and from Hong Kong and other ports of the world for both passengers and cargo operation.

Chongqing Jiangbei International Airport

Chongqing Jiangbei International Airport was expanded in a US$200-million fast-track construction project commencing in 2000 and completed in 2004. It now ranks among the top 10 airports in China, being the largest aviation hub in the Central and Western regions. The design provides for a capacity of 8 million passengers per year in 2010, increasing to 25 million by 2025, and the airport has significantly enhanced the city's strategic status and economic potential. The new terminal serves domestic demand, linking with Beijing Capital International Airport, which is three hours away by air, but its scale means that it will eventually handle a significant number of international flights. Chongqing provides China with a new gateway to the Western Provinces. Such has been the growth in the Chongqing economy that the new terminal is already serving 10 million passengers a year and plans are being put in place to expand capacity to 25 million as a matter of urgency.

Designed by the collaborative team of global design firms Arup and Llewelyn-Davies, the new airport has opened up the industrial West of the country and sets the standard for this new wave of airports.

The economic importance of Chongqing

Chongqing city has the largest area and population in China. With over 30 million people, it is one of the largest cities in the world. It is an increasingly important industrial centre, being home to the national motorbike industry, car production by Ford and mineral extraction by BP. The city enjoys important trade relations with foreign investors, and Britain is the largest source of foreign funding. The new terminal also encourages the development of city infrastructure for the local area, with a new monorail and subway already under construction. Several smaller airports are also being built within the city province.

The design element

The airport terminal has been designed with a curvy roof structure that is meant to symbolize the spine of a dragon, as well as to reflect the hilly landscape where the terminal is located. The key to the design team's success on the project was forming local relationships and combining these with global expertise.

The new terminal design is a departure from the traditional prescriptive airport style commonly used throughout China. Instead, it offers passengers an experience that is instantly recognizable as 'Chongqing', with modern bars and retail outlets over three storeys. Sustainability was a significant factor in the team's selection of materials. The terminal is made predominately from glass, steel and concrete with the majority of materials procured locally. The project was officially opened by the Civil Aviation Authority of China in December 2004.

Beijing Capital International Airport

Construction of the Beijing Capital International Airport (BCIA) expansion programme began in March 2004, and was conceived in response to China's entry to the World Trade Organization. It will be completed in time for the 2008 Beijing Olympics, accommodating 66 million passengers by 2015 and 1.8 million tons of cargo a year. It will be 25 per cent larger than Heathrow's terminals 1, 2, and 4 combined.

The development has two main features: a 420,000 m² third terminal and a third runway. The terminal is being designed by NFAJV, a joint venture team comprising Dutch airport planners NACO, architects Foster and Partners and design engineers Arup, working in support of the Beijing Institute of Architectural Design and Research (BIAD). The consortium also designed and engineered Hong Kong International Airport.

The new terminal has been described as being the 'world's most advanced', not only technologically but also in its concern for passengers and operators. Its roof evokes traditional Chinese colours and symbolism, in harmony with the architecture of Beijing. The terminal building has been designed with few level changes, relatively short walking distances and relatively quick transfer times in mind. The perimeter of the building is fully glazed and the internal space is lit through roof lights and bathed in colour, changing from red to yellow as passengers progress through it.

Creating a unique sustainable identity

The airport will be one of the world's most sustainable, incorporating design concepts such as southeast-orientated skylights to maximize heat from the early morning sun and integrated environmental control systems to minimize energy consumption and carbon emissions.

The climate in North East Asia – reaching up to 36 °C in summer months and –20 °C in the winter – also presents a number of challenges. Airport buildings are huge – very large and very wide, with passengers able to be more than 300 m away from the external wall. Due to the size of the internal space, it is important to get sunlight in through the roof to maximize natural daylight, and to maintain required temperatures and fresh air levels all year round.

The roof lights are designed to keep direct sunlight out in the summer, but let it in during the winter so the building is warmed up in the mornings. The air conditioning systems use natural air wherever possible, giving free cooling for much of the year and permitting chillers to be turned off.

The glazing is shaded by the structure and is tilted to further reduce heat gains. The glass has 'solar control', which reflects the heat-carrying wavelengths while allowing visible light to pass through into the building. The glass also has a low emission coating to minimize heat loss in winter.

Forecasting the future

Beijing Capital International Airport currently has two runways and two terminal buildings with a combined annual capacity of 35 million passengers. By 2008, passenger capacity at the airport is expected to hit 42 million, rising to 66 million by 2015. Additional developments currently taking place include new taxiways, an apron for 97 aircraft parking stands, plus a new cark park and cargo facilities, all covering an area of 1,480 ha.

As part of an international scheme to improve public transport for the 2008 Olympic Games, Arup is also working on other new transportation systems in Beijing. The Airport Express Railway will connect the airport to the Central Business District in the city, and will also link up with what will be China's largest transport interchange. The 790,000 m^2 Dongzhimen Transport Interchange will transport visitors to the Games venues.

Collaboration is key

If there are lessons to be learned from these projects for companies looking to enter the Chinese market, one of the keys has to be a healthy spirit of collaboration. It is an approach that is welcomed by Chinese clients and has been integral to Arup's work in China for the last 30 years. It has been well worth investing the necessary time and effort to build lasting relationships with our Chinese colleagues.

22

Working in China – a personal perspective

Stephen Gill, Stephen Gill Associates

Introduction

At the end of May 2004, I flew to Shanghai at only a few days' notice to manage a Dutch–Sino joint venture (JV) company, the Shanghai Grasso Refrigeration and Engineering Company with instructions to act as an interim general manager whilst a permanent replacement for the previous incumbent could be recruited. The Dutch partner is a large international engineering group and I was employed as a director of one of its UK operations. As I was only expected to be in China for a few months, the engagement was a solo package and my family stayed in the United Kingdom.

The company was a JV formed some eight years previously with a Chinese state-owned refrigeration company with the ownership split 51/49 in favour of the Dutch company. The JV agreement laid down the composition and management of the board and the organization structure of the management team. The position of general manager was a nominee of the Dutch and the assistant manager was appointed by the Chinese partner. The staff comprised approximately 40 people and was made up entirely by Chinese nationals, of which less than a handful spoke English. The company's sales turnover was approximately RMB40 million.

We operated from an office and workshop in Shanghai near to the Hongqiao airport. The company designed and assembled industrial refrigeration packages comprising locally sourced pipe and pressure vessels, together with major components imported from Europe. The packages were predominately for the Chinese market and the company had installations all over China.

However, the 'few months' turned into a year and my initial instructions to 'just keep a watching brief' soon changed as I discovered that the company was, in Western terms, insolvent. During my time there the company was indicted for smuggling (for items that were imported before I arrived), the company was closed and all the workforce was laid off. We then formed a wholly foreign-invested enterprise (WFOE), which opened in new premises nearby employing approximately half of the original number. I was threatened by disgruntled suppliers and ex-staff, and once arrived at the office only to have the doors blocked with me inside and the power cut off (on a cold December morning) until I agreed to pay a neighbouring company's invoice. To cap it all, the former Chinese chairperson of the company was tried and convicted of fraud and accepting brides. The last I heard of him he was serving a 15-year jail sentence.

Every day working in China was interesting and full of fresh situations; combine this with managing a company with as many problems as this one had and perhaps it is easy to see why I faced so many challenges. In this personal account I hope to share a few of the many lessons I learnt the hard way and also make some observations about my experiences. Every person the world over is different and it would be misleading to suggest otherwise. Where I generalize in what follows and use terms such as 'the Chinese', 'Westerners' or any other generalizations, I do so purely for convenience of writing style and to help the narrative flow without lengthy explanations.

Are the problems faced in China unique to China?

Before I arrived at the Chinese company there had been no time to be informed of the company's problems. However, it didn't take me very long to discover them. They included issues of product quality, purchasing, accounting and finance, staff quality and motivation, sales and contractual documentation and stock problems. This is probably not a comprehensive list and it would be simpler to say that there were serious issues with all departments.

Within the group, the company was seen as a problem and had been perceived as such for a number of years. So, why weren't these issues addressed? The reason, and a major contributing factor to the company's ongoing problems, was that the problems were viewed by the management back in Europe as being Chinese problems and related specifically to operating a company in China. I disagree with this view. The problems were all due to poor management and nothing else. A company managed as this one had been, anywhere in the world, including the United Kingdom, would have the same problems.

Staff training and quality can be issues but these, as with all management problems, are issues that can be addressed. If there is a common problem with operating companies in China it would seem to be that management style needs to be different and the approach taken sometimes almost counterintuitive. Therefore, some managers who are very competent in the West fail in China and it is easier to make the excuse that there is a 'Chinese' problem rather than admit a management failure. Working in any country offers some unique challenges. However, all the problems that some companies have experienced and reported cannot truly be laid at the door of some mysterious Chinese problem.

Not for profit

The majority of the workforce that we employed had joined us from the state-owned parent company. They were technically skilled and competent enough in what they were doing and had extensive knowledge of the market. Due to their background or for some other reason, it is difficult to say, they all lacked a commercial awareness at company level that was astonishing. I thought at first that they simply didn't grasp the concepts of profit and loss. However, I soon discovered that in fact the opposite was very much the case; they had an advanced, almost natural instinct to make money for themselves, but it appeared beyond their comprehension that the company was there to make a profit. And if we didn't make a profit, of course, there was no point in the company existing.

It was 'explained' to me that the company was a subsidiary of a very large multinational Western company that was 'very rich'. 'They don't need money' I was told. The company existed only for the staff and the bosses to receive wages and any other benefits that came along.

In company terms, it was said, profit had two purposes. First, the sales people had to show a profit at the point of sale so that the order would be accepted by the company and also so that they could receive their commissions. Of course, the larger the apparent profit, the larger the sales people's commission. An order was generally celebrated because it meant that there was money available. Money would be coming into the company and this meant that there would be more opportunities available to take money out. In fairness, it also meant that there was work to do and there was a sense of pride in the work.

Second, company profit is something that must be reported by the accountants and it was their job to do so. As long as they do so (whether the numbers are genuine or not) everyone is happy. What it boiled down to was that money was viewed in very simple terms and totally from a human perspective. The concept of the company as a separate entity with its own identity existed only as a vehicle for trading. Money was something that we take from the company in any way possible; some of them quite ingenious. Stealing is not only illegal, it is morally wrong; taking money from the company was never stealing and that expression was never used. When I argued against this logic, they smiled knowingly, and claimed that if the company were getting nothing out of the venture, why would they keep on investing?

Communication

Forgive me for stating the obvious, but English is a second language to the Chinese. Although the situation is changing, with many younger people now studying overseas or having access to native English speakers, most of the older generation have learnt their English from the teachers at school who are also Chinese. Some may have learnt it from other Westerners whose first language is not English. The vast majority do not speak any English or only a few words.

That said, some do speak it remarkably well and clearly, with very good pronunciation. So well in fact, that one can forget for a moment to check that they actually understand what they are saying or what is being said to them. It is always worth checking when giving an instruction or even offering advice, that your meaning is understood. Getting them to repeat back what they are about to do can avoid wasted time and reduce the risk of things not being done as requested.

Conversations and meetings conducted in English are often reduced to being spoken in very simple English. This is done with the best of intentions so that all can contribute. It was surprising to me at least, that the Chinese preferred meetings chaired by my Dutch colleagues because the English was more direct. There is the habit in English (particularly when written) to avoid using the same word twice even when the same meaning is intended, so things may be described as 'large', 'big', 'huge' 'significant', and so on all in the space of a few sentences, which can be very confusing.

The level of English is often reduced to simple words and phrases pretty much as one uses them when talking to a child and herein lies the danger. It can become easy to view colleagues as children (no matter what the age) and treat both them and their opinions in that way. It can be difficult but you must explore ways to ensure that you are getting the most from interaction with colleagues and any other Chinese person with whom you come into contact. Inevitably, there are times when a translator is needed. Great care needs to be taken if another member of staff is being used. Often they have a vested interest in what is being said and the translation in both directions may not be exactly as intended.

The same applies to written documents. A manager is brought many letters and documents for authorization and approval. So many that it simply isn't practical to have them all translated. Common business sense warns us to be wary of signing anything (even when solely in English) without fully understanding its contents and implications. This common sense shouldn't be discarded simply because it is in Chinese.

The language barrier

Language is a key not only to verbal communication but it also opens the door to cultural understanding. If the language barrier can be broken down and removed, not only is the working day easier in terms of instructions, messages and other communication, but it can foster understanding as well. This works both ways very successfully. For the expatriate, the learning of even a few words (hopefully more) will be the start of a removal of many barriers, some of which are not even perceived until they are removed, and for the Chinese, it can help to understand the Western culture. Communication is an exchange of information; this can lead to greater understanding.

I did witness some very successful Chinese language training programmes and also some even more successful English language training programmes for staff. The small investment in resources more than paid for itself by the fostering of a better working environment and organizational culture.

The importance of 'face'

Before I went to China I had heard about the importance of 'face' in some of the Far Eastern cultures. I knew enough not to be overly critical of people in meetings and not to expect the Chinese to show their true emotions. In working practice, the element of face took a far more subtle form and for a working Western manager proved very difficult to understand at times. Let me give you two examples.

The power cut dilemma

In only my second week, I received an official letter from the local electricity supply company advising that we would have no power to the factory every Thursday and Friday the following week due to power supply problems in Shanghai during the summer. I had already had some extremely tight production deadlines to meet and the prospect of losing the two days' production was a serious headache. I quickly drew up a plan involving overtime and shift working to pull back the production. I called an emergency management meeting to go through the plan. It was greeted with nods of agreement and confirmation that the plan, with a few tweaks, was workable.

Before the end of the meeting we were interrupted by the arrival of a second letter from the electrical supply company. This fresh letter advised that the two days without power supply would be every week for the next eight weeks culminating in a total shutdown for two whole weeks. There was no way that we could work through this. It was a nightmare. There were massive penalty clauses on the projects that we currently had going through the workshop and we now couldn't possibly achieve the delivery dates. I was stunned and felt numb. The management team offered no support and looked as lost as I did. It was too early to report back to Europe so I adjourned the meeting in order to seek advice from Europe later in the day.

I was sitting at my desk in deep thought when the assistant manager entered. He had been in the management meeting and knew of the problem. After much discussion, he suggested that we could 'do what we always do'. 'What do you mean?' I asked. It transpired that these power cuts had been expected and happened every year. The whole company simply worked on Saturday and Sunday instead to make up the time. It seemed that the staff expected this, were happy to do it and wouldn't require any additional payments as compensation. A simple and effective solution.

Why had none of the management team explained this to me? Because they didn't want me to lose face by going against my plan! I called another emergency meeting and these arrangements were then discussed openly.

Down with mobile phones

It was at the second emergency management meeting of the same day that I finally lost my patience with mobile phones. The Chinese will answer their mobile phone whenever it rings, whatever they are doing at the time. Not only that, but they will complete their whole telephone conversation before hanging up; it doesn't matter how long the call is or how important the meeting that has been interrupted.

Maybe it was because of the stress or maybe because I was disappointed by the lack of constructive participation when discussing the electrical supply problem earlier but I finally snapped and in a very unprofessional, but it has to be said, calm voice, threatened to ram the phone down the throat of the next person who answered the phone whilst still in the meeting. The puzzled looks from the management team and the translated explanation for the ones that hadn't quite understood my meaning although comical to see, showed that my warning had been fully understood. I am sure that this management style did not allow anyone to save face but it did prove effective, judging by the lack of calls at future management meetings.

The expatriate cycle

Sitting alone in quiet restaurants at 10.00 pm is not the only social problem that expatriates face. Anyone visiting China for the first time can't help but be struck by the cultural differences with Europe. You either love it or hate it. Most, if not all of those that I have met or worked with like it and appreciate the differences.

Others go through something that, for want of a better expression, I have called the 'expatriate cycle'. They start by being fascinated, charmed and even amused by the endless differences in the Chinese way of life from what they are used to back at home. There is so much to see and discover for the inquisitive mind. The view from the window of a car when travelling down a busy street can be fascinating and full of surprises. One is constantly noticing new differences and, if one is of an enquiring mind, may even spend time wondering why it is the way it is. This isn't exactly a honeymoon period but may be something akin to it. However, after several months, the question in the mind changes from 'I wonder why they do that?' to 'I wish they would do it as we do'. There is probably a psychological model for this, but the only way I can describe it is that there comes a point when there is a strong desire to return to normality for a while. A short break away can do wonders, but if ignored, the feeling can fester into resentment and the 'I wish they would do it as we do' moves to 'I'm fed up with this and the way they do things'.

Everyone involved in the management of expatriate staff, including the expats themselves, would do well to monitor others and themselves for early warning signs of dissatisfaction or disenchantment. If left untreated, they can cause serious problems to the company and to the individuals themselves.

The cost of expatriate assignments, particularly when compared with local labour costs is extremely high; the cost and the potential damage to the company of an expatriate assignment failure is significantly higher. From what I saw, there is a cycle and so the positive feelings can be restored if the early warning signs are detected and acted upon.

Concluding comments

The newly recruited general manager finally started at the beginning of April 2005. Of course, he started with the new WFOE and not the old joint venture. The handover that I hoped for and would have expected never happened and after a few days of passing over files, I returned to the United Kingdom later that month. Although I was still employed in the United Kingdom by the group company that had been paying me throughout, there was no planning involved in my repatriation. In fact, quite the opposite; I was informed in no uncertain terms that my previously held post was no longer really available. I left the group shortly afterwards and started up my own consultancy. Anyone planning an extended period working abroad needs to consider carefully what they will do once they return home.

I was proud of the condition of the new Chinese company when I left and, although it was very early in its history I understand that it went on to have a successful first year. Unfortunately, it appears that the lessons of the past may not have been entirely learned and, by the end of the second year, problems were becoming apparent so that the company may have a poor third year by any measure.

The best advice that I received whilst in China was from a Danish engineer who had been working there for many years and spoke fluent Mandarin. He said 'Don't trust anyone, not even yourself'. I learned that whilst his advice might seem extreme, there were many times that I wished that the company and I had followed it. For myself, the best advice that I can give is: talk to as many people as possible, look out for vested interests and watch for false assumptions.

Anyone trying to describe working in China is like a blind person trying to describe an elephant to some one else. We can only describe what we touch and feel immediately within our reach without it ever being possible to describe the whole beast. Of course, the animal involved here is not an elephant but a dragon, making the task even more difficult; and so I make no excuses for my observations not only scratching the surface of what I 'touched' but for also being a totally different view of the 'dragon experience' than from the next 'blind person'.

It could be said that my time in China finished my senior career with an international engineering group and gave me some of the worst days of my working life. Would I go back? You bet I would, given the right opportunity. There is something about the people and place that makes it all worthwhile. Love it or hate it, China and the Chinese cannot be ignored.

23

Chinese walls: crumbling fast – the MG Rover story

John Miles, Arup

Background

In July 2007, the China Development Bank stunned the City of London when it paid more than £1 billion to take a stake in Barclays, providing Barclays with the cash to strengthen its bid to acquire Dutch financial institution ABN AMRO. A market analyst exclaimed in the United Kingdom's *Observer* newspaper: 'It is an extraordinary turn of events: Communist China helping a Western bank buy a continental competitor. This gives globalization a new twist'.

The same newspaper reported foreign state-owned institutions and companies as far flung as Qatar and Singapore buying British firms. But, while it may not be unique, the appearance of China on the acquisition trail is a potentially dramatic development for Western economics. China seems to be a special case, partly owing to the vast foreign reserves it has stockpiled, the result of trade surpluses generated by its extraordinary export boom. It is also because of China's assumption that the 'Middle Kingdom' is just that: the centre of the world. With foreign reserves estimated at US$1.3 trillion, and a natural assumption of its rightful place in the world order, it is no surprise that China is on the move.

Any investment portfolio manager would advise China to diversify its reserves out of foreign currencies by investing in assets that yield a higher return than the typical 3–4 per cent of US treasury bills. Anyone who has done business with the Chinese, however, is likely to suspect that China's steady acquisition of minority stakes in Western companies, in the context of its occasional headline buys, has a long-term strategic purpose: that of developing insight into global capitalism and how to run international companies. In effect, China is investing in developing the knowledge and expertise that it lacks in many spheres of economic activity, despite its success in manufacture.

But China is not only investing in developing the 'hard skills' of management and international business. It is also investing in the 'softer' (or creative) skills of design, advertising and brand management. There is increasing brand awareness on the streets of the big cities in China, and the power of brands is beginning to be recognized in the highest circles. Part of China's push to develop a world-class consumer products industry includes a determination to own and manage world-recognized brands.

That this plan is being played out is evident in deals such as the Chinese acquisition of IBM's PC business, and the more recent acquisition of the assets of the collapsed UK car company MG Rover. Both of these moves represented important 'firsts' for the Chinese electronics and automotive industries.

The MG Rover takeover

When it moved to purchase the assets of MG Rover, Nanjing Automobile Company (Nanjing) stepped out of its normal operating environment and found itself briefly in the full glare of the UK media. It was an unnerving experience for Chinese managers and engineers more accustomed to operating in China's strictly controlled media world. As they came to the United Kingdom to make the purchase, they realized they needed experienced UK professional help. Arup was appointed to advise on all aspects of the acquisition and began to build a strong working relationship with the executives, some of whom were doing business in the West for the first time.

Time will tell as to the significance of the deal in terms of Chinese success in managing a global brand. Its significance is clear however, as a milestone, marking the start of China's appearance on the international automotive stage.

Many column inches have been filled with remarks on and analysis of the Chinese takeover of MG Rover. First, it was widely commented that the new Chinese owners were naive. This is not to be confused with any lack of ability. Indeed, many who worked closely with Nanjing's Chinese executives would confirm the opposite: the Chinese working on the takeover were, without exception, talented and well-informed individuals, with a lawyer's grasp of the law and excellent understanding of key issues. What they lacked was any real experience of doing business in Britain: its culture, commercial customs and political structures.

Chinese project management

Yet the gap closed fast. It was both instructive and sobering to see how quickly it is possible to eradicate a competitive disadvantage through sheer effort. The systematic approach taken by the Nanjing executives to understanding the perspectives of government and public bodies, and the way they accustomed themselves to the cultural norms they were facing for the first time, yielded fast results. Those involved in the deal would confirm that if anyone was naive, it was those who made assumptions about how long the gap of understanding would persist, rather than the Nanjing team, who simply dealt with it.

Second, observers have often interpreted unusual moves on the part of Nanjing as cultural clumsiness, born of lack of experience. Yet this is to underestimate the Chinese tendency to bring a singular focus to the task in hand, and combine it with a determination to do it in their own way – which is seen less frequently in Western culture. You might explain 'That isn't how it's done here', but such protestations are likely to be pushed aside, because they want to do it their own way. At first, you think the misjudgement is theirs; that they will come to rue their decision, which has no chance of ending in success. Often, however, what initially looks like intransigence turns out in retrospect to have been admirable single-mindedness. Coupled with an apparently limitless ability to follow instructions, it is hard to criticize when the end result is success, and they get what they set out to achieve.

Third, the Chinese tend to approach things in a serial manner, focusing on or dealing with one issue at a time before moving on to the next. This I think leaves them less able to deal with, say, four problems at the same time that are interconnected and that need to be dealt with in parallel. A Chinese person tends to deal with one problem, and only when that problem is resolved will they turn to the second, and so on. Such a serial approach is frustrating to a Western mind, which habitually picks up problems and deals with them in parallel. Unfamiliar as it may be to a Westerner, it is nevertheless effective.

Such methods and ways of thinking are so much a product of one's culture that it is unsurprising that Westerners find Chinese working methods and approaches confusing. Our culture thinks it is a poor way of doing it, but if you look to China itself you can see that it is a very effective way of getting things done. Working with Chinese people makes one realize just how wide cultural differences can be. It can be difficult for a Westerner to relate immediately to Chinese people, or indeed to make allowances for a different way of approaching business practice. In a Western context, you can say that if people do things differently, they got it wrong. In the Chinese context, maybe not.

Global brand management

All eyes are on how well the Chinese succeed in running international brands like MG Rover. In acquiring MG Rover, Nanjing has won the first battle: the next thing is to win the business. Can they make a success of it in terms of the global business? Success here is less clear, because of the way in which they do things. They will learn how to develop their brand in China, but not perhaps globally – an altogether different prospect. It is not clear at all whether they will make an international success of MG Rover: if we could fast-forward two decades, we would likely see many successes, while any failures will be put down to experience, learned from and used to create successes at a later date. Right now, there is a question mark about their ability to pick up a global brand and ensure that it succeeds in a world more open towards Western branding and icons than Chinese.

Branding is the key issue for global companies, far more than ownership. When global mega-brand IBM agreed to sell most of its US$12-billion-a-year PC group to China's Lenovo for US$1.75 billion in 2005, the sale looked remarkably like a joint venture between the icon of US capitalism and the state-owned[1] Chinese company. Lenovo's headquarters moved to New York, while IBM took on a minority ownership stake in Lenovo. Two former IBM executives were appointed CEO and COO, with a Beijing-based chairperson. The benefits were obvious: IBM had access to potentially the highest-growth PC market in the world, as well as a low-cost manufacturing base. Lenovo acquired the scale it was after, together with well-respected technology and a highly regarded global brand.

Mary Ma, Lenovo's CFO at the time of the deal, articulated Lenovo's intentions: 'For the first 18 months we can use the stand-alone IBM brand unchanged. In the months after that, we can sell co-branded or a brand endorsed by IBM'.[2] Though the company's intentions had been clearly signalled, October 2005 saw Lenovo's UK distributors calling on it to increase the brand awareness of Lenovo before abandoning the much-respected IBM brand over the next two years, or see partner sales suffer. One can speculate as to whether giving up the IBM name was part of the original agreement, which allowed Lenovo to use the name IBM under licence. But the decision taken by Lenovo to ditch the IBM mega-brand, and replace it with Lenovo, turns brand logic as known in the West upside down. The IBM brand was seen as bringing much needed kudos to Lenovo. It made products more attractive to consumers outside China and helped overcome obstacles to the Chinese company selling in the United States and other markets. Whether abandoning the brand, as well as the 'halo' effect it provides was foolhardy, or an audacious entrepreneurial move, is yet to be seen.

In the short term, whether or not Lenovo or the Nanjing Automobile Corporation succeed with their initial attempts at international brand management is open to question. Both simply represent the first steps down a long road. The point is that there are more deals like this to come, and gradually the business world will change. The electronics and automotive industries, and others, too, will change fundamentally, not simply by the emergence of a massive new consumer market, but also by China's ownership, management and direction of globally recognized consumer brands.

What do we draw from these observations of doing business with China? The first lesson is that China's entry into mainstream global business is already happening. It is inevitable that we will see more Chinese activity in the United Kingdom and the Western hemisphere. They may be inexperienced right now, but will catch up quickly and effectively. The United Kingdom has the most open market in the world, and foreign money has been welcome historically. It is likely, therefore, to play host to significant early activity. The comparison with the United States and some Continental

---

[1] The Chinese government owned 57 per cent of Lenovo before the deal, at the closing of which its shareholding was diluted to 46 per cent.

[2] Mary Ma, quoted in *BusinessWeek Magazine* online, 8 December 2004; http://www.business week.com/technology/content/dec2004/tc2004128_5989_tc121.htm?chan=search.

European countries, with their traditions of protectionism and dislike of foreign ownership, is sharp. It is a relatively short time ago – only 2004 – that the US Congress scuppered the takeover of US-based Unocal by China's state-owned oil company CNOOC, as Beijing will remember. But these mechanisms are likely to be transitory, and the forces of globalization will probably open doors all over the Western world for China with the passing of time.

A second lesson is not to underestimate the Chinese, or any other non-Western culture, in the global business world. The people who appear here in the United Kingdom on the behalf of Chinese companies are the brightest of the bright. Their ability may sometimes be masked by the fact that the Chinese do things in a different way from us sometimes. Westerners often interpret 'different' as 'wrong', because that is how it looks to us. Yet that is our own cultural perspective talking, and we would be wise to think twice.

The third lesson is a consequence of the first two. We must learn to accept the Chinese presence as an essential part of doing business in the United Kingdom and internationally, and we must look to ways of dealing with it constructively. Analysts say that the sheer scale of money that the Chinese have at their disposal could have wide-ranging economic consequences for us in the West. If the Chinese invest heavily in UK companies, it will push up prices of the underlying assets, mirroring the effect of an influx of foreign money that we have seen in the London property market and that has affected the rest of the United Kingdom. If this is accompanied by a different way of doing business, the effect on our business culture over the next two decades could be profound. And with change comes opportunity.

24

Managing a business in China – practical problems

Stephen Gill, Stephen Gill Associates

Culture differences

Volumes can (and have been) written about the Chinese culture and the differences between East and West. Learning their 'ways' can take a lifetime, but even a little understanding can be helpful, and any visitor will soon pick up and experience differences.

An element that rarely gets mentioned is that through working with Westerners, some Chinese learn to read and understand our culture and use it in some very subtle ways to their advantage. The unwary Westerner is usually totally oblivious to what is happening. There is a China joke that goes something like this:

> *An Englishman and a Chinese businessman do business in China but soon a dispute arises that needs to be referred to the local Chinese law court. The Chinese businessman showers the judge of the court with gifts and spends more time in pleasing the judge than in preparing his case. The Englishman learns of this and is very happy because he has a natural sense of justice and he knows that he is in the right. No only that, but he views the gifts as bribery*

and this must surely go against his Chinese adversary. The Englishman acts in an honourable and respectful way to the judge and does not insult his integrity by even suggesting any inducements. His case is well prepared; he employs the best and most expensive lawyers and is certain of winning. To his astonishment, the judge rules in favour of the Chinese businessman.

The same two businessmen also do business in England and again a problem arises that needs to go to court. This time it is an English court with an English judge. The Englishman acts in exactly the same way and is once again certain of the court finding in his favour. The Chinese businessman once again showers the judge with gifts, sending him presents and holiday vouchers up until the day of the trial.

Once again the judge finds in favour of the Chinese businessman. The Englishman is in total disbelief as he has been aware of the gifts being sent. The two men meet after the ruling outside the court and the Englishman asks how it is possible that the Chinese businessman won once again. 'I can now understand how you won in China', he says, 'but I am surprised that the gifts you sent influenced the judge here. What is your secret?' The Chinese businessman confides that when sending the gifts to the English judge he had sent them in the Englishman's name!

In the West, we often view a set, rigid, consistent way of working and behaviour as a strength. The merits or otherwise of this is beyond the scope of this discussion, but what becomes clear is that the Chinese exhibit a remarkable flexibility and that they also soon realize that we don't. I used to get what I can only call the 'runaround'. Each working day had its own unique sets of problems, but a typical 'runaround' day would go something like this. I would be concerned that a delivery was going to be late because the workshop was behind schedule; I would go to the assistant manager who would sense that I had an issue to address with him; before I could speak, he would tell me of a problem in the accounts department involving suspected fraud. Of course, this was urgent, so I would go see the accountant and she would tell me of some theft in the stores department, and so on. I would chase around all the departments all day trying to discover some 'crime'. All claims would have enough basis in truth to warrant investigation but none would be that serious. Also, none were really discovered that day; the information had been kept in reserve ready to distract any Western manager that approached.

In our case, the company had been audited every quarter by senior accountants from Holland. Ironically, the three or four days that they were there would be spent 'productively', in their eyes, chasing down these problems without really addressing the real issues.

Accountancy, insolvency, tax and debt collection

As mentioned earlier in my previous chapter, in a Chinese company it is the accountant's job to report a profit. They never want to be the bearer of bad news unless it is about another member of staff. The Chinese have taken creative accounting to new levels.

Bearing in mind that many now work for multinational companies and are audited regularly by international accountancy firms, it is remarkable what I discovered.

It is difficult, if not impossible, for a non-Chinese-speaking person to read through a set of the Chinese accounts unless they speak Chinese. Most of the problems that I uncovered stemmed from debtors being listed several times and the figures against each being inaccurate. For instance, a debtor may be listed by the company name, its city, its industry or any combination of these. Duplication inflates the debtor's figures and so management assumes that more is owed to the company than is actually the case. It also allows all sorts of creative accountancy to take place.

A visit from the tax office is usually an interesting affair and for the outsider it can be a mysterious occasion. The length of visit seemed to relate to the level of hospitality extended. If they were too comfortable they would stay longer and potentially uncover more, or if not welcomed enough, they would make a quick assessment, which would not be a good thing. Not only that but the level of the tax payable could never be explained to me and appeared to my cynical mind to be proportionate to the level of hospitality received. It was therefore all a juggling act, or so it seemed. Let them stay just long enough to have a few meals out and not impose too high a bill.

Whether by luck or otherwise, I discovered within my first month of being in China that the company was to my mind insolvent. At the first opportunity, I telephoned Europe. 'Impossible', was the reply from the other end of the line, 'we audit the accounts ourselves every quarter and to comply with international accounting regulations have the books externally audited every year'. It was left until the next scheduled visit for the group accountant to visit; the same one who had been visiting the company for the last five years.

After looking through the figures and armed with my own findings he could only agree. We were insolvent and by a long way. One might be forgiven for thinking that would be the end of the story and that we would either secure additional investment or would call in the receivers immediately. We did neither. It seems that as long as a company in China can trade, and by this I mean receive money and pay out money, it is still open. Only a judge can declare a joint venture company closed. So, unable to pay creditors and trying to recover debts, we continued for well over another year.

No one the world over likes to be owed money for a long time and then hear that the debtor is struggling to pay, or worse still, not receive payment at all. News of our financial difficulty spread quickly and the range of debt collection techniques used by our creditors was fascinating and remarkable in its range of approaches and effectiveness. At the soft end, one very effective style used by one supplier was to send in a very old lady (well into her 70s I would guess). She was treated with great respect and soon found her way to my office to ask for payment. I explained (through a translator) that we couldn't pay her company at this moment but hoped to pay something by the end of the week. She smiled and nodded, and produced from the small bag that she was carrying a towel and a toothbrush, 'I will stay until then!', she explained, and so she did. Three days and three nights she lived in my office but was the first to be paid as soon as we could.

At the harder end of the debt collection scale were the physical threats to both me and the company's property. I had heard stories that as Westerners no one would actually harm us but I did feel intimidated enough on three occasions to have to call the police. The police did arrive promptly on each occasion and explained that it was a simple matter and that the person making the threats was owed money and that we should pay them; that was the best way to resolve the situation. On the third occasion they did break up a fight that had developed but still left without removing anyone. Although never tested, I didn't feel that the Western status received any special protection in these circumstances.

Another approach was to freeze our bank account and assets to a value slightly in excess of the amount owed. This technique caught me totally by surprise and seemed to rely on the relationship that the supplier had with the local court that granted the freeze. To find our funds suddenly out of reach was bad enough, but court officials could turn up at any time and claim any item (usually specifically chosen by the supplier who had knowledge of the company). This did cause major trading difficulties and with our bank account effectively frozen permanently (as we cleared one payment, another supplier would freeze it again) we had to resort one month to paying the staff direct from Europe.

The company chop

Business letters and documents in the West usually have to be signed to be given legal status. In China, the company chop (a stamp used with an ink pad) rules all. Anyone wishing to control the company must control the chop. Some departments also have chops and these have similar, although naturally lesser status. At an individual level, the bank may only accept cheques, instructions or requests from a company if they have been authorized with the general manager's personal chop.

Once this is understood, it can be better controlled. For a few weeks I thought I was controlling the flow of documents from the company by not signing anything I didn't understand, whilst freely handing the chop to any member of the management team that requested it. When some of these documents later appeared and were shown to be important, my signature counted for nothing and the chop for everything.

Joint ventures

Joint ventures and alliances are entered into for many reasons. They are sometimes described, amongst other things, as a marriage. This description fits very well with my own experience of what happens when things go wrong with a Chinese joint venture. The marriage breaks down over time and ends in a scrappy divorce with both sides fighting over the household possessions and custody of the children. There is also a certain amount of self-denial of responsibility for the current situation and quite often a breakdown in communication and cooperation.

I don't know if there is such a thing as a marriage councillor for joint ventures, but if not, there should be. There is, of course, no shortage of lawyers and financial advisers brought in by the two parties to protect their interests.

It is a messy experience and those involved on the periphery (staff, management and other stakeholders) can go through a torrid time as both 'parents' fight it out. Working through this period can be difficult for all involved and extra company resources and care are strongly recommended to ensure as smooth a transition as is possible under the circumstances and the best hope of a bright trading future.

Labour and staff issues

I understand that the labour laws are changing and so the rules that governed my experiences when firing staff or laying them off may be different now. Informing people that they are about to lose their job is an unpleasant task at the best of times. I can't imagine that it is a nice experience for anyone involved anywhere in the world and in China it is no different. There were times when I was very pleased not to be able to understand what was being shouted at me. I learned that whilst body language can be very intimidating, ignorance of the extent of the verbal threats of physical harm and insults being hurled in your direction do lessen the impact.

When we were closing the company and laying off the workforce (the term redundancy was never used but in my mind that was what we were enacting) we had to pay compensation to those leaving. It appears that, although the company had only been in existence for some eight years, some of the staff had joined us from the Chinese partner and had worked there for many years; in one case over 20 years. It transpired that we were responsible for paying him compensation for the whole 20-plus years.

Although there was a formula for the calculation of the compensation package involved, the discussions and final agreement as to the amount had to be agreed with Party representatives that were sent in by the Chinese partner to oversee the process. In fact, the total amount for the whole workforce was paid to the Party who then, as I understood it, distributed it according to the individually assessed needs of each worker. So, whilst the total was calculated to recognized formulae (plus some extra amount as negotiated for goodwill) the amount that each member received appeared to be discretionary. For instance, we offered new employment to approximately half of the workforce but because their previous contracts were terminated we paid the Party the full amount according to the formulae. However, the Party deemed that because they were being offered fresh contracts with a 'rich Western' company they didn't 'need' to receive the same compensation as someone who hadn't received an offer, even though the amount that we paid out was the same.

Staff salary is often referred to by the monthly amount. If someone has a salary of RMB3,000, this means that this is their monthly pay. It is common to pay a thirteenth month as a bonus and so someone with a salary expectation of RMB3,000 may actually looking to be paid RMB39,000 per year.

The Chinese have some long holiday periods, particularly at Spring Festival (Chinese New Year) and at Mid-Autumn Festival. It is common for them to spend this time with their families and there is a mass exodus from the major cities back to the respective home towns. This can cause travel problems; also, the prolonged shutdowns can be disruptive if the company is working on international projects. However, the staff will typically work at the weekend before and after the holiday periods to make up the time.

I found that the vast majority of the people with whom I came into contact through work were polite, courteous, friendly and hard-working. Contrary to what I had expected before I visited, I also found them very quick to get excited and animated in discussions and arguments with each other, which were not only noisy but sometimes mildly violent. These bursts of conflict were often short and intense but just as quickly forgotten. A fight on the doorstep first thing in the morning seemed to have been forgotten by lunchtime.

In praise of food

As a final observation about business in China, much is written in the guidebooks about the Chinese love affair with food. It is sometimes said that if it is true that we in the West eat to live, in China they live to eat. This has two impacts on anyone working in China. One, as already noted, is the importance of meals in a business relationship. Meals can be extravagant lengthy affairs and are a good way to form and cement a business relationship. The other is the importance of meal times for the staff. Working through a lunchtime or staying late in the office can be difficult as some of the staff I worked with almost stopped functioning even very shortly after an expected meal time. Restaurants are full at 6.00 pm and it is not uncommon to find a Westerner eating alone while the staff sweep up around them at 9.00 pm. Times are changing fast as cities become more Westernized but the love of food has stayed the same.

25

Case studies in manufacturing joint ventures

China Britain Business Council

This chapter consists of the case studies of six successful joint ventures or wholly foreign-owned enterprises (WfoEs) in China where the foreign investors are UK companies. All six are abridged texts selected from company profiles first published in various editions of the *China-Britain Business Review* from 2005 to 2007. The UK companies whose China stories are recounted are:

- Rolls-Royce;
- Sigma Precision Components;
- Westwind;
- Strix;
- BLP;
- Hornby.

Rolls-Royce

Rolls-Royce today no longer has any association with the luxury automobile marque and has concentrated on 'high-technology power and propulsion equipment for land, air and sea' to become the world's second-largest civil aeroengine manufacturer today. Indeed, it was the sale of aircraft engines that first brought Rolls-Royce into contact with China, more than 40 years ago. In 1962, the company supplied 'Dart' engines to Viscount airliners then operated by the sole Chinese airline at that time, CAAC (Civil Aviation Administration of China).

Rolls-Royce continued to supply engines after Vickers was replaced by Trident aircraft in the 1970s, but the more important development occurred the following decade when civil aviation underwent an extensive programme of modernization. China started replacing its Russian-built aircraft with those made by Boeing and then later by Airbus. With the promise of considerably more business, Rolls-Royce set up an office in Beijing in 1983.

The modernization process also led to the establishment of separate regional airlines, operating in China and later, in some cases, internationally. This created new clients for Rolls-Royce. Over the next two decades, the company sold engines to Air China (the country's flagship carrier), China Southern, China Eastern, Sichuan Airlines and Yunnan Airlines. More recently, it has sold its products to Hainan Airlines and in 2006, in what is probably its biggest coup to date, it won an order by Air China to supply Trent engines for 15 Boeing 787 'Dreamliner' aircraft, a deal valued at more than US$80 million. By the end of 2006, there were more than 200 Rolls-Royce-powered aircraft operating in China, making total engine business worth around US$4 billion.

Manufacturing

Rolls-Royce is not only engaged in selling: it manufactures turbine parts in a joint venture in Xi'an set up in 1995, and trains airline maintenance staff at a training centre in Tianjin, jointly owned with CAAC. The other key aspect of selling engines to the Chinese airlines is provision of after-sales service.

Competition in the developing market

Rolls-Royce's principal competitor, GE, has also been pushing hard-to-win orders from China, as has the third aircraft engine manufacturer, Pratt & Whitney. That is hardly surprising when, on Rolls-Royce's own estimates, over the next 20 years, airline traffic in China will grow by 9 per cent, creating a requirement for 2,300 new aircraft a year. The immediate task for Rolls-Royce is to increase its market share of the business in China to match its worldwide market share.

The move towards larger wide-bodied aircraft, incorporating engines of a larger diameter, may help tilt the advantage in Rolls-Royce's favour. That is because Trent engines, which are designed round three shafts rather than two, can be more easily scaled up using the same design. According to Rolls-Royce, the other manufacturers have to make more extensive adjustment when scaling up. The Dreamliner will use two engines, not four, which at 112 inches will be of a much larger diameter than Rolls-Royce has ever used before.

Unusually for China, Rolls-Royce does not face any domestic competition. Although China has some aircraft and engine capacity, it is not a player in the commercial aircraft market. Civil aerospace is a global market in which China is just one important purchaser. As a result, Rolls-Royce does not need to undertake final assembly and testing in China. However, it has developed a supply network and is tapping into China's growing network of top engineers. The most promising area of growth in the supply chain activities is materials, notably special steels.

Marine equipment

The increase in shipbuilding in China also offers attractive opportunities. The Asian shipbuilding market, worth some £19 billion a year, is broadly divided between Japan, Korea and China. Now the world's third largest shipbuilder, China aspires to be the largest. The new shipyard on Changxin Island near Shanghai built at a cost of US$2.6 billion, which opens in 2007, will be the biggest in the world.

Since acquiring Vickers in 1999, Rolls-Royce is now the world's largest supplier of marine equipment by value. In contrast to the civil aerospace market, for the marine sector it pays to be close to the market. It would be uneconomic to transport the heavy equipment over long distances to shipyards where it is installed in ships. For this reason, Rolls-Royce opened a 9,000 m² factory in November 2005 in the Nanhui district, across the bridge from the Yangshan deepwater port. This was the company's largest investment in China to date, of between US$8 million and US$10 million. Rolls-Royce believes that its outlay should be recouped within three years. The factory is primarily an assembly operation, supplying winches and other equipment used in commercial marine vessels, as well as rudders and deck machinery. About two-thirds of the parts are supplied from China, with the more technically advanced equipment (mostly the motors) imported.

The energy sector

Finally, Rolls-Royce has an interest in the energy sector, supplying power for the oil and gas industry, and for distributed electricity generation. The company won the prize contract (worth US$150 million) to provide gas turbines, compressors and controls compression equipment for the first phase of the West to East China gas pipeline, down which some 12 billion m³ of natural gas will be pumped. However, with that work completed, Rolls-Royce lost out to GE for the second phase of the project. No doubt there will be more opportunities in future as China switches increasingly to natural gas to meet its growing energy needs.

Sigma Precision Components

Sigma Precision Components (Sigma) makes parts for the aerospace sector. It has only been in existence for three years but already has big ambitions for its China facility. Sigma identified Chengdu as the ideal location for its manufacturing facility. As one of the largest aerospace centres in China, it offered a wealth of talent from local universities and some significant cost advantages over other Chinese cities, particularly in the East and South of the country.

Another important factor in the choice of Chengdu was its infrastructure and the speed at which the new company was able to establish itself. Formed in late 2004, Sigma had opened a representative office in Chengdu by May 2005. A year later it had secured funding from the UK company, Avingtrans plc, to invest in a manufacturing facility in Chengdu; and by September it had applied for and secured a licence to operate as a wholly foreign-owned enterprise (WFOE) and had signed the lease for the facility.

After two months spent fitting out the facility, the first CNC (computer numerical control) machine tools were delivered in December 2006. For the first quarter of 2007 the focus was on implementing an aerospace-quality management system and 'ERP' (enterprise resource planning) system. Some non-aerospace components were built to test the effectiveness of the quality systems. Full AS 9100 (aerospace) approval was secured in March 2007, with the certification audit conducted by Bureau Veritas Quality Inspection from Shanghai. The facility opened in April.

Of course, not all companies can move so fast when setting up a business in China but the experience of Sigma certainly contradicts the view that bureaucracy in China inevitably forces a slow pace. Kevin Donnelly, co-founder and general manager of Sigma, found that the authorities in the development zones were very supportive. Sigma is based in the export-processing zone (EPZ) of the Chengdu High-tech Zone and has frequent reviews with its management team to discuss any issues. Most problems have been rectified within days. Donnelly pays tribute also to the CBBC, which provided much advice and assistance in setting up the business.

Being located within one of the Chengdu EPZs means that there is no duty to pay on the imported materials, once the manufactured parts have been exported out of China. The agreed administrative processes are quite challenging, but Kevin Donnelly says that once you get used to the system it is possible to make things work without too much pain. Customs are also generally supportive.

Sigma currently has a staff of 30 in Chengdu, whittled down from several hundred applicants. The company has already begun to manufacture and export components mostly to customers in Europe, but in the long term, it sees China becoming more important as the aerospace market in China continues to develop rapidly. Sigma is a key element within Avingtrans aerospace division and provides significant competitive advantage in global aerospace markets.

Like all thriving FIEs in China, the management made time to learn as much as possible about Chinese culture and manages relationships very carefully. Kevin Donnelly considers that they are probably better equipped now to maximize opportunities that are available through working more closely with their network of contacts.

Westwind

Westwind, a company that makes highly specialized parts for drills, is tapping into the growing market in China for manufacturing printed circuit boards.

Background

Many businesses assume that to have a presence in China you need a gleaming new factory built at a cost of millions, or even a prestigious office in the increasingly expensive cities of Beijing or Shanghai. But, for Westwind, the Poole-based specialist engineering company, all it needed was a workshop with space enough for two people.

Westwind designs and manufactures 'air-bearing spindle systems', specialist parts that offer high-speed, low-vibration and extreme rotational accuracy, without the need for lubrication. These spindles have found increasing usefulness when drilling microscopic holes at very high speeds (with drills now capable of rotating at 25,000 revolutions per minute) and, specifically in printed circuit boards (PCBs), which are becoming increasingly miniaturized.

Westwind has built up its business supplying spindles to original equipment manufacturers (OEMs). Part of the company's international reputation derives from the quality of its products, but another equally important part is the attention it pays to after-sales service. Because the spindles are designed to such high specifications and yet are put to extreme high-intensity use, the need to maintain them is paramount. Not surprisingly, the company operates a number of service centres around the world.

The appeal of the East

It was inevitable that sooner or later Westwind would become involved with China. China is becoming an important centre for PCB manufacture, in Dongguan and round Shanghai, specifically in the town of Kunshan (between Shanghai and Suzhou).

More and more of Westwind's spindles have been incorporated into drills being used in China. Maintaining them involved either shipping the parts out of China to one of Westwind's service centres, which was expensive, or having them serviced by local operators over whom Westwind had less control. The principal customers of Westwind, the OEMs, therefore suggested to Westwind that it would be practical – and more cost-effective – if they established service operations in China.

Going it alone

Westwind's first thought was to collaborate with agents already used by one key OEM customer. However, negotiations with the agent foundered because of Westwind's insistence on building stringent performance measures into the arrangements.

Added to that, Westwind was not that keen on setting up a joint venture, based on its past experience in other countries where it had been bogged down in internal conflicts, rather than concentrating on external issues. The logical path was for Westwind to go it alone.

First stop, CBBC

Westwind approached the CBBC for advice and guidance, attending some CBBC events, including a seminar about Jiangsu Province, and generally informed itself about the best approach. Initially, all the company needed was a workshop of comparatively small size. Westwind quickly identified the area around Shanghai as being the most appropriate for its business, since that was where most of the new investment in PCB manufacturing was being directed. The choice of the exact location for its new operation involved selecting a site in one of the numerous trade zones specifically geared to attracting foreign-invested operations or, alternatively, setting up in Kunshan, the heart of the PCB manufacturing area.

Because the investment was likely to be small, the free trade zone option soon fell by the wayside. The possibilities in Kunshan also failed to impress once the company learned of inconsistency of power supplies and a less-than-adequate infrastructure.

Singapore in China

The ideal solution for the company soon presented itself in the form of the Singapore Suzhou Township, in effect a joint venture between the Chinese and Singapore governments to create a mini-version of Singapore in China, complete with highly developed infrastructure, a welcoming business environment, acres of space and Singapore-like efficiency.

The Westwind team met the township administration, who seemed genuinely keen to welcome its investment, recognizing that although the initial investment was small, Westwind might well expand in future. CBBC took care to understand Westwind's business and to help accommodate the company in the right premises.

On top of that, the township had people with excellent English and an efficient administration, which helped to ensure that enquiries were quickly responded to. The township authorities also took over the whole process of applying and obtaining a business licence, which came as a relief, having heard some horror stories from other British firms of how long it had taken some businesses to get their licence. The Singapore Suzhou Township handled it all very efficiently, which certainly put the minds of Westwind's management at ease.

Strix

The core business

Strix, the manufacturer of control systems for over two-thirds of the world's kettle markets was formed in 1981 by a prominent British inventor, John Taylor, who invented the first kettle control with automatic steam switch-off. The device has subsequently protected millions of kettles against accidental dry switch-on or boiling dry.

However, the Strix company is more than an inventor and manufacturer. It also helps brand owners source from OEMs. In this respect, what Strix does is to project manage; as systems engineers for kettles, it doesn't make the elements, for example, but designs them to be an integral part of the kettle. Strix now employs 1,000 people, of whom 600 are in China, and holds over 600 patents, with annual sales over £10 million.

Strix and business opportunities in China

As China has risen to become a major manufacturing force, fuelled by inward investment and years of 'opening to the outside world', so it seemed logical to bring China's manufacturers together with the major kettle companies. At the same time, there was a strong business case for moving some of the assembly of kettle control systems then being carried out in the company's Isle of Man factories to China for logistical reasons, to be close to the kettle OEMs and to support their assembly requirements.

In 1997, the company invested in a factory in Guangzhou, which it set up as a WFOE. The facility was expanded and then moved to a larger greenfield site operation in 2003, which is now the company's principal assembly operation. Some component manufacturing is also done there.

The next development phase will be to further expand assembly and component manufacture in China, although the design and development of new products will continue to be centred in the Isle of Man.

China now makes 85 per cent of the world's kettles, which therefore puts it absolutely centre stage as far as the world's kettle brands are concerned. Perhaps of great interest is the potential domestic market. Some 10 million kettles are sold each year in China, which is a tiny fraction of the overall population. The prospects of more millions buying kettles is enticing, although it may take some time to persuade a nation used to drinking boiling water from a thermos flask to switch to automatic kettles.

Unsafe practices

China may be good for making a typical household product such as kettles, but it is certainly not ideal when it comes to the protection of intellectual property. The biggest problem Strix faces is counterfeiting, although it does everything to try to deal with abuse of its IP. The company talks to Customs authorities, informing them of the differences between its products and those of the counterfeits; it takes out court cases; it commissions third-party counterfeit testers; and it lobbies both at a national and at a European level, all of which cumulatively help. But it is very difficult to prevent the copyists from doing their worst.

More worrying still, the unscrupulous illegal manufacturers sometimes engage in what might be called smear campaigns to allege that Strix products are faulty. They do this by asking their employees to buy a kettle containing a Strix safety system and then claiming that the product went wrong. The chief executive, Brian Amey, hopes that as consumers come to realize the difference in quality and when the authorities start to take action, the proportion of genuine products will rise again, as it did in the Russian market.

The practice of voluntary recall by the manufacturer or retailer is still a long way off in China but would certainly work in Strix's favour. Ultimately, the best solution lies with consumers who come to insist on better-quality products and, in the case of kettles, ones that are completely safe.

BLP

In October 2006, the furniture-making company, BLP, held a grand opening of its huge factory in Suzhou where it is now turning out large volumes of kitchen cabinet doors a month. Getting to this point has been something of an eventful journey.

Three years or so ago, BLP's directors first thought about the possibility of investing in a China manufacturing operation. Founded nearly 100 years ago and now a leading manufacturer of what are called 'membrane-pressed' cabinet doors, as well as other parts used in furniture, BLP has a large manufacturing operation at Doncaster in the United Kingdom. However, as with most manufacturing businesses, the competitive advantage offered by China was a major incentive.

With the rapid growth of the middle class in China, many of whom are buying their homes and fitting them out, there also seemed to be a potential market for the company's products in China itself. In recent years, 'do it yourself' has become a huge industry in China, evidenced by the number of B&Q stores.

Chinese options

In September 2003, BLP Chairperson Malcolm Cohen and his colleagues went to China. With the help of CBBC, they visited and sounded out seven different potential sites, based on a series of criteria (skill base; costs of set-up and operations and proximity to ports) before deciding on the Suzhou New District (SND) (the short-form name of Suzhou New and National High-tech Industrial Zone). Suzhou won out because it offered a skilled labour force, a reasonable cost base and an attractive financial package. SND was also enthusiastic that BLP was offering significant employment with its investment.

The objective was to have the first products coming off the production line by summer 2006. That timetable almost immediately proved to be too ambitious, since there was a difficulty with acquiring land use rights. SND had granted BLP these leasehold rights over the site in early 2004 but the land in question had not yet received the required central government approval to be re-designated for industrial purposes. That prevented the land certificate being issued, which, in turn, meant that a bank loan could not be completed.

This coincided with a credit squeeze, which led to a substantial delay and difficulties in finalizing bank facilities in Suzhou. Both issues were eventually resolved, but they resulted in about six months' delay to the project, as well as a substantial additional cost. There were to be more problems.

Building up contacts

While the plant was being built and all formalities finalized, BLP took the opportunity to generate some goodwill: fostering relations, developing *guanxi* (relationships) and establishing links with the local Suzhou university. It also dipped into its pocket, starting a scholarship scheme to fund four 'able but needy' students to study English at the university's School of Foreign Studies. The scholarship included the offer of work in the summer holidays and an opportunity to work with BLP on graduation.

Starting up

That goodwill was certainly tested to the full while the factory was being built. There were plenty of obstacles to be overcome, mostly minor, but some of them more frightening. Among the major problems was poor construction, which resulted in a crumbling floor and a faulty roof, as well as failures in the electrical and fire prevention systems. What had happened was that the reputable contractor with whom BLP had signed the construction contract had subcontracted part of the work without permission from BLP and in breach of the contract. Added to that, the contractor changed the specification halfway through. All of this took extra time: to renegotiate the contract, to have the unlawful subcontractor thrown off the site and to carry out repairs.

The second challenge arose as BLP endeavoured to import equipment for the factory. The intention had always been to have 'global sales' of the manufactured products, both to markets inside and outside China. Importing equipment would therefore normally attract duty. However, BLP was persuaded to set up in SND on the basis that the factory would have 'encouraged project status', which allowed for exemption from paying VAT and import duty.

That was not the way the Customs office saw it and they threatened to levy full VAT and import duty on the equipment. While the two Chinese organizations argued back and forth, BLP found itself caught in the middle, and the equipment was impounded at the docks.

A third problem arose concerning the use of a special boiler brought to burn waste wood and generate electricity. Officials at SND decreed the boiler was not suitable and that, in its place should be installed a fossil-fuel-burning boiler. BLP got its way, however, after explaining that its choice of boiler offered environmental benefits.

After much huffing and puffing, the plant was finally occupied in April 2006 and finished that summer. Today, the plant is operational, but challenges persist, not least in hiring and training staff. BLP found it more difficult to hire good managers and is relying on more expatriate managers than it had budgeted for.

The BLP plant in Suzhou is 625,000 ft², employing 400 workers (about a fifth of the target number by the third year if successful) and in three years' time should be manufacturing some half a million doors a week. To date, BLP has invested about US$30 million, about half the approved overall investment.

In retrospect, Malcom Cohen admits that he hadn't expected it to be so hard. However, he is still strongly of the opinion that the investment has been worth it. By the end of 2007, the factory should be running at break-even level and the huge investment could be recovered within the next few years. All the advice BLP had received had been to go down the WFOE route and he is pleased that they did so.

Hornby

In the late 1970s, Hornby, the model train manufacturer, employed some 2,000 people on its extensive site in Margate, on the east coast of Kent in the United Kingdom. The company had been through a number of changes of ownership but remained a quintessentially British company, based in the United Kingdom and selling its products to the UK market.

Through the next decade, the children's toy market underwent some dramatic change, with the introduction of video games, other toys of a more high-tech nature and then, after that, the arrival of the PC on a mass scale. Such change had an inevitable downward effect on Hornby's sales. But what happened next is a remarkable illustration of the benefits of moving production to China. It is true that there are fewer jobs in Margate, but overall, the company is bigger, certainly measured in turnover and profits, and has now made huge inroads into overseas markets. Sales have all but doubled since 2001 to reach £45 million, and profits are about £8 million.

China or bust

It was about 10 years ago that the company's then executive chairperson noted with concern that Hornby's competitors had moved manufacturing into China. They were gaining market share, seemingly as a consequence of this step, and his analysis was that Hornby needed to follow suit.

As it happened, Hornby already had a China connection through a Hong Kong company called Sanda Kan Industrial, which had produced parts for the model trains and associated train set equipment. Sanda had indicated that it was keen to develop the relationship further, and would be able to identify a manufacturer across the border in Guangdong, to help make the complete model trains.

Sanda Kan's facility was in Dongguan, which is halfway between Shenzhen and Guangzhou. Because the making of model trains is such a specialized business, involving unique tools, it was decided to ship the tools out to China, in effect transferring manufacturing wholesale.

The process of transferring tools and equipment began in 1997. At that point, Hornby was then employing some 750 people in Margate, of whom about 600 were involved in manufacturing. The initial thought was that the manufacture of Scalextric model cars, which Hornby also undertook, would remain in the United Kingdom and the model trains be made in China. However, Scalextric, too, was moved to China. In all, some 1,500 tools were shipped to China over a period of five years. A second manufacturer was found, also in Dongguan.

In January 2001, Frank Martin took over as chief executive, having built a career working for companies in the toys and consumer products manufacturing business. Hornby had gone public in 1986 and investors had picked up the trend of oscillating company profits. The new chief executive's mandate was to 'try to chart a steadier course'.

Advantages of China production

The China end of the business was certainly going to plan. Interestingly, the main reason for moving to China was not to cut costs, although that was an incentive, but rather to use the cost advantages to improve the quality of the products. Hornby's business is driven by innovation. It needs to deliver new products that people want, especially locomotives. However, each new product introduced to the market has high investment costs in terms of design and development of the prototype.

Tooling costs in China were found to be about half what they were in the United Kingdom. In figures, to tool a new locomotive in the year 2000 would cost around £200,000 in the United Kingdom, but when done in China would cost about £100,000. In short, the China business offered the scope for devising more new products. Rather than bringing one new model to the market every four years, as had happened up to that point, it then became possible to launch two or even three new models a year. That had knock-on effects for revenues, because each new model generates related sales in models associated with the locomotive (eg, carriages, trackside buildings and so on) as collectors develop their collections.

China has also provided Hornby with the advantage of higher specification, allowing for greater intimacy and detail in the model trains and cars. The sophistication is helping the company to produce and sell some remarkable products, including a locomotive that is actually steam-driven, using electricity drawn from the track to heat up water.

Moving up a gear

The models have moved up a gear, literally, with the introduction of digital controls so that, for example, with the Scalextric car, the controls operate an individual car rather than simply increasing or decreasing power to the track. This means that cars can race one another on the same track (the technology for this was developed by a Cambridge company, Scientific Generics, now Sagentia – see Chapter 26).

Again, this seems to go against the prevailing wisdom that China can manufacture cheaply but is not geared up to manufacture top quality. Hornby's experience is quite the reverse. Frank Martin says that if it is technically possible, Hornby's manufacturing partners will find a way to do it.

The reasons for not moving all processes from design and engineering as well as manufacturing to China is that Hornby needs to maintain a connection to the home market and to keep engineers close to the products that they are engineering. Some three-quarters of Hornby and Scalextric sales are in the United Kingdom.

Frank Martin also highlights the importance of the good relationships that have been established, both with the Hong Kong partner and with the manufacturing operations. The Chinese partners recognize that if Hornby's business grows, then their business will grow. They are not looking to go it alone, because they know that together both can benefit.

By the same token he is sure that there is little, if no scope for theft of the Hornby intellectual property (even if the Chinese were minded to do so) because Hornby owns the tooling, the brands and has the sale and distribution expertise. In that respect, Hornby is in a much different position from, say, soapmakers selling in the Chinese market.

Another interesting facet of the China business is that the manufacturers operate to international health, safety, environmental and ethical standards set by the International Council of Toy Industries (ICTI). Altogether, some 600 toy factories in China have been audited, according to the British Toy and Hobby Industry, which is a member of the ICTI.

Production is increasing at Hornby's Chinese manufacturing operations, and there are now four separate factories turning out Hornby model cars and trains. A steady stream of containers leaves China for the United Kingdom, with Hornby train sets (all pre-packed and wrapped) and Scalextric cars (which are packaged in the Kent factory). Each year the company takes delivery of some 300, 400-ft containers, each container holding goods worth about £150,000. Hornby currently employs about 130 people in the United Kingdom, all based at its Margate factory.

The market steams ahead

Meanwhile, on the demand side, a highly significant development in the Hornby business was the securing of the exclusive right to make the Harry Potter Hogwarts Express in 2001. Even though that particular model only ever accounted for around 5 per cent of sales, it generated huge publicity and helped revive the brand as Frank Martin knew it would. It woke people up to the joys of model trains and cars, and helped Hornby with its major retailers. Among these are Toys Я Us and Argos.

With the Chinese manufacturing secure – and with an all-important competitive advantage – the company contemplated a big push into new markets, particularly in Europe and the United States, which has just under half the world market. Germany has by far the biggest market for model railways in Europe.

Hornby embarked on a series of acquisitions. In 2004, the company bought a company in Spain and, following that, the entire assets of the Italian model manufacturer, Lima Spa, which had gone into liquidation. Through that, Hornby acquired some 10,000 tools, which were shipped over to the United Kingdom and are gradually making their way to China.

Additionally, Hornby discovered some priceless models that had been stored in unmarked boxes, among which were some items that would have any collector drooling. These may eventually be put in a Hornby museum. The following year Hornby acquired a distributor in France.

The company now says that it has built up the broadest brand portfolio in the world, including, Lima, Rivarossi, Jouef and Arnold, as well as Hornby. It is not all thanks to moving to China, but the company reckons that it was one of the best moves it has ever made.

Part 5

Service provision and trade with China

26

A bridge from the West to Chinese manufacturing

Tim Moore, Sagentia

Introduction

Anglo–Chinese business partnerships stretch back many centuries, but the recent growth of the Chinese economy, and the growing sophistication of its workforce, has placed many of these relationships on a different footing. China is no longer 'just' the home of cheap, low-cost manufacture and a seemingly bottomless pool of labour. As home-grown Chinese engineering talent comes on stream, product design and development is increasingly outsourced by Western companies keen to cut costs and stay competitive in challenging home markets. Many outsourcing relationships, however, are not a smooth ride. A lack of cultural awareness, and the sheer physical distance of China from Europe, can result in problems of staffing, quality control and, crucially (and most costly) lost IP. A poor understanding of what a Chinese partner will deliver has seen many Western companies unwittingly establish a new competitor as they hand over responsibility for the design, development and manufacture of their product line.

The structure of Chinese manufacturing

To understand the nature of the problem, one needs to understand the structure of Chinese manufacture, which falls broadly into three categories:

- OEMs (original equipment manufacturers) are the 'traditional' outsourced manufacturing facility, producing a product to a given design with no contribution to product development. There is limited risk to IP if the right OEM is selected, especially if the OEM depends upon outsourcing contracts from large blue chip, Western firms, and if the right procedures are put in place for IP protection.
- ODMs (original design manufacturers) both manufacture and assist in product design and development. This second service often appears to be 'free', and so it is easy to hand over increasing responsibility to the ODM. However, if design and development work is not paid for specifically, and the IP is not protected by appropriate contractual arrangements, the IP belongs to the ODM. Western companies often run into difficulties with ODMs, as designs and ideas that they thought they 'owned' are used by the ODM on its own account.
- OBMs (own brand manufacturers) often spin out from ODMs, producing and marketing products under their own brands, sometimes basing the design on what the ODM has developed for Western customers. Chinese OBMs are a growing force in the world economy. Many are now buying Western companies in order to obtain brands swiftly and gain a market presence that might otherwise have taken years to establish. Western companies doing business in China need to be very aware of the danger of gradually handing over product knowledge to Chinese suppliers with the potential to become OBMs – because these may well be future competitors.

SGAI – on-the-ground control

In 2002, Sagentia, one of the world's pre-eminent technology management and product development companies, was managing new product development and Chinese-based manufacture for leading brand model-maker Hornby. As the project progressed, it was clear that a growing percentage of Sagentia's consultancy costs were being inefficiently spent on cultural mismatches and so – encouraged by Hornby – Sagentia made the decision to open an office in Hong Kong, the first UK-based technology consultancy to do so. To make sure the new enterprise would deliver, the office became SGAI (pronounced see-guy) – a joint venture between Sagentia and AML, a leading Hong Kong-based electronic products manufacturing company. AML already employed an extensive and highly skilled workforce (over 4,000 people) and ran certified facilities (around 330,000 ft^2 of production space) in mainland China.

Operating as a joint venture from the very beginning has proved the key to SGAI's significant success. Dr Tim Moore, SGAI CEO, was a consultant at Sagentia at the time, and remains partly based at Sagentia's office in Cambridge, in the United Kingdom:

We knew that many of our clients would significantly benefit from using Chinese resources, but it was no longer proving cost-effective to use a UK-based management service. Despite this, our clients were facing real barriers to operating successfully in China, and in particular were suffering from the effects of their own displacement from their manufacturing base, especially in terms of quality control. Our depth of market awareness, technical and scientific expertise and knowledge of the entire process was unavailable in China at that time and there was little help for companies wanting someone to physically manage an outsourced project through from start to finish. SGAI's unique end-to-end offer filled this gap.

From AML's perspective, SGAI was also the best way to do business with the West. AML/SGAI COO, Dr K.M. Chow, comments:

To operate in China, merely getting a local partner doesn't work. We believe that setting up a joint venture is the only way, as when your partner is also your co-investor, you can guarantee that both parties will perform to the best of their abilities in order to make sure the business is a success.

AML was hungry for Western business, but also wanted to develop its innovative capabilities, and saw Sagentia, with its Cambridge base and scientific heritage, as able to help it achieve this goal. Dr Moore says:

In many ways, AML is very similar to Sagentia. It is client focused, its goal is to achieve higher margins through delivering real innovation, and it is an award-winning company; producing high-quality electronic devices for a range of industry sectors.

AML provides the cultural know-how and on-the-ground presence essential to make a real difference to Western clients. Dr Chow:

A local partner offers local support in many ways. It provides day to day management of an outsourcing project, allowing both parties to focus on their core competencies, as well as making sure business is done the Chinese way, which is more cost- and time-effective.

But for SGAI to succeed, it had to reflect both the Chinese and the Sagentia business ethos. Dr Moore comments:

The Hong Kong business community is very tight-knit and very risk-averse. SGAI, however, was born from a consultancy famous for its innovative, entrepreneurial work, and it was important that the new company reflected this entrepreneurial spirit.

The choice of joint COO was therefore crucial, and Dr Chow was deliberately appointed because of his energetic and ambitious personality, cultural sensitivity and entrepreneurial approach.

Hard-won success

SGAI is now a successful, profit-making business, but this success has been hard won. Staffing was a particular issue, with a turnover of up to 30 per cent in the first few months of trading. Job-hopping is not considered unusual in China, and with so many companies opening their doors, opportunities are legion. To address this problem, an incentive scheme was put in place, there was considerable investment in facilities and the profile of SGAI was raised in the community as a whole. An important marker in this process was the naming of SGAI as one of the first winners of the Cathay Pacific Awards, set up to recognize business dynamism in Hong Kong and China. As a result, SGAI is now considered an employer for whom talented, experienced people want to work, offering a career with the prospects of travel, promotion and exciting client development.

There were also early issues of quality control. These issues have dogged Western companies for decades, but are often the result of the mindset of the Chinese manufacturing base, which does not always recognize that the cost required to ensure better quality can eventually translate into significantly larger profits. Forward-thinking Chinese companies, such as AML, already recognized the benefits improved quality control can bring, and have exploited Sagentia's expertise in QA processes and procedures to improve the quality of design, development and manufacturing processes throughout, thereby providing further reassurance for clients in the West.

Protecting IP

A major problem for many Western companies is the protection of IP when outsourcing to China, and this is another key benefit of using SGAI and its Hong Kong location. An understanding of China's history is important when considering IP protection. Communist rule engendered a culture where individuals could not own ideas – these all became the property of the state, as it was considered to be for the greater good of the country if knowledge was shared. The concept of IP as a valuable asset was therefore unrecognized. Although Chinese legislation to protect IP has now been put in place, the necessary cultural shift has not happened so quickly. Hong Kong, however, built on the 'British model', has valued IP from the start. It has put in place legislation for its protection, and understands its nature and value. SGAI, with its base in Hong Kong, is therefore ideally placed to benefit from a culture that values IP highly, whilst still being able to access the manufacturing benefits of mainland China.

How to do business

Hornby was the first client to benefit from SGAI's management skills, although Hornby already had its own product, development and manufacturing contacts, which it continues to use. Now, almost all of Hornby's R&D is handled in China, with products exported back to be sold in the West. Dr Moore again:

Frank Martin, the Hornby CEO, spotted a need for Western technology and design but at Far Eastern costs and hence saw the concept of a joint venture, such as SGAI, as one way to achieve this by acting as an R&D centre and a bridge to manufacture with barriers to losing IP. His foresight has proved to be correct – Hornby can now produce novel and innovative products quickly, efficiently and at low cost, which helps them beat the competition.

SGAI is an excellent example of how to do business in China to the mutual benefit of everyone involved. The Chinese government knows that being the world's lowest-cost manufacturer is not necessarily the best place to be, and actively wants Chinese business to 'grow up', especially in terms of design, innovation and a market-centric approach. SGAI is helping the country meet this target of moving up the value chain – another reason why it won the Cathay Pacific Award for 'Innovation and Dynamism'. But SGAI has also had a fundamental effect on Sagentia, placing it at the forefront of consultancy in the 'sweet spot' between East and West, between innovation and manufacture. SGAI was profitable within eight months of opening its doors and now accounts for 5 per cent of Sagentia's turnover, with a target of generating up to 50 per cent in two to three years time.

Dr Chow concludes:

The key to success when operating in China is mutual trust. Both parties have to understand each other in depth, remain open-minded, respect each other's culture, customs and traditions. A joint venture must also be allowed to operate without too much interference from the parent companies – if the result is a transparent, profitable business, then there should be no need for interference. We have quarterly board meetings, present summaries of our market forecasts and business results, and our ultimate aim is to fulfil our commitments and exceed our board's expectations.

27

Exporting trucks from China – a lost opportunity

Jonathan Reuvid

Introduction

In principle, sourcing products from China is probably less hazardous in the case of higher-value technical and industrial products than it is for low-value consumer goods purchased in bulk. For all products, there are world-class shipping services from the major Chinese container ports, including the national Chinese shipping line COSCO, as well as others such as Maersk and AMT. Shipping documentation and procedures and documentary credits conform to the International Chamber of Commerce (ICC) standards allowing for the release of payments on receipt of goods via major international banks both for exports and imports. Therefore, the financial mechanics of import and export trade are relatively risk-free.

Quality issues

The problems that arise are mainly related to quality assurance and the negotiation of the original commercial contracts. For Western manufacturers and wholesalers or retailers of consumer goods (such as clothing and toys) who are sourcing products from

China because it is low cost and labelling goods with their own brands for distribution in Western markets, the quality issues are particularly serious. The Chinese suppliers are selected primarily on the cost criteria and the product specification may not be too rigorous. Provided that the samples are satisfactory, Western buyers are often ready to purchase in bulk, paying only cursory attention to ensuring that quality assurance procedures and regular inspection checks are in place. Although the Chinese suppliers may be qualified to the relevant ISO standard and subject to periodic checks by the regional quality standards inspection bureau, the frequency of such checks is uncertain and it is not unknown for unscrupulous suppliers to forge inspection certificates or to subcontract production to even less qualified factories in remoter areas. The recent spate of product rejections on health and safety grounds, particularly the case of toys purchased from China and marketed by Mattel, highlights the problem.

The Chinese government is keen to exercise tougher QA control on its export manufacturers but lacks sufficient inspection resources at present and the suicide of factory owners whose products are returned is sad but serves no useful purpose. The problem is also exacerbated by Western customers' continuous pressure to drive down already cheap factory prices even further, which encourages Chinese manufacturers to cut corners and to use inferior raw materials.

The solution is largely in the hands of the Western customers who should introduce tougher product specifications that include raw materials, more rigorous supplier qualification and regular factory inspections by their own agents. Finished goods inspection and sample testing at the port of departure by one or other of the international inspection agencies can also be introduced to reduce the risk of defective products being shipped. All of the measures add significantly to the landed cost of sales and have to be factored into market pricing. They may cause reductions in gross margins but that should be an acceptable cost for purchasing from the cheapest manufacturing sources available.

These problems are far less acute in the case of consumer durables to which retail customer warranties are attached, and quality assurance routines both in the factory and by the trade customer are more rigorous. They are even less in the case of high-value industrial products where adherence to specification and product quality are paramount in gaining export market share. Higher gross margins for both manufacturer and buyer support the cost of greater quality assurance at all points in the supply chain.

Commercial issues

In negotiating export sales and distribution arrangements the focus of attention is likely to be on the terms of contract rather than quality issues. This was certainly the main concern in the case study that follows of an abortive project to purchase Chinese-manufactured trucks for distribution in the Gulf and Middle East.

The heavy-duty truck project

The same US investment banker with strong Middle East connections who visited China in 2004 to search for a chicken broiler production partner (see Chapter 16) was also introduced to a manufacturer of heavy-duty trucks in North East China. He was impressed by the quality of the product, which had been raised over the previous five years with the development of a state-of-the-art cab and chassis, including air conditioning, which is a prerequisite for sale in Middle East and African markets. The most marketable feature of the trucks was the engine manufactured under licence to the designs of a long-established and highly regarded Western truck manufacturer and compliant to Euro-2 exhaust emission standards with the prospect of upgrading to Euro-3 standards within two years. The steering, braking and suspension systems were also manufactured under licence, to the designs of leading US multinational component manufacturers.

The US banker recognized immediately that there were promising markets in the Middle East and the Gulf for the Chinese trucks and asked whether the distribution rights were available. He was assured by the senior vice-president sales of the Chinese truck company that there were no distribution arrangements in place, although a handful of trucks might have been sold in the region. On this basis the banker returned to New York with product specifications and freight-on-board (f.o.b.) export prices, promising to return as soon as he had researched the markets where he had clients and associates engaged in automotive distribution.

Researching the market

The banker quickly established that the largest potential market would be Saudi Arabia, with smaller market opportunities in the Gulf States, a lesser market in Egypt for heavy-duty trucks, and other possible markets in the Magreb countries of North Africa and perhaps Pakistan. In Saudi Arabia, an investment conglomerate with which he had a longstanding business association held the national distributorships for the top leading German and Japanese truck manufacturers, which it operated through a network of service centres. The Chinese trucks would be complementary to the existing trucks with a quality specification that fitted well between those of the heavier German and lighter Japanese products. Moreover, the f.o.b. price of the Chinese product was less than half the cost, insurance and freight (c.i.f.) cost of the comparable German product. The Saudi group expressed a keen interest but was sceptical that a commercially acceptable deal could be struck. It was agreed that the banker should return to China to open negotiations and that if all went well the London-based vice-president would fly out to inspect the Chinese plant and product and, hopefully, sign a contract. It was estimated that the first year's sales could be as much as 1,000 trucks. At a unit price of £30,000 the potential value of the business was significant. Before returning to Beijing, the banker also established that there was a similar interest from an investment group in Oman.

The negotiation

Back in Beijing the banker and an associate met with the Chinese vice-president and his staff in a hotel suite hired for the occasion where they were well received. In a friendly atmosphere the banker unfolded his distribution plan for the Middle East region, mentioning by name the distributor in each country that he hoped to engage.

Among the Chinese managers present was the director of export sales who took copious notes. The banker added that to coordinate the operation he was ready to set up, at his expense, a regional sales office for the distributorship in Cairo where he maintained a second home.

The meeting moved on to a discussion of first year sales and to how many trucks the banker and his clients would commit themselves. The banker suggested a first order of 100 trucks, building up to a minimum of 1,000 trucks by the end of the second year. It was at this stage that the Chinese export sales director delivered his bombshell. They already had a customer in Riyadh, he told the meeting, who had recently ordered five trucks against the offer of an exclusive distributorship for Saudi Arabia if he purchased a further 95 within two years. This news was a complete surprise to the vice-president as well as the banker. Although the export sales director reported to him, he had not chosen to tell his superior. The situation deteriorated further when the written agreement with the Riyadh customer was produced. The conditional offer of the Saudi distributorship was in a legally binding form. The export sales director further revealed the existence of several other small trial orders into other Middle Eastern territories to which no distributorship offers had been attached.

The meeting ended with both sides saying that they would try to find a way to resolve the impasse but the unwelcome information cast a considerable cloud over the lavish pre-arranged dinner that followed at the banker's expense. The Chinese vice-president was slightly embarrassed but not at all apologetic.

The final détente

In the week that followed the banker consulted with the vice-president of his Saudi client in London. On investigation the Riyadh customer was found to be a small dealer with a single service outlet. The Saudi client offered to buy out the Riyadh dealer or grant him an agency if the Chinese truck company was prepared to renegotiate his contract.

The banker suggested that the problem could be eased if the truck company entered into a joint venture partnership with him for a regional distributorship, which would override existing arrangements and could appoint new sub-distributors in each country.

All suggestions were to no avail. The Chinese export sales director refused to back down and was supported by his vice-president. To make matters worse his assistant approached the Beijing office of an Omani company that the banker had identified in an attempt to sell trucks direct. It was also discovered that the export sales director was paid commission on all completed export sales and feared the loss of his commission on the five trucks that had been ordered. Of course, his attitude was short-sighted because he could have earned far more in commission from sales to the major Saudi group.

If there is a conclusion to this unfortunate case study, it may be to take particular care when dealing with the senior management of state-owned companies. Do not assume that they are fully briefed on the activities of their subordinates. In this case, the vice-president sales had abdicated rather than delegated his responsibilities.

Floating over the top of his export sales department, he had no idea of the business that his managers were doing.

Back in London, the vice-president of the Saudi group was philosophical about the outcome that he said was consistent with his experience of trying to do business with China. The story was relayed around the leading trading companies of the Gulf and this incident probably put back the truck company's export development plans for the Middle East by several years.

28

Opening a reinsurance operation in China

*Ian Faragher, Lloyd's Reinsurance
Company (China) Limited*

Introduction

In November 2005, Lloyd's got the green light from the Chinese regulator to set up
an onshore reinsurance operation in China. The announcement, made by China's
President Hu Jintao during a state visit to Britain, marked an important day in Lloyd's
history. It gave us the opportunity to establish an onshore operation in one of the
world's fastest developing insurance markets, in a country forecast to be the world's
second largest economy.

Eighteen months later, after putting all the operational plans in place, Lloyd's
Chairperson, Lord Levene, officially opened our office in Shanghai with the city's
Executive Vice-Mayor Feng. Today, a number of Lloyd's businesses are participating
in the operation, and we are seeing new risks pass through it every day.

So, what did we learn from the whole experience? What were some of the key
challenges we faced while setting up in a country that is increasingly taking centre
stage in the global economy? And how exactly does our operation out there work?

Lloyd's has provided offshore reinsurance capacity to the Chinese insurance
market since the 1970s in areas such as marine and aviation. Over those decades, a
relationship of mutual support has developed, so at the turn of the Millennium, Lloyd's

consulted the firms who operate in the market to get their views on the opportunities in China.

A key finding from this consultation was that underwriters believed that continued economic growth and infrastructure development would result in more demand for specialist onshore reinsurance. This view remains, as research carried out earlier this year revealed that 80 per cent of Lloyd's underwriters named China as offering the most significant growth opportunities in 2007.

Market entry

So Lloyd's decided to set up an operational presence in China, enabling its underwriters and brokers to work more closely with Chinese insurers, offering them the benefit of their expertise backed by the security of Lloyd's capital. But it wasn't straightforward. Lloyd's unique market structure presented challenges when seeing how it could fit into the country's regulatory framework.

It was a complex process, but in March 2005, the Chinese Insurance Regulatory Commission (CIRC) indicated that it would look upon a model based on a subsidiary of the Corporation of Lloyd's favourably. So a month later, we formally approached them proposing that we do just that – set up our own reinsurance company in China, something that Lloyd's had never done before. This model was accepted, leading to President Hu Jintao's announcement in the winter of 2005. But the good news we received that day was not the end of the journey – it was only the beginning.

Negotiations with the regulator

According to Chinese regulation, Lloyd's had one year to set up its reinsurance company and show the CIRC that it was operationally ready. We spent the following 12 months in negotiations with the regulator to see how we could interface a subsidiary of Lloyd's based in China with the London market.

We agreed a business model with the market, reserved a name for the company – Lloyd's Reinsurance Company (China) Limited (LRCCL) – employed a team of top people and confirmed Shanghai as the location for our office, no easy task given that both Shanghai and Beijing offered significant advantages. We also gave a lot of thought to the right technology for the operation, ensuring that a core reinsurance system and the means for efficient electronic placing of business were in place to make it as easy as possible for Chinese insurers to place risks with Lloyd's in China.

In March 2007, we were granted our licence, and in April we held the official opening ceremony at our office in the Azia Centre in the Pudong District of Shanghai.

The market opportunity

We don't expect to see huge financial benefits overnight, but as China continues to develop, and as we continue to build our relationships there, we believe that over time it will provide a wealth of opportunity. China is, after all, already one of the world's largest economies, ranking fourth when the official exchange rate is used, but second in terms of purchasing power. It is forecast to overtake the United States and become the world's largest economy in real terms by 2040. This growth has been driven by dramatic inflows of foreign direct investment, which has risen from US$38 billion in 1995 to US$72 billion in 2005. And, as a result of this, the insurance industry has flourished. Chinese non-life premium has quadrupled in the past decade. In 2006 alone, China's overall annual insurance premium grew by 18.8 per cent to US$24.4 billion.

Entering China is clearly the right decision, but every step of the way we have made clear that the 'long-term' nature of the opportunity it provides should be an important consideration for insurers. While it is true that the natural tendency of governments is to develop their domestic insurance industries, the Chinese government is in fact opening up in accordance with its World Trade Organization obligations. China is recognizing the importance of foreign investment, and it needs insurers to support its development and underpin its economy.

At this point, the foreign entrants combined in China have so far only managed to amass a 1 per cent share of the primary market, but we firmly believe that this will change. The basic infrastructure required to run an insurance market is now in place and is being constantly refined.

The Chinese market is transforming, and foreign insurance entities will continue to play a vital role in this development. The important message for international investors is to understand the strategic choice they are faced with. When combining the current challenges of developing China's insurance market with the potential of reaping substantial rewards in the medium term, the conclusion to draw is that now is the time to make a long-term commitment to China.

The opportunities are clearly there. China's domestic insurance and reinsurance market is thriving. The significant demand for infrastructure, as well as growing property ownership and an increasing awareness of legal and property rights, are combining to underpin increasing demand for specialist insurance products.

The Chinese non-life insurance market has therefore expanded at an annual rate of close to 12 per cent over the last 10 years. If insurers are to make the most of its opportunities in the long term, it is vital that they establish a presence there now, as we have done at Lloyd's.

But once the commitment to do this has been made, there are still a number of challenges to face. For example, culturally, Chinese businesses have relied on the state to protect them rather than purchasing insurance cover, and generally, there is low consumer awareness of insurance. This is certain to change over time, but as insurers it is vital that we make people aware of the services, experience and expertise we can provide, particularly to such a rapidly developing country. Insurance in China is still often sold rather than bought.

This is particularly true of an organization like Lloyd's, where we thrive on insuring the world's toughest risks. Much of China's economic development is taking place in areas of catastrophe risk and exposure such as earthquake, flood and windstorm-prone areas, and coastal regions – all areas that Lloyd's specializes in. But overall, all lines of business will be crucial to China's development, and we foresee demand increasing significantly for specialist liability, property risks and business interruption.

Staff recruitment

Another challenge facing multinational organizations in China involves getting the right people for the job. The rapidly expanding economy brings with it rapidly expanding demand for experienced and talented people, meaning that good people have a lot of choice about where they want to work. And this isn't just an issue for insurance. Fortunately for Lloyd's, our powerful brand and unique status as the world's leading specialist insurer has allowed us to attract and recruit a unique team in China from a good range of first-class corporations.

Looking at another issue, it is important that we continue to support the development of broker distribution in China. We recognize that a great deal of reinsurance business is placed directly, and of course will not ignore the opportunities that brings. But over time, we see brokers as our predominant method of distribution. At Lloyd's, we also believe that local companies will become increasingly aware of the benefits a broker can bring – especially to speciality placements.

Operating an onshore reinsurance company in China

So how exactly does Lloyd's onshore reinsurance company in China operate? It has been incorporated in China as a foreign-invested reinsurance company. Capitalized by the Society of Lloyd's, it provides a vehicle through which Chinese insurers can access the specialist underwriting capabilities of the Lloyd's market for their reinsurance.

Lloyd's managing agents can get involved in the operation in one of three ways. First, they can base an underwriter in Shanghai, which four businesses have already done. Clearly this is a great way to maximize the opportunities presented by Lloyd's China, and gives them a good start building their own respective brands in the country. We recognize the importance of this, and so Lloyd's China has been set up to provide branding opportunities for managing agents via branded underwriting divisions. It is, after all, a country where good relationships and a good reputation are key to success.

Second, Lloyd's businesses in London can get involved in Chinese risks through an electronic placing system. We have adopted state-of-the-art technology to ensure that the operation runs as quickly and efficiently as possible. We use Xchanging's processing software genius as our core reinsurance system in China, which enables users to log on as either a Chinese- or English-speaking user, viewing screens and developing reports in the appropriate language.

We have also bought a global licence from trading service provider RI3K that enables business to be placed in an efficient, cost-effective and secure manner. This will assist us in the transfer of technology into China, especially as we start to offer electronic placement capabilities to the local insurance market.

And third, managing agents can close a London-placed risk directly through the offices of Lloyd's China, which has advantages to local ceding companies under Chinese law.

If a particular risk attracts a lot of attention from a number of syndicates, we do our best to ensure that all interested underwriters get a chance to participate wherever possible and appropriate. But in order to be successful, syndicates will need to do more than simply wait for business to be shown to them in London. They will have to be proactive and build relationships in the local market. Standard market business is not likely to be attractive, so successful insurers will have to build up their own reputations as speciality players and do the work to develop niche product lines.

At Lloyd's, we are not in China to drive that development, but we are there to facilitate it. We have the experience and capabilities to help navigate the Chinese market and regulatory environment. For example, the Chinese legal environment is something that the foreign business community often finds difficult to understand. It is still developing, but there is no question that it is becoming increasingly sophisticated. At Lloyd's, we took on international law firm Deacons and benefited enormously from its experience of the Chinese legal environment. It is certainly worth getting the right specialists in to help you navigate the maze when entering this dynamic country.

Conclusions

It is also absolutely vital that businesses looking to set up in China do their research and understand the political landscape. A lot hangs on government policy, so it is important to understand what the government's priorities are and how your business can fit in with them. You have to be flexible. As I outlined earlier, we went through a lot of negotiations with the Chinese authorities before we successfully found a way into the market, and it involved setting up a company – something that we had never done before. You have to keep an open mind and consider all the options. It takes time, but it's worth it.

China is an impressive country, but it is still growing, and it takes time to develop the right relationships. Lloyd's now has an impressive business based there, but that is also growing, and we are now busy further promoting it throughout the country. We have learnt that, to set up in China, it is all about knowledge and relationships. You have to have an acute understanding of the country – its rules, its regulations and its government's policies. And you have to develop the right relationships over time.

I am delighted to say that we have done this successfully at Lloyd's, but after getting the regulatory approval and setting up the office, we now have a further journey ahead of us. We are now busy promoting our business and ensuring that we provide the right insurance products at the right time – products that are compatible with China's emerging risks and that support its growth. We have 300 years' experience of doing this throughout the world, and are now perfectly placed to do it in China.

29

The independent director in China

David Steeds, Steeds & Co

Introduction

When Chinese companies come to London, or other overseas stock exchanges, to raise capital, it is a normal requirement of the listing authorities and the providers of capital that two or more non-executive directors be appointed to the board. Such non-executive directors are appointed for their independence and wide business experience including:

- independence from management;
- independence from the major Chinese shareholders;
- knowledge of international corporate governance best practice;
- wider international business skills and experience.

They are on the board to be independent directors, which is what they will be called here. One of them may be appointed chairperson; another will chair the audit committee. It is a lonely business being the only independent director on any board and there should be at least two on any publicly quoted company board.

This chapter is based on involvement as an independent director with bringing three Chinese companies to a listing on AIM (the London Stock Exchange's junior market). This involvement with China has been fascinating, demanding and rewarding.

But it is not for the faint-hearted; China's ways of business are very different from those in Western countries and independent directors are not part of that tradition!

On appointment

Planning to float – get in there early

Chinese companies are persuaded to come to London to raise capital because it has been difficult up to now for private companies (as opposed to state-owned enterprises) to raise money within China. The Chinese company wants capital: the overseas advisers want fees. Recruiting the independent directors is often left until the process is well under way. This is a mistake as it takes time for the newly appointed independent directors to be fully accepted by the company team. One needs time to develop relationships in China. Chinese companies often have no one in the United Kingdom to represent their interests, so this is a role the independent director is very well placed to carry out.

Many of the challenges facing Chinese companies in listing on a public stock market apply equally to all companies going through this daunting process, but it will seem even stranger to the Chinese, particularly if they do not speak English.

Before a company commits to listing it is important to explain the restrictions on management and on shareholder freedom of action that follow from becoming a public company, particularly the following:

- Shares owned by existing shareholders will be subject to restrictions and cannot be sold or transferred without the agreement of the NOMAD (the Nominated Adviser or investment banker and stockbroker required by the AIM rules).
- Significant business decisions will need to be discussed with and approved by the independent directors.
- Major changes to the business, such as the issue of more shares, mergers or sales, will need to be agreed by all shareholders in a shareholders' meeting.
- The financial position of the business will be made public every half-year and the results subject to a rigorous external audit.
- Management remuneration will need to be agreed with the independent directors and disclosed in the annual report.
- The senior management will need to spend time with the major outside shareholders and City analysts every six months explaining the results and the way the business is developing.

The listing process imposes huge demands on management's time. The CEO and CFO will need to spend a number of weeks in London, so it is important that they agree how the company will be run during their absence.

There is a trade-off between share price on admission to AIM and ongoing investor relations. The Chinese in particular are used to negotiating the highest price for their wares and find it difficult to understand why they should not sell shares in the company at the highest possible price. However, it is better to have satisfied shareholders whose shares have gone up in value rather than shareholders who have suffered a loss on their shares. As the founders are normally selling few, if any, shares on listing, their own interests are best served by the shares going steadily up in value, rather than starting high and then dropping.

Advisers

Before appointment, check that the advisers are well qualified and committed to doing a good job for the company. Advisers' fees can easily become a cause of friction, leaving the independent director in the middle, with a conflict between duty to the company and sympathy for the advisers with whom the director may well want to work again in the future. So, be sure to adhere to the following:

- Agree engagement letters with advisers. Ensure their listing fees and commissions are reasonable and in line with market rates and that all costs are clearly set out and understood by the Chinese side.
- Advisers' fees, in the event that the listing is aborted, should also be clear.
- Ensure Chinese management and shareholders understand the ongoing costs of being listed, which are typically between £200,000 and £400,000 per annum. This includes the costs of NOMAD, auditors, financial PR and the independent directors.
- It is a good idea to develop a schedule with three columns for full fees, abort fees and ongoing costs.

Chinese companies can be very keen on getting a good deal, even from trusted advisers. This can make them seem over cost-conscious. For instance, there is more changing of auditors in China than elsewhere. The benefit of an auditor who knows the business, can add value and will do the audit cheaper next year as a result is often not appreciated. Lower audit costs are more important to the Chinese. Concern about costs applies particularly to foreign independent directors, who are seen as expecting huge salaries for part-time work (more than the Chinese earn full-time). It pays to be mindful of and sensitive to this difference in remuneration.

There is a history of over-ambitious forecasts by Chinese listed companies; profit forecasts can get talked up to support company valuations. The management then do not like to lose face by admitting they will not achieve the forecasts. In the interests of good relations with the City, management should understand that it is imperative to produce plans that they are confident are realistic and attainable.

London advisers are also prone to overstate the capital they can raise. There is still a limited number of institutional investors who are prepared to invest in small, illiquid emerging market companies with whom they have difficulty communicating and undertaking due diligence. The independent director can be caught in the crossfire between a company that has not delivered on its forecast and advisers who have not delivered as much capital as promised, each blaming the other.

Cultural realism: China does business differently from the West

Directorships of Chinese companies are not for the timorous, as standards of corporate governance are less developed than those in the West and China has its own ways of doing business. In China, there is an emphasis on consensus (without the outsider foreigners!), which can result in following the leader without question. This is often alien to Westerners, who see robust challenge and discussion as the way to thrash out the best business solution. In contrast, the Chinese are less comfortable with open challenge and discussion. So smaller pre- or post-meeting discussions are even more important than usual to build agreement.

The Chinese are not used to independent directors. One needs to earn their respect and trust even more than on Western boards. In China that takes time. Remember:

■ A Chinese participant will rarely say 'no' to anything – this is seen as impolite.
■ Be careful about assuming that 'yes' means 'I agree'. It may just mean 'I have heard you'. At worst it may mean 'I don't want to be impolite by disagreeing with you directly'.
■ Do not expect Chinese participants to admit they have made a mistake at a meeting. That would be to lose face, which is very un-Chinese. This makes it very difficult to handle problems such as poor results.

On the other hand, China has some of the world's most dynamic entrepreneurs who are very good at making money and are perfectly capable of using outside ignorance of Chinese culture to get their way.

Chinese society is very hierarchical and there is much upward delegation. Staff will most likely continue to take orders only from the boss even if the board has authorized other directors to take action. Consequently, Chinese staff do not easily accept the need for the division of duties and internal control that good corporate governance normally requires.

Here are some examples of ways in which China does business differently:

■ Customers will expect to deal with the CEO, which means that it is difficult for him or her to avoid acting as the sales director.
■ The collection of receivables can be a major problem. In the old managed economy where all businesses were state-owned, there was no incentive to collect cash as it all belonged to the state. This is slowly changing, but collecting cash needs constant attention.
■ There is much less attention placed on health and safety at work. Many working practices would be considered unsafe in the West. Independent directors may want gradually to raise the awareness of safety issues.

Ongoing management issues

Corporate governance

Under the AIM rules, AIM companies are not required to comply with the *Combined Code 2006 on Corporate Governance*, although they are encouraged to do so where possible. However, they are expected to comply with the *Corporate Governance Guidelines for AIM Companies* published by the Quoted Companies Alliance (QCA), which are less onerous.

In March 2007, the National Association of Pension Funds (NAPF) published its own guidelines for AIM companies that are generally consistent with the QCA guidelines. NAPF expects companies at the top end of the AIM market capitalization range to comply with the *Combined Code* or else explain their non-compliance. Very small companies should provide good levels of disclosure in their annual report and accounts. Companies in between are expected to apply the highest standards of corporate governance consistent with the size and complexity of their business.

Most Chinese AIM companies state they intend to comply with the *Combined Code*, though in many cases the compliance is less good in practice. Some sound approaches are:

■ Ensure that the company properly reports whatever its corporate governance is in practice – not what it aspires to.
■ Consider whether it needs improvement. This will depend partly on its size (see the NAPF guidelines above) and partly on the risks in its business.
■ Keep things in perspective. Investors will be more concerned to have a successful investment rather than an investment with first-class corporate governance but poor returns.

The audit committee is a Western concept. Particularly in small companies, the Chinese have difficulty accepting that the audit committee appoints the external auditors and must approve the accounts before they are published. Reviews of internal controls and risk management are even harder for them to comprehend. The solution is to make progress slowly; get the management information and reporting right before dealing with risk management.

In similar vein, the remuneration committee can be seen as none of the business of the independent directors. Surely it is up to the CEO to decide the remuneration of his immediate subordinates? As the directors' contracts will have been agreed before the listing, there is no urgency to hold a remuneration committee meeting afterwards until it is time to review top-level remuneration. As long as the management accept that their contracts can only be changed with the agreement of the independent directors, it may be better to concentrate on ensuring the business is running well.

It is unlikely to be sensible to set up a nominations committee for AIM companies unless they are very large. New board appointments should be agreed by the whole board.

Board meetings

Much of the independent director's effort in the aftermath of listing will be to ensure the proper functioning of board meetings and good and timely board reporting. First, a schedule of meetings must be agreed:

■ Although much of an independent director's business is now transacted by e-mail, regular formal meetings remain important, particularly while management adjusts to life in a listed company.
■ The independent directors must expect to visit the company in China at least twice a year at the company's expense (agree class of travel up front!). The CEO and CFO will need to meet investors in Europe at least once a year, twice for bigger companies. Board meetings should be arranged to coincide with these visits.
■ However, be careful about board meetings in the United Kingdom of listed offshore holding companies, which might cause the company to become subject to UK tax.

Second, rules for the sensible conduct of meetings need to be established:

■ Ensure good telephony. Videoconferencing does not seem to have yet caught on in China and the quality of the phone lines is not good. Make sure the company has the best possible equipment.
■ Skype is becoming more widely used and may provide a cheap and easy way of communicating.
■ Ban mobile phones during board meetings. Some people throughout the world (but particularly in China) do not seem to be able to turn their phones off!
■ Insist that financial and operational reports are circulated to directors well before the meeting. It is often an ongoing struggle to persuade management to brief the board properly. Given the problems of telephone meetings, the more information that can be circulated beforehand, the better.
■ Agree who is taking minutes. Depending on the language capabilities of the management team, it may be easiest if one of the independent directors takes the minutes. Otherwise, ensure that someone appropriate such as the company lawyer can take good minutes in English. Keep the English as simple as possible and sentences short to make them more easily understood by Chinese readers.

Many of the challenges facing independent directors in implementing acceptable corporate governance are common to all companies moving from private ownership to listed company status and becoming accountable to international investors. It is sensible to make haste slowly.

Accounting issues and the role of the CFO

One of the major differences in the way Chinese companies are organized concerns the status of the finance department and the chief financial officer (CFO). In a managed economy controlled by the Communist Party and where all businesses were state-owned, accountants were bookkeepers who kept the score and nothing more. As a result there is a shortage of well-trained accountants in China and the status of the finance department is likely to be lower than that of the marketing, production and technical departments. There may well not even be a CFO. In contrast, in Western companies, the CFO works alongside the CEO to agree and implement business plans and to control the company.

It is important to ensure there is a strong CFO, preferably someone who speaks English and understands International Accounting Standards ('IAS' but often referred to as 'IFRS' – International Financial Reporting Standards), who can communicate with the board and outside investors. However, they must also be someone to whom the CEO will listen and who will be accepted as part of the management team, otherwise they will not be able to do their job.

The audit committee chairperson must expect to devote his or her initial efforts to helping the company come up with a clear, useful and informative format for the monthly accounts. The company's budget and plan should then be put into a similar format analysed month by month.

Both budgets and monthly accounts should be on a consolidated basis for the group including intermediate holding companies and overseas costs because this is the basis on which the group's results will be published each half-year. The Chinese accounts staff may well need help to produce this.

The introduction of IAS has involved all companies in much work and made company reporting more complicated. The situation is exacerbated for Chinese companies that will not have been used to audits and consideration of accounting policies. They will require considerable outside support in preparing their first set of accounts under IAS, whether from the external auditors or other experts. It is important to ensure adequate time is allowed to meet the AIM reporting deadlines, which are three months after the half-year end and six months after the year end.

Most Chinese companies will have two or more sets of books: one for the tax authorities and one for international investors. It is sensible to try to persuade them to run one set of books (normally for Chinese tax purposes) with a separate set of entries to adjust to IAS and to reflect items that are either not relevant or not allowed for tax purposes.

Agree in which currency the company will report its results. Many Chinese companies, unless they undertake much direct exporting or importing, should consider using the renminbi (RMB or yuan) as the great majority of their transactions will be in renminbi . This will make reporting much easier for the finance department. As the renminbi becomes accepted as a major international currency by overseas investors, more Chinese companies are reporting in it.

Language and culture

Chinese culture has a long history and deep roots and it merits taking the opportunity to learn something about it. The culture varies across the country. China is a continent-sized country with a wide range of cultures, language, openness to outsiders and so on:

- Learn some Mandarin – it makes the Chinese feel you are trying and helps you understand them. Besides, it is an ancient and beautiful language.
- The Chinese (like the French) are more formal in addressing other people. If in doubt it is better to use a title and family name, for example, Mr Li, rather than a first name.
- Ensure there is someone capable of interpreting for board meetings. It is difficult to contribute to a meeting if you arc also translating, particularly if the translator is the Hong Kong-trained CFO, whose Mandarin may not be so fluent.
- Try to learn Chinese culture – wish them Happy New Year each spring when the lunar New Year starts. Don't give white flowers – white is the colour of death. Eight is a propitious number in China (the same word with another tone means prosperity); it is no coincidence the Beijing Olympic Games were planned to start on 8 August 2008! Watch out for the number eight in future dates of national importance.
- Remember China goes on holiday for a week over the Chinese New Year, Labour Day (1 May) and National Day (1 October).
- Use chopsticks and enjoy the food – but be careful about doing business over meals unless your hosts wish to. Almost every sip of drink is prefaced with a short toast (*gan bei* means 'bottoms up' so only say it if you are ready to finish your glass!).

Finally

Be realistic about what you can achieve as an independent director in China and you can play a small part in integrating China into the world's economy. You will be rewarded with an inside view of a rapidly developing major economy as it returns to the place it occupied 200 years ago as the world's largest economy.

30

Computer software outsourcing to China

John Pickup, Avington Systems Ltd

Introduction

Outsourcing software development and software writing to China, or in fact to any country, is a potentially emotive concept. Keeping jobs and skills in the United Kingdom and concerns about leakage of proprietary information due to lax intellectual property rights (IPR) protection are often cited as reasons for not outsourcing. The reaction can be that the work might be cheap, but the work may not be very good – how do you control the quality of the work?

In fact, if one wants to look for them, there could be plenty of reasons for not outsourcing work. And there are companies that are quite content with a slower development cycle, without the perceived hassle of working with an outsourcing organization – particularly in a distant country. However, there are an increasing number of companies that are keen to innovate, to drive technology hard, to beat competition from anywhere in the world and to grow aggressively. They see leading-edge software solutions as a key to a profitable source of business or to overcome or head off a competitive threat. These are the companies that will take advantage of the globalization of software development and look hard at China.

The key drivers for software outsourcing

The main reason for outsourcing is an urgent business need to get a new application up and running quickly – to provide better customer service or to launch a new product. National and international competitive pressure is driving down the time to market.

Very often, a software development project is estimated to require more than the available people resource in an organization. If this is the case, there are various alternate ways forward. A company can hire more developers, bring in contract staff or work with a software outsourcing organization. There are costs and benefits associated with each route but, increasingly, companies that are growing quickly are turning to software outsourcing as a means of supporting that growth.

There are many factors driving this direction. Good development skills are scarce and expensive. In the United Kingdom it is becoming increasingly costly and cumbersome to hire additional staff – especially if the need for these people might fluctuate. Report after report bemoans the growing shortage of software engineers and developers in the United Kingdom. As a recent example, silicon.com reported (21 May 2007) comments by John Suffolk, the government's chief information officer on the growing IT skills shortage. Suffolk said that it is difficult for businesses to find graduates with relevant skills, for example, in systems architecture: 'deep enterprise architects are hard to find, and there aren't many in the world', he said. The report continues to state that the technology industry needs an influx of more then 150,000 people per annum, according to e-skills UK and Gartner. According to the Higher Education Statistics Agency, the number of computer science graduates in 2005/06 was just some 34,000. Another report puts that figure at 20,000, which highlights an even greater shortage. Even if properly qualified people can be found, faced with an urgent business need, the sheer cost, complexity and the time it takes to hire people militates against hiring permanent employees.

An objection to outsourcing – the difficulty of working with a company on a different time zone, can, when properly managed, be a distinct advantage. A British company in the electronic control field has software development sites in the United Kingdom, the United States and China. They have good software project management and development projects move forward continuously during the 24-hour day.

If a company thinks totally globally, seeing the world as a market, there is an advantage in working with software houses in other parts of the world – gaining access to a different set of creative, lateral thinking skills outside an organization. In fact, the ideal outsourcing relationship is one where both companies jointly develop projects, each partner contributing their separate but complementary skills – a relationship built up over time, so that additional resources can be deployed quickly to meet fluctuating demand.

Why China?

Currently, the bulk of the Chinese outsourcing business comes from Japan and the United States. There is a strong Japanese presence in certain areas of the East Coast – Dalian in particular. Outsourcing from the United States is growing, probably due to the large number of Chinese students who have studied in the United States and are now moving up in management in aggressive entrepreneurial companies. In the United Kingdom, traditionally, for historical and cultural reasons, India with its similar educational system and English language ability among the educated elite, has been the destination of choice for software outsourcing. But now China is moving very fast as a software destination. In fact, IDC forecasts that 'Chinese cities will overtake Indian cities by 2011 due to massive investments made (eg infrastructure, English language, Internet connections etc) that are favourable to offshoring'. Indian software companies are themselves outsourcing software development to China. Bill Marcus, a technology commenter based in Shanghai, reports that major Indian outsourcers are building up their Chinese operations. Infosys Technologies has committed to spending US$65 million over the next five years on consultant campuses in Shanghai. Other Indian vendors Wipro and Tata are also investing in Chinese facilities. Software development is a very competitive service industry in China. There are some 13,000 registered software companies, with 500 having more than 1,000 employees.

China has a huge pool of good IT skills. Accurate like-for-like figures are difficult to find, but it is reported that China is producing some 800,000 software engineering graduates annually (*Developing the Future*, 2007, report series on the industry, commissioned by Microsoft). These graduates are eager to find work, to earn money and to better themselves.

An increasing number of software companies are focusing on providing software development and writing services for foreign companies. Currently, foreign clients account for some 10 per cent of total revenue, compared with 70 per cent for India. But that is changing rapidly; the Chinese government is putting increased focus on the software industry, as the Eleventh Five Year Plan to 2010 indicates. China's software industry recorded an increase of 23 per cent year-on-year for the first half of 2007, according to a Chinese Ministry of Information report released on 29 July.

In December 2006, the Chinese Ministry of Commerce (MOC) announced it was to develop 11 outsourcing base cities to build up the country's outsourcing service. The MOC plans to 'encourage 100 multinationals to shift outsourcing services to China and foster 1,000 large and medium-sized service outsourcing enterprises'. The first base cities would be Shanghai, Dalian, Xi'an, Shenxen and Chengdu. Others are Beijing, Tianjin, Jinan, Nanjing, Hangzhou and Wuhan.

The government is aiming for a fourfold increase in its service outsourcing export volume during the period of the current Five Year Plan. So, there is a large and growing focus on software outsourcing in China. Any company considering outsourcing software development to China knows it is swimming with the tide.

There are many different ways of working with software outsourcing organizations, depending on a client's business need and resources as the following case studies show.

Case study A – IKANO Financial Services

An example of a company that knew exactly what it wanted to achieve but did not have the in-house resources to deliver a solution in the preferred timescale is IKANO Financial Services. It provides consumer finance product to multiple retailers in the United Kingdom and in Europe and it needed a new application processing system to handle applications for various types of customer credit, including store and credit cards. Clearly, the system had to be robust, to deliver a predetermined response time and be able to cope with peak traffic volumes. Having designed and documented the business specification, IKANO made the decision that, rather than hire additional staff to do the coding, it would use an outside resource and it awarded the work to a software house in Beijing. The work was completed satisfactorily, on time and on budget. IKANO had no difficulty integrating the code into their existing systems, having bought the source code and written the interfaces. Maintaining the code over some years has not been a problem.

At the other end of the spectrum, other companies look to Chinese software houses to design a complete solution to a business opportunity, taking advantage of the increasing creativity and ingenuity of Chinese software developers.

Case study B – a complete solution

An example of this is a British company that provides information for bodybuilding clubs. The company had no detailed requirement specification, only a general idea of what it wanted to achieve. It wanted to help motivate the members' passion for bodybuilding by enabling data to be input into and queried from a PDA, a mobile phone or a website. Data synchronization was an important requirement, as was data protection. Working closely with the client by phone, MSN and e-mail, an elegant system architecture was developed by a Chinese software house ensuring a stable and secure, but user-friendly system. Secure remote access of the website was achieved, enabling bodybuilding enthusiasts easily but securely to share and compare information about their progress. The Chinese software house came up with a very creative solution, which despite its complexity, was delivered on time and within budget. It is now being successfully marketed as a standard software solution for the health industry.

Traditionally, the Chinese have been typecast as being very good at following a well-defined requirement – and doing it more cheaply. Education has been based on rote learning and to ask questions and challenge ideas was seen to be somehow critical of the teacher. Especially with the widespread internet, this is now changing. The culture is becoming more innovative: across the board there is a move from 'made in China' to 'developed in China'. This is particularly true regarding software development.

Although, of course, there is still the facility to get software written inexpensively and well to a tight predetermined specification. But it can be even more rewarding to involve a Chinese company in the logic, specification and architecture of a solution – genuine creative problem-solving. In fact, the World Intellectual Property Agency announced in August 2007 that China filed over 170,000 patents in 2005, a third up on the year before. China is now ranked third in the world after Japan and the United States in IPR registration.

The examples in the case studies illustrate the theme of an address that Bill Gates, Chairman of Microsoft Corporation, gave at the Bo'ao Forum for Asia in April this year. He is quoted as follows:

> *The advances in Asia are incredible... it's amazing to see it in person... to go to the universities to see how the classes have become very world-class in their capabilities. Microsoft started a research center here in Asia just 10 years ago. The results have been quite amazing, among the best work in the world. Not only is Asia benefiting from technology, but Asia will be a major source of the breakthroughs and advances of technology... There was a survey done in the United States that asked where the next Bill Gates will come from. Sixty per cent of the United States said that the next stunning success would come from Asia. I think it's true and amazing that it's so well recognized that the investment and changes here are leading to very innovative work.*

British companies need to tap into this growing and innovative resource of ideas. Their world-wide competitors are doing so.

Another advantage of China is its robust and pervasive telecommunications infrastructure. For example, it is estimated that with a forecast of some 80 million broadband subscribers this year, it will overtake the United States as the largest in the world (VNU Business Publications).

General business costs are lower than in India. In fact, Indian software house are themselves outsourcing to China. Costs are increasing in the big East Coast conurbations, Beijing and Shanghai, with salaries rising at 10 per cent to 15 per cent, but the Chinese government is encouraging software development in Western China, for example Chengdu, where costs are much lower, and employees are just as committed.

Perhaps the single most telling reason for outsourcing software to China is the Chinese work ethic. It is difficult to quantify, but the thoroughness, drive and sheer commitment to success is tangible to anyone exposed to it.

Issues and concerns

For those companies who have never outsourced their business abroad, it is all too easy to think of reasons for not outsourcing software to China. The following are the concerns usually raised.

Lack of IP protection

A recent conference stated:

> *Five years after China's accession to the WTO, most companies generally agree that the Chinese government has begun to put in place a more healthy and transparent IP environment. However, the legislative framework for IP protection and administrative enforcement in China still has some way to go before becoming truly efficient. (China Intellectual Property Summit, July 2007, Shanghai)*

Although there is clearly a distance to go, IP protection is very much a focus of attention. Chinese companies are increasingly taking each other to court where IP is alleged to have been breached, the courts are becoming more experienced in handling these issues and the Chinese government is rigorously tackling IP issues.

The leading companies bidding for international work are very mindful of the overseas concern about IP protection and take rigorous steps to enforce it. They realize the importance of reassuring their clients that they take IP protection very seriously and are very strict in enforcing it. Good IP protection also follows from low staff turnover.

In considering an outsourcing partner, a thorough IP protection plan is a good measure of a company's competence. Of course, a good non-disclosure agreement is essential; then companies have various ways of protecting the client's work. One company has a secure office for each client's work with password access, with confidential document control. Each employee has a confidentiality contract backed up by continuous training and education.

Poor English skills

Language skills and the opportunity to travel overseas can do much to keep employees happy. All graduates have to pass a national language test and those with Chinese English Test (CET) Level 6 have a good working knowledge of English. Some companies have an 'English only' policy so that all employees can converse with their overseas clients. In fact, there is a certain cachet attached to working with a software house with overseas clients, which helps with employee retention. Many senior managers have travelled extensively and so know English well; they also know how Western companies tend to operate. Other companies are foreign owned – usually US, so language facility is not an issue.

Poor employee reliability

Job-hopping is a problem in the IT industry, with turnover rates of up to 15 or 20 per cent, but it can be controlled in well-managed companies. Staff can be retained with a good salary and promotion package. One software company, with a well-managed English language programme, is reported to have kept annual turnover to just 3 per cent and yet in one year they reportedly received 20,000 resumés from job applicants.

Of course, staff retention is the greatest challenge in the affluent East Coast cities. Further west, where the quality of life and the environment are important factors, it is not such a problem.

A company's internal processes may not be good enough

Look for a Capability Maturity Model (CMM) or Capability Maturity Model Integration (CMMI) level. The CMMI and its predecessor CMM, is a measure of the effectiveness of the systems and processes within an organization. The higher the level – up to a maximum of Level 5 – is an indication of how seriously a company takes its internal processes and their improvement and how robust are its systems. It gives a measure of a company's commitment to quality work, including IP protection.

Quality of the code

Good enough for IBM, Microsoft, Intel, Siemens, Nokia... who all have major software development facilities in China. And more are coming. The aim of the Chinese government is to encourage 100 multinationals to shift their offshore outsourcing services to China and to foster 1,000 large and medium-sized service outsourcing enterprises in China (Ministry of Commerce [MOC] News Release December, 2006).

The time difference issue

With proper planning the time difference can be a positive advantage; software projects can be kept moving for more hours of the day.

Keeping track of what is happening

Clearly, reassurance about close communication is important. Companies use direct internet access, VOIP, MSM and so on to achieve this.

Emotional objections such as 'exporting jobs' or 'keeping UK salaries down'

Frankly, these objections do not stand close analysis. There is a desperate shortage of good IT skills in the United Kingdom. In fact, companies that source their resources from the most cost-effective locations in the world, tend to be those companies that are growing fastest, are competing most strongly and therefore tend to be a growing source of employment.

The next stage

As companies grow along with their software development needs, the next stage could be the setting up of an offshore development centre – either in conjunction with an existing software house or as a wholly foreign-owned enterprise (WFOE). Many Chinese cities are competing very hard to get inward investment that leads to employment growth. Many of them now have software parks, and some cities are promoting their start-up incubators where foreign companies can start up with minimum investment and bureaucracy. Although the Chinese government is moving towards a uniform corporate income tax rate of 25 per cent in January 2008, there will still be a tax rate of 15 per cent for high-technology companies; also, a 150 per cent R&D expense deduction for new technology enterprises.

Conclusion

Analysts predict that China will become the world's biggest provider of software outsourcing (MOC News Release, 14 December 2006). So go for it! Take advantage of the fastest-growing large economy in the world. Work with this huge reservoir of highly skilled, highly motivated and creative people. Companies that do this are best placed to compete and succeed at a global level.

Note: *With thanks to Dr. Anna Pang, Avington Systems Limited and Chris Cheung, China Britain Business Council, Beijing, for their helpful input.*

31

Case studies in trade and services

China Britain Business Council

Like Chapter 25, this chapter consists of a series of six case studies involving British companies, this time in trade with and the provision of services to China. As before, each case study is an abridged version of company profiles that have been featured in issues of *China-Britain Review*. The six companies in this second compendium are:

- Virgin;
- Watts Urethane Products;
- Menzies Aviation;
- CEL International;
- Sassan Ceramic Designs;
- Sheffield United.

Virgin

From December 2005 Virgin became not just the only airline to fly daily between Shanghai and London but pipped British Airways, its arch rival, to become the first British airline to fly daily anywhere between Mainland China and the United Kingdom. No wonder Sir Richard Branson, Virgin's founder, boss and supremo, flew out to Shanghai to celebrate.

It had been a whirlwind journey for Virgin in China. Virgin only thought of the possibility of flying to Shanghai as recently as 1998, which – given the lengthy negotiations and procedures – was comparative recent. The first and obvious question: 'Why Shanghai?' Virgin had identified Shanghai both as an entry point into China and as a growing, exciting city and destination in its own right.

First mover advantage

There was another very important reason why Virgin was keen to select a city that is fast reviving its pre-war reputation as the 'Paris of the East'. Shanghai, as well as being a vibrant city that Virgin believed would make an excellent market, was unique for the airline in that it was the first time that Virgin had started a new route as the first British carrier. In all previous cases, British Airways had started a new route and Virgin had followed in its wake.

Exciting it may have been, but launching a new route presented considerable challenges. First, for the very fact of it being China. All foreign businesses are faced with the full range of obstacles – from uncertain application of laws and regulations to bureaucratic procedures – but those facets of doing business are exacerbated when it comes to starting a new air route. For one thing, it involves a mutual swap of landing rights, permitting Chinese carriers to take up a corresponding landing slot in London.

Second, even after securing the flying rights, Mainland China presented a completely new market for Virgin. The airline had already been flying the Hong Kong route, but it was accepted that the Mainland would present a new type of market. Persuading a whole new market to fly an untried and untested airline requires an intensity of promotion to convince would-be purchasers not just of aspects, such as reliability and comfort, but also winning people's trust about safety.

Getting the price right

Increasingly, too, issues of pricing form a key component of business strategy for any airline in the world, not just in China. Budget airlines do not exist yet in China, but for a nation that has only comparatively recently become used to flying both in and out of China, and where average income is still far below levels of the West – despite the rapid increase in economic growth in recent years – price remains the overwhelming factor. By happy coincidence, the red corporate colours of Virgin played very well in a culture in which red is associated with many good things, including happiness and celebration.

After starting the new route in 1999, the number of passengers rose steadily, but the returns on the investment were slow in coming. This was largely due to the fact that the company had to invest resources and establish the infrastructure to operate the route but yet was only flying, initially, twice a week, which increased to four times a week two years after that. To draw a comparison, this is like hotels operating their business with only 25 per cent of the hotel available.

Flying to stay afloat

The first few years were a struggle, as Virgin's General Manager for China, Chris Humphreys, readily admits. Some within the company even suggested that the China market was a step too far and that the airline should cut its losses and withdraw. However, the view prevailed that Virgin should stay the course and wait for the returns to come. It was new territory in all senses and the lessons gained from developing a new route to China would provide valuable lessons for other new routes in future.

The decision was not assisted by external events, which conspired to make the business more challenging still. The Twin Towers attack of September 2001, the SARS crisis of 2003 and the Gulf War of the same year all had a significant impact on international travel, particularly from the United States. In the case of SARS, the impact was more direct, since SARS originated in China and spread quickly to Hong Kong.

But, as the old adage goes, a crisis was turned into an opportunity. Virgin considered how best to respond and decided that it would continue flying, despite the commercial losses that would inevitably accrue. During SARS, Virgin's crews volunteered to stay in China rather than in third countries unlike many other EU carriers. This gave rise to a welcome perception of the airline's long-term intentions. And, indeed, the decision was taken to make a point that Virgin was committed to its market, no matter how serious the conditions, and was not, literally, a fly-by-night carrier. Virgin was here to stay. As it happened, the situation was not at all bad. Even though passenger numbers were decimated, cargo continued to be transported.

Enter the competition

Following the resolution of the SARS crisis, business picked up again; only this time the airline now had to contend with greater competition on the London–Shanghai route. China Eastern started in 2004, matching Virgin with four flights a week, and the following year, British Airways, which had been flying to Beijing only, added Shanghai to its roster, flying five times a week. That was why it was so important that Virgin was able to up its service to a daily flight from December 2005. Finally, it could offer its customers, especially business travellers, a choice of being able to fly whatever day they wanted.

Not that it became plain flying. The market remains highly competitive. It is also seasonal, so that in the summer months airlines can probably fill planes twice over, but bookings are less assured in winter. The difference is accounted for almost entirely by the number of Chinese passengers. In the summer, some 90 per cent of passengers are Chinese (students and teachers heading to the United Kingdom for English language courses). In the coming summers that percentage could be higher, now that the United Kingdom has been given 'authorized destination status', allowing Chinese tour groups to go there on holiday. But that is by no means a certainty, for a number of reasons. The first is the high cost of a UK visa, which can add as much as 25 per cent to the cost of a visit.

Vouching for tourists

More problematical still is the requirement that tours can only be arranged by accredited travel agents, who themselves are required to vouch for each and every one of their tour groups. Should just one of their tour groups decide to jump ship, the travel agent can instantly lose its accreditation. Not surprisingly, some have been reluctant to take the risk.

Finally, taking tour groups may not even be that profitable. A squeeze is exerted by travel agents who control the tour group market, and highly price-sensitive consumers who, perhaps not unnaturally, want the very best deal. But this can create huge difficulties for the carriers as tour groups block-book seats and then cancel or switch them at the last minute – often on the basis of an RMB10 per passenger price difference. Lufthansa have stopped taking tour groups for that very reason.

A more promising route, perhaps, lies with attracting Chinese businesspeople and the better-off Chinese tourists on to flights at any time of the year, and not just the summer. Virgin's own data reveals that during the winter months the numbers of Chinese and overseas passengers are roughly equal, revealing a potential gap in the market.

The rise of Chinese outward investment is, therefore, a welcome development. Invest UK, which has an office within the Shanghai consulate, is encouraging more Chinese companies to open in the United Kingdom. According to Chris Humphreys, both UK Trade & Investment and the Welsh Development Agency are also 'working their socks off'.

Broadening the business

China is a key market for Virgin and not just in the airlines sector. Virgin is hoping to open its first megastore in Shanghai and is looking to branch out into mobile phones, soft drinks, hotels, health clubs and other retail outlets.

Meanwhile, Virgin is hoping to add Beijing to its Mainland China routes and to fly twice daily between London and Hong Kong. It would like more flights overall from China but that depends on the landing slots at Heathrow, which, in turn, may depend on Heathrow building a third runway. Virgin is acquiring more aircraft to create extra capacity on its China routes.

Watts Urethane Products

Demand in China for almost any product is growing fast and the rising economy is providing opportunities for all sizes of companies from the very largest to the smallest. For example, Watts Urethane Products, which, among other products, makes squeegees used in the silk screen printing business, has explored the potential of the China market and is very optimistic about the opportunities.

Polyurethane is a remarkable substance. A blend of three different polymers, polyurethane can be as hard as steel and as malleable as rubber, depending on the mix. It is a useful material because it doesn't rot or need painting, can be moulded and, better still, can easily be produced in large quantities.

One company, based in Lydney in Gloucestershire, has certainly capitalized on this invention. Watts Urethane Products, part of the Watts of Lydney Group, has been making, mixing and processing what it calls 'castable' polyurethane for over 25 years. The company's factory makes anything from street furniture and wheels (for anything that needs wheels, not just vehicles) to the biggest growth area of its business, squeegees, mostly used in silk screen printing. The business breaks down, roughly into one-third wheels and tyres, one-third squeegee blades and one-third general engineering.

China business

Watts sells its products all over the world, and China was always a market in its sights. Selling to China meant having an agent in Hong Kong. As can sometimes happen with agents, however, Watts had the sense that sales, although satisfactory, were less than they should have been. In particular, the company felt that the agent was not making the most of the potential for squeegee blades in CD printing and in the electronics sector. The company's Technical Sales Director, Mike Saunders, explains that it was not that the agent was doing anything wrong. Watts just felt he could be doing more. But, Mike Saunders explains, they had to be careful how they suggested this to him, because the company had built up a very good relationship, which it didn't want to upset.

The first step was for Mike Saunders to explore the potential in the market for himself. Some market research revealed that there was potentially strong demand for squeegees, particularly in the electronics sectors. He visited the all-important printing trade fair and exhibition in Shanghai in 2003, and in Tianjin the following year, which yielded a distributor for the Watts products. During this development, towards the end of 2003, Watts joined the CBBC and very soon after took a 'Launchpad' desk in Shanghai. The aim was to build up a customer base in China.

A face-saving compromise was reached, whereby the existing Hong Kong agent would continue to market the 'Watts' brand of squeegees, whilst Watts itself appointed another agent to sell a new brand of squeegee product into China called 'ORA'. As Mike Saunders concluded, China requires dedication, perseverance and an ability to overcome any number of challenges.

Menzies Aviation

Menzies Aviation, the Edinburgh-based group specializing in all matters related to aviation and airports signed a joint venture with the Chengdu Airport Authority in 2003. Reflecting on the boom in aviation in the Chinese market, General Manager, Chris Hutchinson, states that the company was definitely in the right place at the right time. And what is the most encouraging aspect for him is that growth is sure to continue.

Early days

It was in 2000 that the company first came into contact with the China market through its acquisition of Ogden Aviation, which gave it a presence in Hong Kong and Macau. The next step was an expansion into China. Rather than opt for the major airports, Menzies Aviation decided to pursue opportunities in the 'secondary level' airports.

The company alighted on Chengdu for several reasons: the so-called 'go West' policy of the central government that offered some incentive and tax breaks; the relative standing of Chengdu airport (which then ranked sixth and seventh for passenger and cargo throughput respectively); and, finally, the Chengdu Airport Authority that impressed Menzies as being one of the most progressive and innovative in China. A good partner was essential, because there is no opportunity for a WFOE in this industry.

The final deal with the Chengdu Airport Authority involved Menzies investing US$2 million for a 40 per cent stake, providing tenure for 10 years with a five-year extension option. Subsequently to that, the JV has spent a further RMB4 million (about £260,000) on new ramp vehicles all made locally.

The joint venture in operation

The joint venture opened for business in the first days of 2004 and the first 12 months were pretty hectic. The joint venture, which provides passenger, cargo and aircraft handling and aircraft line maintenance as well as ground support equipment maintenance has been operating at full capacity almost from the word go.

By early 2005, throughput of cargo and mail was running at 600 tonnes a day, of which 90 per cent was domestic. In total, Shuangliu (the name of the Chengdu airport) handled some 210,000 tonnes of freight in 2004. A new 100,000 m^2 cargo terminal was then built for opening in 2007. Passenger numbers are also growing, rising from 7.5 million in 2002 to 10 million in 2004 and were on track to reach 11 million in 2005.

In terms of the impact on the Menzies business, the joint venture handles between 30 and 70 departures a day, depending on the season, the busiest times being the summer and the three national holiday 'golden weeks'. Such expansion put enormous pressure on the JV resources. Traditionally, the growth surge would have been covered by hiring extra staff, but working closely with the new management team and staff, the extra work was absorbed without any increase in headcount at all.

For the following year and anticipating further growth, the JV took on a group of university and college graduates and took advantage of the winter season to train and develop them. They also advertised for engineering staff.

Quantity is one aspect, but so is quality. Menzies is keen that the operation sets and abides by high standards. Targets are set that allow for continuous improvement, and there are incentives to help performance improve. Industry standards such as AHS 1000 are also being established and installed to allow for better measurement and reporting.

The joint venture was expected to post a small operating profit for its first year, but such was the surge in business, coupled with increased flexibility and efficiency in the workforce, strict cost monitoring and stronger financial and management controls, that the profit forecast was revised upwards. The profits were put to good use, allowing the JV to invest more in equipment and people.

By the beginning of 2005, there were 60 daily departures, and the big question was when Shuangliu would start taking on direct flights to Europe and the United States. Five carriers (Martinair, Air France, Lufthansa, Gulf and Air Philippines) were known to be interested at that time. The passenger terminal was expanded in 2004 and there are plans to build a second runway in 2010.

CEL International

At one time a division of the Courtauld Group, CEL International can trace its presence in China back further than most, to the mid-1960s. In 1965, on the strength of projects the company had managed in Poland and the Soviet Union, Courtauld was invited to manage a project to equip and fit out an acrylics plant in Lanzhou in Gansu Province. In very difficult circumstances, that project was successfully accomplished and, remarkably, at a profit.

Subsequently, business developed further in the early 1990s when, with the liberalization of the economy under Deng Xiaoping, foreign investment became easier, and Western companies started building production facilities. This presented new opportunities for CEL.

In 1998, Courtauld was acquired by Akzo Nobel, the Dutch company, and two years later, CEL became a separate, independent company, following a management buyout. Today, CEL International is a dedicated project management company, providing engineering, design, procurement and construction management in complex projects mostly in the 'process' industries. The company has acquired a track record for managing projects in the chemicals, fast-moving consumer goods (FMCG) and pharmaceutical industries. More recently, CEL has expanded and diversified into biotechnology and environmental consultancy. The company has a staff of 285 and manages projects with a total capital value of more than £150 million a year.

China business

The return to the China market was signalled by the fulfilment of a project to build China's first foreign-invested paint plant in 1991. That project convinced the company that it needed a permanent presence in the country. After a year with a desk in the CBBC Shanghai office (the forerunner of today's 'Launchpad' scheme), CEL set up its own office in 1994. Gerry Shen, who was CEL's first employee in China, is still with the company today.

CEL then gradually built up its business in China. Chinese engineers were taken on, and relationships established with a network of contractors and designers whom CEL pulls in on different projects. All engineering disciplines exist within the company, or can be readily accessed, including: instrumentation and control; process, mechanical and electrical engineering and civil and structural engineering. On top of that, CEL is equipped to provide basic architecture and pre-project work. CEL has an alliance with a company called IntraLink, which advises on market entry strategies and undertakes market research.

Design collaboration

Key to the company's China strategy has been to form a partnership with a Chinese design institute, and this has resulted in a close collaboration with the Sinopec Nanjing Design Institute (SNDI). SNDI is a progressive medium-sized design institute employing around 600 engineers and has an excellent reputation through its main specialization in the chemical and process industries. CEL treats SNDI as if it were a joint venture partner. It is a good relationship and provides comfort and assurance for CEL's clients that the company has an established cooperation with a reputable design institute in China.

The decision was made to base the CEL business in and around Shanghai, since that is where there is a concentration of plants and factories that need processing expertise, but CEL has managed projects in many different parts of China. Some projects in the Yangtze Delta area include:

- An application support centre for aerospace sealants and coatings based in the Suzhou New District, on behalf of PRC.
- A manufacturing facility for nickel salt in Kunshan, Jiangsu Province for International Nickel (Jinco).
- A manufacturing and packing facility for tablets in Syzhou for GlaxoWellcom.
- A plant in the Suzhou New District for the Dutch company Stahl, its most advanced anywhere in the world, making coatings (acrylics, pigments and lacquer emulsions) for leather and other substances. The plant was built and equipped from start to finish within a year.

CEL is looking to the next phase of its own expansion. It has established a WFOE, upgrading from a foreign representative office, and has taken new office space in the Xujiahui area of Shanghai. The head of CEL in China, Simon Maguire, moved to Shanghai in September 2005, after 10 years of flying in and out of the city.

Being a WFOE Chinese company enabled CEL, for the first time, to receive orders in renminbi, directly take on staff in China and be taxed like a local company. With full localization in the foreseeable future, CEL in China will then be run by local management, have local staff and fulfil local contracts.

Growing client base

From a strategic point of view, the change in local status also paves the way for the company to expand into the local market. Currently, the company's client base is almost exclusively drawn from multinationals setting up operations in China, but it is aiming in the longer term to work with more Chinese clients. An opportunity may lie in the growing practice of Chinese businesses themselves to invest overseas. Take, for instance, pharmaceuticals, a growing sector within the Chinese economy. Chinese pharmaceutical companies will need expert assistance and advice, particularly to chart a way through the complex European and US regulations, if they wish to sell or invest in either of these regions.

CEL is all too aware that its competitors also see China as the market of the future, and that it will face constant challenges. In China, however, history counts for a great deal, and the successful accomplishment of the Lanzhou project nearly 40 years ago will always stand CEL in good stead.

Sassan Ceramic Designs

Jingdezhen is renowned for its ceramics, a magnet for Sassan Ceramic Designs, which designs, makes and sells porcelain lamps. Getting the business up and running was as intricate and refined as the designs on its products.

The lure of Jingdezhen

In any other pottery town in the world the transaction would have been straightforward: you have the money, I'll supply the goods. But Jingdezhen isn't just deep in the heart of one of China's most conservative provinces; it was once the centre of the porcelain universe, for centuries the manufacturing base of exquisite imperial ware, benefiting from ready access to unique raw materials and levels of artisanship far in advance of anything the West could then imagine. John Stuart Clark, the co-founder of Sassan Ceramic Designs, and his partner should have expected that their glaze supplier, Mr Huang, would be a Grand Master of the Arts and Crafts. It wasn't simply that he needed to know what his celadon glaze would be applied to in order to proffer sound advice. He wanted to build a relationship to get to know them, where Sassan sourced its clay, whose studios they were working in and, most importantly, which kiln they would employ to fire their pieces. 'No, I'm sorry', Mr Huang said, looking disconsolate, 'but the kiln in the sculpture factory – its *chi* (life force) is not good for my glaze'. It took three visits, a change of kiln master and the drinking of a lot of Yaoli tea before the partners walked from the Master's workshop with a pot of his sumptuous celadon in their hands.

Some of this ritual is symptomatic of the Chinese way of doing cordial business, but in Jingdezhen, Western entrepreneurs face the added resistance of a mutually suspicious history. Jingdezhen porcelain first arrived in Europe as ships' ballast for tea clippers. The passion with which the 17th-century aristocracy embraced China's 'white gold' triggered a feverish search for the Grand Arcanum. While the emperors held the 'barbarian' merchants at bay on the coast, Jesuit missionaries with access inland were enticed to wheedle out the production secrets of the pure white china of China.

All the important secrets had been uncovered by the 19th century, by when pottery towns in Britain, France, Germany and the United States were producing their own fine porcelain or close equivalents. But in Jingdezhen there remains an inherent distrust of the 'white ghosts' (as Westerners were called) and firm conviction that they still hold secrets that we are keen to walk away with. Time and again in their dealings, Sassan witnessed small evasions indicative of their suspicions. They were bluntly accused of 'spying' and their translators were treated as 'collaborators'.

Sassan's ceramics business is on the small side of the SME spectrum. Known in the trade as artist designers, they bridge the gap between studio ceramicists and production industries like Spode and Wedgwood. Specialists in porcelain lighting, each Sassan piece is uniquely hand-crafted from a small-batch production core for an exclusive market. Sassan's trips to China were in search of a workshop that could produce consistently high-quality cores for its designer. Weeks into their second trip, Sassan was still struggling to make sense of how the Jingdezhen potteries, and therefore, the town, operated.

Three hundred miles as the crow flies southwest from Shanghai, Jingdezhen is a mountain backwater dealing in a specialist commodity still highly prized in the West. While boasting sizeable industries producing Changhe helicopters and Suzuki automobiles, ceramics represent two-thirds of Jingdezhen's economy and employment.

Quality issues

On her first foray, Sassan's designer, Sandy Bywater, located herself at one of the two international workshops exploiting the reputation of the town to entice visiting artists from overseas. Hoping to use this as a springboard into the workshop system, she quickly discovered that the claims of the grandly named Sanbao Ceramic Art Institute were not matched by the reality of what they provided (or rather didn't) on the ground.

This first sortie revealed that Jingdezhen does have a major problem with quality control, and the authorities openly acknowledge the need to raise standards. They have invested millions in expanding the Tao Yuen Ceramics Institute, building a vast new campus in under a year, lobbying the state authorities for university status. While this might have an impact a decade down the line, right now, finesse is a victim of the migration from the countryside. Lured by higher incomes, whole families have relocated, served time in separate workshops learning different trades, then left to form their own companies that undercut prices by skimping on quality.

And the town's reputation for fine but functional pottery took a hammering in the mid-1990s when Beijing gave the nod for the privatization of huge complexes like the Guangming Porcelain Factory. Factored into hundreds of specialist workshops, it is now almost impossible to source anything requiring more than one workshop's skill and retain any consistency. To use computer jargon, there is no 'cross-platform capacity'. Thus, each component of a tea set, for example, needs to be sourced from a different workshop. When examining the set, discerning eyes can instantly detect disparities in the glaze, minor disproportions between cup and saucer, small incongruities between finishing touches – the sort of subtle aesthetic clashes that give the overall appearance of a shoddy product.

Aware that European retailers throw their arms aloft in despair at the slightest suggestion than any element of a high-end ceramic product might have been factored in the Middle Kingdom, Sassan knew that easing co-produced lamps into the designer market was going to involve a major challenge to Western prejudices.

The way forward

Sassan returned to Jingdezhen with its own 'secrets', prepared to play the game of 'You show, I'll show'. It generated invitations to run drawing workshops for ceramic designers who had never lifted a pencil; it revealed 'trade secrets' and sensible short-cuts known to every ceramics student in the West, but was a blinding light in Jingdezhen. Sassan gave English lessons to interested parties who might prove useful in future business dealings and, to top its efforts at ingratiation, it located itself in the family-run Ming Qing Studios, headed by the esteemed Grand Master Liu Yuan Chang.

Larger, less flexible businesses might not have had the time, but Sassan's product is unique for a niche market open for what a marriage between European design and Chinese artisanship could create. And that market extends to the Far East, because Chinese ceramicists are stymied by a lack of creative vision. Innovation, where education and training is by rote, is hamstrung by an irrational adherence to traditions that are totally unreflective of modern China.

Despite being created by ages-old technology, Sassan's prototypes were finally embraced as 'new technology'. However, the bubble burst when Sassan bumped into somebody unconnected with its business carrying one of its cores down the street! In an industry built on copying the old masters, IPR is a headache the local authorities are reluctant to even recognize.

Jingdezhen is a different country from anywhere on the coast, and no amount of legal documentation will intimidate the copyists. At present a sound relationship with its suppliers is Sassan's best hedge against rip-offs – one that spells out the parameters and penalties in the contract, one built on mutual respect and shared ideas. In a system that has bred and exploited distrust of thy neighbour since 1949, one can't underestimate the power of friendship or the lengths Western businesses might need to go to in China to nurture it.

Time is a major player in forging a business relationship. If it seems that Sassan's dealings with the Jingdezhen ceramics industry has plunged it into a quagmire of obstacles no progressive business needs, Sassan had no alternatives. Unlike many who venture into the Far East, it was not simply looking for cheap output and higher returns. While Sassan could simply export the exceptional raw clay to the United Kingdom, the Chinese have on site an industry that was once second to none but is now floundering under quality competition. John Stuart Clark likes to think that Sassan's mission is recognized by Jingdezhen's potters as one that gives as much as it takes.

Sheffield United

When it bought Chengdu Five Bulls, Sheffield United became the first foreign club to acquire a team in the People's Republic of China. In the off season, Sheffield United fans are still able to follow their club's fortunes, not in Bramhall Lane but thousands of miles away where Sheffield United also owns 90 per cent of the Chengdu Five Bulls Football Club.

It has all happened very fast for the Northern England club, which gained promotion to the Premiership in 2006. The first contact came in 2000 through Tony Xu, an agent acting on behalf of the club, when the club was looking for a sponsor for the club shirts. The club negotiated a £200,000 sponsorship, spread over two years, with a Chinese company, Desun, which makes apple juice cordial.

In the course of the negotiations, Kevin McCabe, who was chairperson of Sheffield United, visited China for the first time. He went with the preconceptions that many people have of China and discovered instead a place that was, in his words, 'Westernized, similar to the British society and a people with tremendous commercial enterprise'. While in China he also thought that there might be some opportunities for Sheffield United's other lines of business in property and leisure. Initially, he was motivated by the prospects in property, not in 'direct development' but in trading and buying with a view to leasing or selling. In conjunction with a joint venture partner, properties were bought in the Southern city of Shenzhen to provide serviced apartments and serviced offices.

Wherever he went in China, the subject of football would inevitably come up, and people Kevin McCabe met were most interested in his position as chairperson of Sheffield United. He was bombarded with proposals, most of which he rejected, but he did accept an offer to take on the running of a football academy in Hainan, which was also connected to a sponsorship deal for the Junior Academy in Sheffield.

Then in January 2005, the Blades (the name for the Sheffield United team) signed the renowned Chinese footballer, Hao Haidong, to their squad. Hao Haidong, who had played more than 90 times for China, was taken on not so much to play first-team football but to do some coaching for young Chinese footballers and, more generally, to serve as a bridge to China. Subsequently, Sheffield United agreed to acquire Li Tei from Manchester City to strengthen the connection with top Chinese footballers.

The following July, the Blades went on a pre-season tour of Shenyang, X'ian and Hangzhou with Hao Haidong in the team. The trip was a great success, making money for the club and, more importantly, introducing Sheffield United to a wider audience in China. It played strongly in the club's favour that Sheffield United is actually the oldest football club in England and Bramall Lane (where Sheffield United plays) is considered to be the home of association football.

As he watched the games and went to different grounds, the businessperson in Kevin McCabe observed a glaring gap in the market. 'They have the stadiums in China, but they didn't know how to fill them or use the retail potential', was his analysis. With the property business developing well, he shifted his focus to football.

Taking the bull by the horns

Tony Xu also has good connections with the Chengdu Football Association. Through that body, McCabe came across the local side, the Chengdu Five Bulls football club, founded in 1996 and at that point hovering in the middle of the country's second division. But what made him take a greater interest was the fact that the club played in a 40,000-seat stadium in the heart of Chengdu city itself. The club was the owned by a tobacco company, a situation that didn't make sense to Kevin McCabe.

He also thought that the potential for developing retail space attached to the stadium was enormous. The elements were in place to make not just a successful football club but also a successful business. He therefore put in a bid to acquire the club. As it happened, the tobacco company then sold its shares in the club to the Chengdu Football Association, making an approach from a foreign football club that much easier.

The deal that was struck was that Sheffield United bought 90 per cent of the Chengdu club for an undisclosed sum said to be 'minimal', leaving 10 per cent with the Chengdu Football Association. The stadium was not included in the purchase price but the club has the use of it whenever it wants, together with the training facilities.

From then on, there has been a two-track approach to developing the club. In purely football terms, the objective is to build a better football team that will seek promotion and then challenge for the top spots. Li Bing, a former Chinese international forward was named head coach, supported by two assistant coaches brought in from Sheffield. Kevin McCabe believes that having a top coaching team is vital. On top of that, the new club plans to spend about RMB20 million to build a brand-new team for the 2006 season. The team name remains Five Bulls, but the club is renamed Chengdu Blades Football Club. The club is aiming to obtain sponsorship approaching £1 million a year, and to start developing merchandising.

The club is now working at opening themed retail stores and 'Blades bars' in Chengdu to Westernize the operations of the football club. And, of course, the key objective is to get more people to watch the club from Chengdu's own population of 11 million in a province of more than 100 million.

And that was before Sheffield United won promotion to the Premiership. Since the Blades have gone up, the team is being watched by an audience of tens of millions in China since Premiership matches are broadcast there.

Within two or three years, Kevin McCabe fully expects to have recouped the initial investment, after which the Chengdu venture should generate good returns. Meanwhile, back in Sheffield, there is a language school attached to the Sheffield Academy, which means that young Chinese players coming to Sheffield can learn English and further their education, while being given football coaching.

International accountancy and law firms with offices in Mainland China

Accountancy firms – Beijing and Shanghai offices

Deloitte Touche Tohmatsu CPA Ltd
8/F Office Tower 2
The Towers
Oriental Plaza
1 East Chang An Avenue
100738 Beijing
Tel: +86 (10) 8520 7788
Fax: +86 (10) 8518 1218
Website: www.deloitte.com

30/F Bund Center
222 Yan An Road East
200002 Shanghai
Tel: +86 (21) 6141 8888
Fax: +86 (21) 6335 0003

Ernst & Young
Level 16, Tower E3
Ernst & Young Tower
Oriental Plaza, No 1
East Chang An Avenue
Dong Heng District
100738 Beijing
Tel: +86 (10) 5815 3000
Fax: +86 (10) 8518 8298
Website: www.ey.com

23/F The Centre
989 Chang Le Road
200031 Shanghai
Tel: +86 (21) 2405 2000
Fax: +86 (21) 5407 5507

Grant Thornton
Unit 1212, 12th Floor
Tower B, Full Link Plaza
18 Chaoyangmenwai Avenue
Chao Yang District
10020 Beijing
Tel: +86 (10) 6588 6655
Fax: +86 (10) 6588 8575
Website: www.gti.org

Unit 1603
16th Floor, Novel Plaza
128 Nanjing Xilu
200003 Shanghai
Tel: +86 (21) 6327 2200
Fax: +86 (21) 6358 8966

KPMG
8th Floor, Tower 2
Oriental Plaza
1 East Chang An Avenue
100738 Beijing
Tel: +86 (10) 8508 5000
Fax: +86 (10) 8518 5111
Website: www.kpmg.com

50th Floor, Plaza 66
1266 Nanjing West Road
200040 Shanghai
Tel: +86 (21) 5359 4666
Fax: +86 (21) 6288 1889

Mazars
1608, Tower E1
Oriental Plaza
1 East Chang An Avenue
100738 Beijing
Tel: +86 (10) 8518 9780
Fax: +86 (10) 8518 9781
Website: http://mazars.com.cn/

Xinmei Union Square
Floor 6
999 South Pudong Road
Pudong
200120 Shanghai
Tel: +86 (21) 6859 8060
Fax: +86 (21) 6859 8070
Website: http://mazars.com.cn/

PriceWaterhouseCoopers
26/F Office Tower A
Beijing Fortune Plaza
7 Dongsanhuan Zhing Road
Chaoyang District
100020 Beijing
Tel: +86 (10) 6533 8888
Fax: +86 (10) 653 8800
Website: www.pwc.com

11/F PriceWaterhouseCoopers Center
202 Hu Bin Road
200021 Shanghai
Tel: +86 (21) 6123 8888
Fax: +86 (21) 6123 8800

Law firms – Beijing and Shanghai offices

Adamas
Shenku Yard
Ritan Park
Chaoyang District
100020 Beijing
Tel: +86 (10) 8563 1202
Fax: +86 (10) 8561 2433
Website: www.adamas-asia.com

Suite 608 Dynasty Business Center
457 Urumqi Road North
Jing'an District
200040 Shanghai
Tel: +86 (21) 6240 0302
Fax: +86 (21) 6249 0501

Allen & Overy
Suite 522
China World Tower 2
1 Jianguomenwai Avenue
100004 Beijing
Tel: +86 (10) 6505 8800
Fax: +86 (10) 6505 6677
Website: www.allenovery.com

18F Bank of Shanghai Tower
168 Yin Cheng Middle Road
Pudong
200120 Shanghai
Tel: +86 (21) 3896 5000
Fax: +86 (21) 3896 5050

Baker & McKenzie
Suite 3401, China World Tower 2
China World Trade Center
1 Jianguomenwai Dajie
100004 Beijing
Tel: +86 (10) 6535 3800
Fax: +86 (10) 6505 2309
Website: www.bakernet.com

Unit 1601, Jinmao Tower
88 Century Avenue
Pudong
200121 Shanghai
Tel: +86 (21) 6105 8558
Fax: +86 (21) 5047 0020

Clifford Chance
Room 3326 China World Tower 1
1 Jianguomenwai Dajie
100004 Beijing
Tel: +86 (10) 6505 9018
Fax: +86 (10) 6505 9028
Website: www.cliffordchance.com

40th Floor, Bund Centre
222 Yan An East Road
200002 Shanghai
Tel: +86 (21) 6335 0086
Fax: +86 (21) 6335 0337

CMS Cameron McKenna (representative offices)
Room 601–89, 6/F Executive Tower
W3 Oriental Plaza
1 East Chang An Avenue
Dongcheng District
100738 Beijing
Tel: +86 (10) 8518 2585
Fax: +86 (10) 8518 1820
Website: www.law-now.com

Unit 2801, Plaza 66
Tower 2
1366 Nanjing Road West
200040 Shanghai
Tel: +86 (21) 6289 6363
Fax: +86 (21) 6289 9696

Eversheds
Units 501–502, Platinum
233 Taicang Road
Luwan District
200020 Shanghai
Tel: +86 (21) 6137 1088
Fax: +86 (21) 6137 1099
Website: www.eversheds.com

Freshfields Bruckhaus Deringer
3705 China World Tower 2
1 Jianguomenwai Avenue
100004 Beijing
Tel: +86 (10) 6505 3448
Fax: +86 (10) 6505 7783
Website: www.freshfields.com

34th Floor
Jinmao Tower
88 Century Boulevard
200121 Shanghai
Tel: +86 (21) 5049 1118
Fax: +86 (21) 3878 0099

Herbert Smith
Units 1420–1419
China World Tower 1
1 Jianguomenwai Avenue
100004 Beijing
Tel: +86 (10) 6505 6512
Fax: +86 (10) 6505 6516
Website: www.herbertsmith.com

38th Floor, Bund Center
222 Yan An Road East
200002 Shanghai
Tel: +86 (21) 6335 1144
Fax: +86 (21) 6335 1145

Linklaters
Unit 29, Level 25, China World Tower 1
1 Jianguomenwai Avenue
100004 Beijing
Tel: +86 (10) 6505 8590
Fax: +86 (10) 6505 8582
Website: www.linklaters.com

16th Floor, Citigroup Tower
33 Hua Yuan Di Qiao Road
Pudong
200120 Shanghai
Tel: +86 (21) 2891 1888
Fax: +86 (21) 2891 1818

Lovells
Level 2, Tower C2
1 East Chang An Avenue
Dongcheng District
100738 Beijing
Tel: +86 (10) 8518 4000
Fax: +86 (10) 8518 1656
Website: www.lovells.com

11th Floor, Shanghai Kerry Centre
1515 Nanjing West Road
200040 Shanghai
Tel: +86 (21) 6279 3155
Fax: +86 (21) 6279 2695

Paul Weiss
Unit 3601, Fortune Plaza Office Tower A
7 Dong Sanhuan Zhonglu
Chao Yang District
100020 Beijing
Tel: +86 (10) 5828 6300
Fax: +86 (10) 6530 9070/9080
Website: www.paulweiss.com

Rouse & Co International
Unit 1403, NCI Tower
12A Jianguomenwai Avenue
Chaoyang District
100022 Beijing
Tel: +86 (10) 6569 3030
Fax: +86 (10) 6569 3040
Website: www.iprights.com

Room 2601, Central Plaza
227 Huang Pi Road North
200003 Shanghai
Tel: +86 (21) 6375 8811
Fax: +86 (21) 6375 8060

Simmons & Simmons
33rd Floor, Plaza 66
1266 Nanjing Road West
200040 Shanghai
Tel: +86 (21) 6249 0700
Fax: +86 (21) 6249 0706
Website: www.simmons-simmons.com

White & Case
9th Floor, Beijing International Club Office Tower
21 Jianguomenwai Avenue
100004 Beijing
Tel: +86 (10) 8532 9800
Fax: +86 (10) 6532 6720
Website: www.whitecase.com

Room 220, Shanghai Bund No 12 Bldg
12 Zhingshan Dong Yi Road
200002 Shanghai
Tel: +86 (21) 6132 5900
Fax: +86 (21) 6323 9252

Zhinglun W&D Law Firm
19/F Golden Tower
1 Xibahe South Road
Chaoyang District
100028 Beijing
Tel: +86 (10) 6440 2232
Fax: +86 (10) 6440 2195/6440 2925
Website: www.zlwd.com

British Chambers of Commerce in China

British Chamber of Commerce in China
The British Centre, Room 1001, China Life Tower
6 Chaoyangmenwai Avenue
100020 Beijing
Contact: Nigel Clark
Tel: +86 (10) 8525 1111
Fax: +86 (10) 8525 1001
E-mail: communications@pek.britcham.org

British Chamber of Commerce in Guangdong
Room 1015, Main Office Tower
Guangdong International Hotel
339 Huanshi Dong Road
510098 Guangzhou
Contact: Jeremy Sargent
Tel: +86 (20) 8331 5013
Fax: +86 (20) 8331 5016
E-mail: bcc-gd@ihw.com.cn

British Chamber of Commerce in Shanghai
Unit 1701–1702 Westgate Tower
1038 Nanjing Xi Lu
200040 Shanghai
Contact: Ian Riley
Tel: +86 (21) 6218 5183
Fax: +86 (21) 6218 5193
E-mail: admin@sha.britcham.org

British Chamber of Commerce South West China
Room L, 7/F Sichuan International Building
206 Shuncheng Avenue
610015 Chengdu
Contact: Paul Sives
Tel: +86 (28) 8652 1196
Fax: +86 (28) 8652 1056
E-mail: cbbcd@mail.sc.cinfo.net

China Chamber of International Commerce
Qingdao Chamber
European Affairs Division
Contact: Peter Hu
Tel: +86 (532) 8389 7995/ 8389 8153
Fax: +86 (532) 8389 8251
E-mail: info@82invest.com

British universities and business schools offering Chinese Studies

Abertay University
University of Abertay Dundee
DD1 1HG
Tel: +44 (0) 1382 308 000
Fax: +44 (0) 1382 308 877

Bath University
Foreign Languages Centre
Bath BA2 7AY
Tel: +44 (0) 1225 323 844
Fax: +44 (0) 1225 323 686
E-mail: flc@bath.c.uk

Birmingham University
Centre for Modern Languages
Contact: Miyoko Yamashita
E-mail: M.Yamashita@bham.ac.uk

Bristol University
Centre for East Asian Studies
8 Woodland Road
Bristol BS8 1TH
Tel: +44 (0) 117 954 5577
Contact: Emma Holland
E-mail: Emma.Holland@bristol.ac.uk

Cambridge University
Oriental Faculty
Sidgwick Avenue
Cambridge CB3 9DA
Tel: +44 (0) 1223 335 106
Fax: +44 (0) 1223 335 110

University of Central Lancashire
Lancashire Business School
Dept of Strategy & Innovation
Tel: +44 (0) 1772 894 703
Contacts: Robin Miller, Feixia Yu
E-mail: Rmiller1@uclan.ac.uk; Fyu@uclan.cac.uk

Durham University
East Asian Studies
Elvet Hill
Durham DH1 3TH
Tel: +44 (0) 191 374 3231
Fax: +44 (0) 191 374 3242
E-mail: e.a.studies@durham.ac.uk

Edinburgh University
Scottish Centre for Chinese Studies
8 Buccleugh Place
Edinburgh EH8 9LW
Tel: +44 (0) 131 650 4227
Fax: +44 (0) 131 651 1258
Contact: Margaret Gall
E-mail: Margaret.gall@ed.ac.uk

Glasgow University
Department of Economic and Social History
4 University Gardens
Glasgow G12 8QQ
Tel: +44 (0) 141 330 6616
Contact: Dr Catherine R. Schenk
E-mail: c.schenk@socsci.gla.ac.uk

Lancaster University
Lancaster Centre for Management in China (LCMC)
Lancaster University Management School
Lancaster LA1 4YX
Tel: +44 (0) 1524 594 059
E-mail: chinacentre@lancaster.ac.uk

Leeds University
Department of East Asian Studies
Leeds LS2 9JT
Tel: +44 (0) 113 233 3462
Fax: +44 (0) 113 233 6741
E-mail: eastasian@leeds.c.uk

Liverpool John Moores University
Liverpool L3 5UZ
Tel: +44 (0) 151 231 3388
Contact: Dr Qing Cao

London School of Economics
Asia Research Centre
Houghton Street
London WC2A 2AE
Tel: +44 (0) 20 7955 7229
Fax: +44 (0) 29 7955 7399

The University of Manchester
Centre for Chinese Studies
Lime Grove Building
Oxford Road
Manchester M13 9PL
Tel: +44 (0) 161 306 1621
Fax: +44 (0) 161 275 3031
Contact: Karen Wang
E-mail: Karen.wang@manchester.ac.uk

Newcastle University
School of Modern Languages
Old Library Building
Newcastle on Tyne NE1 7RU
Tel: +44 (0) 191 222 7441
Fax: +44 (0) 191 222 5442

University College Northampton
The China & Transitional Economics Research Centre
Boughton Green Road
Northampton NN2 7AL
Tel: +44 (0) 1604 735 2163
Fax: +44 (0) 1604 721 214
Contact: Richard Sanders
E-mail: Richard.Sanders@northampton.ac.uk

Nottingham University
Institute of Contemporary Chinese Studies
University Park
Nottingham NG7 2RD
Tel: +44 (0) 115 846 6322
Fax: +44 (0) 115 846 6324
E-mail: chinese-studies@nottingham.ac.uk

Oxford University
Institute for Chinese Studies
Walton Street
Oxford OX2 2HG
Tel: +44 (0) 1865 280 430
Fax: +44 (0) 1865 280 431

School of Oriental & African Studies
East Asia Department
Thornaugh Street
Russell Square
London WC1H 0XG
Tel: +44 (0) 20 7637 2388
Fax: +44 (0) 20 7436 3844

Sheffield University
East Asian Studies Department
45 The Arts Tower
Western Bank
Sheffield S10 2TH
Tel: +44 (0) 114 222 8400
Fax: +44 (0) 114 222 8432
E-mail: ses@sheffield.ac.uk

University of Wales Lampeter
Centre for Chinese Studies
Ceredigion SA48 7ED
Tel: +44 (0) 150 422 351
Fax: +44 (0) 1570 423 423
Contact: Professor Xhinzhing Yao
E-mail: x.yao@lamp.ac.uk

Warwick University
Department of Politics and International Studies
Coventry CV4 7AL
Tel: +44 (0) 24 7652 3486
Contact: Charlotte Lewis
E-mail: charlotte.lewis@warwick.ac.uk

Westminster University
Chinese Department
School of Social Sciences, Humanities and Languages
309 Regent Street
London W1B 2UW
E-mail: hunagd@westminster.ac.uk

Useful business and trade organizations in the UK and China

In the UK

China Britain Business Council (CBBC)
Head Office
1 Warwick Row
London SW1E 5ER
Tel: +44 (0) 20 7802 2000
Fax: +44 (20) 7802 2029
E-mail: enquiries@cbbc.org

CBBC Scotland Office
30 George Square
Glasgow G2 1EQ
Tel: +44 (0) 141 204 8322
Fax: +44 (0) 141 204 8354
E-mail: office@cbbc.org

CBBC Manchester Office
International Trade Centre
Churchgate House
Oxford Street
Manchester M60 7HJ
Tel: +44 (0) 161 237 4090
Fax: +44 (0) 161 1341
E-mail: giles.blackburne@cbbc.org

CBBC Yorkshire and Humber Office
White Rose House
28a York Place
Leeds LS1 2EZ
Tel: +44 (0) 113 247 1584
Fax: +44 (0) 113 247 1111
E-mail: jessica.zhan@cbbc.org

CBBC East of England
Pightle Cottage
School Street
Foxearth
Suffolk CO10 7JE
Tel: +44 (0) 1878 310 245
E-mail: chris.cotton@cbbc.org

Chinese Consulate General
Manchester
Denison House
49 Denison Road
Rusholme
Manchester M14 5RX
Tel: +44 (0) 161 224 8672

Edinburgh
Tel: +44 (0) 131 316 4789
Fax: +44 (0) 131 334 6954

Embassy of The People's Republic of China
Economic & Commercial Counselor's Office
Cleveland Court
3 Leinster Gardens
London W2 6DP
Tel: +44 (0) 20 7723 8923
Fax: +44 (0) 20 7707 2777
Website: www.mofcom.gov.cn

Visa Section
31 Portland Place
London W1N 3AG
Tel: +44 (0) 0891 880808
Website: www.chinese-embassy.org.uk

Export
Export Credit Guarantee Department
PO Box 2000
Exchange Tower
Harbour Exchange Square
London E14 9GS
Tel: +44 (0) 20 7512 7000
Fax: +44 (0) 20 7512 7649
Website: www.ecgd.gov.uk

Technical Help for Exporters
BSI Standards
Tel +44 (0) 20 8996 7111
Fax: +44 (0) 20 896 7048
E-mail: info@bsi-global.com

Trade Partners UK China Desk
Bay 553, Kingsgate House
66–74 Victoria Street
London SW1E 6SW
Tel: +44 (0) 20 7215 4957
Fax: +44 (0) 20 7215 8797

In China

British Council China
The British Centre, Room 101
China Life Tower
8 North Dongsanguan Road
Chaoyang District
100004 Beijing
Tel: +86 (10) 6501 1903
Fax: +86 (10) 6590 0977
E-mail: enquiry@britishcouncil.org.cn

British Embassy & Consulate General
British Embassy, Beijing
Commercial Section
11 Guang Hua Road
Jiangguomenwai
100600 Beijing
Tel: +86 (10) 6532 1961/5
Fa: +86 (10) 6532 1937/8/9
Email: siobhan.gill@fco.gov.uk

Shanghai
Suite 301 Shanghai Centre
1376 Nanjing Xi Lu
200040 Shanghai
Tel: +86 (21) 6279
Fax: +86 (21) 279 7651
E-mail: natalia.xia@fco.gov.uk

Guangzhou
7th Floor Giangdong International Hotel
339 Huanshi Dong Road
510098 Guangzhou
Tel: +86 (20) 8335 1354
Fax: +86 (20) 8333 6485
E-mail: guangzou.commercial@fco.gov.uk

Chongqing
Suite 2801 Metropolitan Tower
68 Zourong Road
400010 Chongqing
Tel: +86 (23) 6381 0321
Fax: +86 (23) 6381 0322
E-mail: bcgchq@public.cta.cq.cn

Hong Kong
6th Floor, 1 Supreme Court Road
Hong Kong
Tel: + (852) 2901 3182
Fax: + (852) 2901 3066
E-mail: commercial@britishconsulate.org.hk

China Britain Business Council (CBBC)
CBBC Beijing
The British Centre
Room 101 China Life Tower
16 Chaoyangmenwai Street
10020 Beijing
Tel: + 86 (10) 8525 111
Fax: +86 (10) 8525 1001
E-mail: beijing@cbbc.org.cn

CBBC Shanghai
Unit 1701–1702 Westgate Tower
1038 Nanjing Road West
200040 Shanghai
Tel: +86 (21) 6218 5183
Fax: +86 (21) 6218 5193
E-mail: shanghai@cbbc.org.cn

CBBC Chengdu
1705B, 17/F Block A Times Plaza
2 Zongfu Road
610016 Chengdu
Tel: +86 (28) 8652 1700
Fax: +86 (28) 8652 1056
E-mail: chwengdu@cbbc.org.cn

CBBC Wuhan
Unit 11 6/F Wuhan International Trade Commerce Centre
297 Xinhua Hou Road
430022 Wuhan
Tel: +86 (27) 8577 0989
Fax: +86 (27) 8577 0991
E-mail: wuhan@cbbc.org.cn

CBBC Shenzhen
Tower A International Chamber of Commerce Building
Fuhua Yi Lu
Futian District
518048 Shenzhen
Tel: +86 (755) 8219 8148
Fax: +86 (755) 8229 3159
E-mail: shenzhen@cbbc.org.cn

CBBC Qingdao
Room 503, 5th Floor
121 Yan An San Road
266071 Qingdao
Tel: +86 (532) 386 9772
Fax: +86 (532) 386 9329
E-mail: qingdao@cbbc.org.cn

CBBC Nanjing
Room 2514
50 Zhinghua Road
210001Nanjing
Tel: +86 (25) 5231 1740
Fax: +86 (25) 5223 3773
E-mail: nanjing@cbbc.org.cn

CBBC Hangzhou
A-809 Zhejiang World Trade Centre
122 Shuguang Road
Hangzou
310007 Zhejiang
Tel: +86 (571) 8763 1069
Fax: +86 (571) 8763 0961
E-mail: hangzhou@cbbc.org.cn

CBBC Shanyang
Room 901 Tower II City Plaza Centre
206 Nanjing North Street
Heping District
110001 Shenyang
Tel: +86 (24) 2334 1600
Fax: +86 (24) 2334 1858
E-mail: shenyang@cbbc.org.cn

Contributors' contact list

Arup Group
13 Fitzroy Street
London W1T 4BQ
Tel: +44 (0) 20 7755 4311
Contact: Ben Richardson
E-mail: ben.richardson@arup.com

Avington Systems Limited
PO Box 82
Winchester
Hampshire SO21 1WA
Tel: +44 (0) 1962 779 894
Contact: John Pickup
E-mail: john@avington.com

Centre for Intellectual Property and Management
Business School, Bournemouth University
Talbot Campus
Fern Barrow
Poole
Dorset BH12 5BB
Tel: +44 (0) 1202 965212
Contact: Professor Ruth Soetendorp
E-mail: rsoetendopr@bournemouth.ac.uk

China Britain Business Council
1 Warwick Row
London SW1E 5ER
Tel: +44 (0) 20 7802 2000
Contact: Humphrey Keenlyside
E-mail: humphrey.keenlyside@cbbc.org

The Culture Partnership
Vital People Ltd
288 Bishopsgate
London EC2M 4QP
Tel: +44 (0) 203 170 5665
Contact: Joan Turley
E-mail: joan@vitalpeople.co.uk

HSBC Holdings plc
China International Business Development
8 Canada Square
London E14 5HQ
Tel: +44 (0) 20 7992 1183
Contact: Amanda Gu
Direct line: +44 (0) 20 7992 5084
E-mail: amanda.gu@hsbcib.com

Invest Hong Kong
6 Grafton Sytreet
London W15 4EQ
Tel: +44 (0) 20 7499 9821
Contact: Alasdair Crewe
E-mail: alasdair_crewe@hktolondon.gov.hk

KPMG Huazhen
50th Floor, Plaza 66
1286 Nanjing West Road
Shanghai 20040
Tel: +86 21 2212 2888
Contact: Ning Wright
Direct Line: +86 21 2212 3602
E-mail: ning.wright@kpmg.com.cn
Contact: Linda Lin
Direct line: +86 21 2212 3525
E-mail: linda.l.lin@kpmg.com.cn
Contact: John Lee
Direct line: +86 21 2212 1819
E-mail: john.lee@kpmg.com.cn

Lloyd's Reinsurance Company (China) Ltd.
33rd Floor, Azia Centre
1233 Lujiazui Ring Road
Pudong
Shanghai 200120
Tel: +86 21 6162 8200
Contact: Ian Faragher
E-mail: Ian.Faragher@lloyds.com

Jonathan Reuvid
Hethe Management Services
Little Manor
Wroxton
Banbury
Oxfordshire OX1 6QE
Tel: +44 (0) 1295 738070
Contact: Jonathan Reuvd
E-mail: jreuvidembooks@aol.com

Rouse & Co. International
Unit 1403
NCI Tower, No. 12A
Jianguomenwai Avenue
Chaoyang District
Beijing 100022
Tel: +86 10 6569 3040
Contact: Joshua Whale
Direct line; +86 10 6569 3030
E-mail: jwale@iprights.com

Sagentia Limited
Harston Mill
Harston
Cambridge CB22 7GG
Contact: Emma Drake
Tel: +44 (0) 12223 875200
E-mail: emma.drake@sagentia.com

Steeds & Co.
1 Littleworth Avenue
Esher
Surrey KT10 9PB
Tel: +44 (0) 1372 465909
Contact: David Steeds
E-mail: steeds@globalnet.co.uk

Stephen Gill Associates
Stanton Lodge
Aston on Trent
Derby DE72 2AH
Tel: +44 (0) 1332 793399
Contact: Stephen Gill
E-mail: stcvc@stephengill.eu

Withers LLP
20th Floor
Gloucester Tower
The Landmark
Central
Hong Kong
Contact: Guy Facey
E-mail: guy.facey@withersworldwide.com

Index

Index of advertisers